Awakened Wisdom

A Guide to Reclaiming Your Brilliance

PATRICK J. RYAN

Awakened Wisdom Experiences® Inc. ("AWE™") is a global training, coaching and personal development organization. If you are interested in discussing the use of our proprietary materials please contact us about certification as an AWE™ coach. AWE™ services may only be provided by certified AWE™ service providers.

Published by: Awakened Wisdom
            patrick@awakenedwisdom.com

ISBN 978-0-9842363-0-5

Cover photo by Patrick Ryan
Design and Layout by Vancouver Desktop Publishing Centre Ltd.
Printed by Lightning Source

The paper used in the production of this book will be offset through support for the planting of trees and other initiatives.

Dedication

With the deepest gratitude to Mary, for your love, companionship, and for the wisdom that you bring to every amazing adventure that we take on.

With Love,
Patrick

PRAISE FOR AWAKENED WISDOM

"Patrick's profound yet practical models undo the belief that there is something out there to be found to complete us. *Awakened Wisdom* helps readers quickly connect with their own heart intelligence and what it really means to be human."
—*Marci Shimoff, # 1* NY Times *bestselling author,* Happy for No Reason *and* Chicken Soup for the Soul

"After having read many of the great spiritual works of our time, I can honestly say that *Awakened Wisdom* is definitely among the very best."
—*Dr. Peter C. Rogers author* Ultimate Truth: Book I

"Patrick is a new teacher that everyone needs to know about. In his new book, he shares wisdom, principles and clear action steps that will help anyone navigate the personal, professional or even global changes we are facing. You will look at yourself and your life very differently after reading *Awakened Wisdom.*"
—*Ariane de Bonvoisin, bestselling author of* The First 30 Days

"Everyone who is on the path of self-discovery will benefit from Awakened Wisdom's fresh and authentic approach to living a life that is congruent with their own personal brilliance."
—*Mike Robbins, author of* Be Yourself, Everyone Else is Already Taken

"A practical yet powerful tool to connect you with who you really are. A fantastic read for anyone who is open to discovering more about who they are and how to tap into their brilliance!"
—— *Shawn Miller*

"Every once and again a book comes along that speaks to me and provides me with a greater view on making my journey in life a more magical and heartfelt experience. Awakened Wisdom: A Guide To Reclaiming Your Brilliance is one such book. I love the teachings Patrick Ryan offers here and the way he presents them. Be kind to yourself and make time to experience the gifts of this book, each one of us deserves that."

— *D. Schwartz*

Pragmatic and Timely

"I loved the way this book takes the ancient teaching of Buddhism , Native , Sufi and other Wisdoms and weaves then into a practical modern guide to awaken the higher states of consciousness and it does so in an elegant and heartfelt way."

— *Mary Diamond*

"While drawing on ancient learnings, Patrick Ryan has made the concepts relevant to a contemporary audience. The shifts he presents are profound, but also approachable and practical in a current busy life. I feel joyful and grounded, and called forth to life in a new way. I am truly grateful for the wisdom in this book."

—*Colleen O'Rourke*

"*Awakened Wisdom* gives the how-to of being present in the moment that Tolle only says is possible. In a friendly, story-filled text, Ryan offers the tools to move through each moment awake. The book is a gift to those who are drawn toward the flame of full aliveness.

—*David Carr, D.Div, spiritual counselor, co-leader with Laura Davis of Writer's Journey Retreats*

Compelling

"I find "Self-Help" and "Spirituality" books to be a dime-a-dozen . . . not the case with *Awakened Wisdom*'s author Ryan. He is not only wise, generous and insightful but a clear and relatable writer. A must have." —*Joy Glasser, Minnesota, USA*

A Must-Read

"Ryan's book is easy to read, compelling and practical. His writing takes the reader on a journey into a new layer of Self, yet it is relatable no matter what your experience with this genre. A must-read for anyone interested in uncovering the best part of them self."
                                                                              —*Lisa Goren*

"Patrick Ryan takes us to a higher level of consciousness through this transformative book. Everyone needs to read this book and go through the *Awakened Wisdom* Experience's Reclaiming Your Brilliance workshop. Believe me. You will be so glad you did!"
                                                                              —*Julia Lau*

Practical and Profound

"*Awakened Wisdom* provides insight for the wondering soul in all of us in these times of uncertainty and distress. This book is a practical and profound guide. Read it, study it, feel it, and do yourself and your loved ones a favor."
                                        —*Santiago Garcia De Leaniz, Madrid, Spain*

"For a book that is intended to guide you on your spiritual journey, it is very clear and easy-to-read. The wisdom is also very practical. I dove in and I'm enjoying the experience."
                                        —*Julie A. Spezia,California, USA*

"Patrick Ryan has wisdom far beyond his years. His work, *Amazing Wisdom* is insightful and makes you question every word and interaction you have and what it evokes in your relationships. It is a delight to read, jam-packed with much to learn about yourself. "
                                        —*Sharon Madeiro, Greene, Rhode Island, USA*

"Wherever you are on your journey in life *Awakened Wisdom* is a must read. Patrick Ryan is a masterful teacher, who leads us on a journey of amazing discoveries. Patrick's book is a brilliant tool for tapping into your own wisdom and bringing your own brilliance to the world." —*E. Gwen Semenoff*

"Brilliant book! Patrick has a wonderful way to bring us closer to our authentic self, while inspiring us to live a purposeful life guided by our divine essence, our intuitive self. A great book that will guide you how to start living an awakened life!"
— *Raymond Hippolyte, California, USA*

True Understanding

"After attending Awakened Wisdom it was awesome to have this book to re-absorb the weekend. A true understanding can be had on just how you can find, make and keep peace with all that you are and to bring that forward every day in a way that serves you and your relationships."
—*Kathie Sue, British Columbia, Canada*

"Another helpful pointer to truth. The author (I prefer "teach" in this case) provides guidance on finding and fulfilling personal dreams, during which, an exciting and moving process of self-discovery and self-healing is experienced. Eventually we will fulfill our collective destiny, which would be the ultimate goal for all our dreaming and all our efforts, life time after life time."
—*D. Zhao, British Columbia, Canada*

"I feel blessed to have this book and to have experienced the AWE weekend in Vancouver. It's been an avenue of reconnecting with my dreams, my voice, my curiosity and, bigger than all of these, my faith. The book and the work is simple and profound and continues to grow with me. Thank you Patrick for creating this book and this work!
—*Maughan Mariani*

Acknowledgments

Over the period of time that it took to write this book, I had the privilege to travel and work with some very extraordinary people all around this world.

From Istanbul to London to Dubai, Israel to Egypt, Burma (Myanmar) to Thailand and Japan, and of course around Canada and the United States.

I wrote this book in each of these cultures. This was fortunate as I was able to present and to dancehammer, that is to discuss, these ideas with vigorous and straightforward people. I was very pleased to witness how effective and resonant these ideas were across so many places.

Awakened Wisdom Experiences (AWE) is the organization I founded to bring these and many other offerings out to the world. AWE is committed to serving the awakening of a higher level of consciousness around the planet. We believe that when people are grounded in their Divine Essence and aligned around the ideas presented herein that we meet each other with respect and good intention. And from there anything is possible, according to the wisdom and creativity of our Divine Essences.

I am very grateful to my beautiful and generous wife, Mary Diamond, who believes in my calling and who shares her wisdom, as well as our time, with the world, as I travel far and wide. She has also brought her gifts of insight and creativity as support to the work of Awakened Wisdom.

I am thankful for the strong support of Einav Tadmor in Israel who has committed her energy to getting these teachings out throughout her country as well as Europe. Einav is brilliant and is constantly calling us all forth in a gentle and determined way as she works to bring groups of people together to hear and receive these teachings. She is a Peace Worker on the planet.

I would not be able to move forward if the organization were not so well held from behind the scenes. For that service I am grateful to Arvind Shenoy, who guides the not-so-simple matters of finance and accounting and who has become my friend in the process. I am also lucky to have Megan Hanson as my "pit crew chief," taking care of the details as only she can.

As Awakened Wisdom has toured around the world, there are many people who have contributed. Thank you to Pemma Fox, Abi Shilon, Yossi Eilot, Hide Enomoto, Wael Borhan, Lina Nahaas, Sue Belton, Boris Prigmore, Mika Sato, Kelly Carlin-McCall, Denise Burke, Cynthia Ridley, Kate Roeske, Coby Kozlowski, Kyoko Seki, Jennifer Shelton, Isolde Huijbregts, Meisha Rouser, Izumi Yamamoto, Morrie and Sher Sacks, Darren Roberts, Deborah Smith, and Flash, to name a few.

I want to acknowledge my editor, Brooke Warner, whose magic touch has supported the writing of this book in invaluable ways.

This would not be complete without acknowledging all my past colleagues at the Coaches Training Institute, with whom I have journeyed over ten years around this planet. It is through many of our experiences together that I have learned much about what is needed to be a human out on the planet as a teacher and leader—thank you.

I am not trying to pass on any particular tradition, and yet there are some teachers who have had a profound influence on me and, therefore, on the offerings of Awakened Wisdom.

First and foremost, I am grateful to Sayadaw Thin Bury, the teacher who took me in and opened me up to so many teachings that go beyond the spoken word. I send my prayers to the people of Burma, who at the time of this writing are still held under the grasp of a military junta that is caught in a deep distortion.

My gratitude also goes out to White Eagle, Wind Eagle, and Rainbow Hawk, the keepers of The Beauty Way teachings, and to the many other teachers I have been fortunate to meet and work with over the years.

And, of course, I wish to thank all the participants who have attended the Awakened Wisdom programs over the years. It is through you that I have seen these teachings come to life. You have shared your dreams and purposes and dared to ask big questions. It is because of you that we at Awakened Wisdom have continued to commit our Selves to furthering this work out in the world.

Gratefully,
Patrick Ryan

Contents

PART TWO:
THE EIGHT STATES OF AN AWAKENED LIFE©

Foreword

"This is all your fault," is what I wanted to shout down to Patrick Ryan while I stood on a very small platform forty feet up a redwood tree. A few minutes earlier, before climbing up there, I had so much fear about this exercise that I had channeled the energy of my four-year-old self and tried to cry my way out of it—a strategy that had kept me safe, yet ultimately unfulfilled, my whole life. Patrick, ignoring my archaic strategy, had smiled at me and patiently asked how far up I was willing to go (I had originally said, "to touch the platform"). Then he politely asked if I was willing to reassess my goal once I got there. I had said sure, relieved that he was not going to bully me into anything I didn't want to do, and so I'd started to climb. I quickly climbed up the pegs at the bottom of the platform and realized right away that I would be very dissatisfied if this was as far as I went. I saw that I did want to actually stand on the platform, but had no idea how to get up there. Patrick simply guided me by pointing out where the next pegs were, and before I knew it I was standing on the platform. That's how straightforward Patrick's teachings are—before you know it, you are exactly where you want to go.

Once I was up there, I realized that wanting to stand on the platform and actually standing on it were two very different things. I now stood facing and clinging to the tree. The platform was hardly some kind of luxurious space one would want to spend a sunny afternoon picnicking on, but instead it was practically nonexistent (barely bigger than a skateboard deck) and therefore terrifying. I was sure I was going to die. Never mind the fact that I was fully secured in a climbing harness with four people on the ground holding the rope that would hold me if I fell—I was absolutely sure I would be dying in the next few moments. All I wanted to do was to send a number of ripe and juicy expletives Patrick's way for making it so damn easy for me to get up here. However, I knew I couldn't blame him, because I had signed up for this very moment six months earlier when I first met him and saw the power and grace of his Being. I'd casually said to him, "I want what you have." He suggested I come do a leadership course with him, and so I did. That's how special Patrick Ryan's teachings are—you will find your Self in their presence for only a few moments and immediately be ready to face your biggest, oldest, most unhelpful unconscious beliefs about your life.

Standing on that platform, I had no idea how I was going to turn around and do what I needed to do to finish the exercise, which was to walk out onto a plank and jump off the end of it. My mind was blank. My body was petrified. My heart was beating a million miles an hour. And so I asked for help. "Patrick, how do I turn around?" A second nature action that people do every day without thinking now completely eluded me. "Turn your feet to the right," he said calmly. And so I did, and there I was, turned around facing away from the tree and looking out into the most beautiful redwood forest. That's how paradigm-shattering Patrick's teachings are: he helps you to take a step toward the direction you want to go, and before you know it, a whole new view opens up.

But next came the moment of truth. I was now forty feet up, on a tiny platform, and I knew that I was here because I really, really wanted to learn something once and for all—that my fear about my life was an illusion. And so I looked down at Patrick and said, "My fear, right in this moment, my fear, it's just an illusion, right? It just isn't real, is it?" And he said, "Yes, Kelly, it is just an illusion. You are perfectly safe." That is how powerful Patrick's teachings are—they will unflinchingly stand toe to toe with you on the brink of the biggest aha moment of your life. He will tell you the truth so that you can finally be free.

I then made my way out to the end of that plank and jumped out and into the air, changing my life forever—just another day with Patrick and his teachings.

Even though you won't be physically climbing up any redwood trees with Patrick while reading this book, you will be metaphorically. Reading this book is like having Patrick, with all his deep compassion, great wisdom, and fierce commitment, at your side calling you forth towards your awakened life. His Awakened Wisdom will teach you how to connect with your highest self, maintain that connection, and create a path guided by the highest self so that you can finally live the big life that you know you were put here to live. I know this because I have worked with his Awakened Wisdom model and it helps me daily. It keeps me clear, on track, and moving forward. I am thrilled that it is now available for the whole world to take in and be transformed by.

—Kelly Carlin-McCall, writer, performer, change agent
September 2009

PART ONE

Being Human

A Prayer to Open

I acknowledge great Divine, creator of the Universe
That we are in a Dance of interrelatedness together
Deeply connected, in fact, we are One
It is your brilliance that shines through me
I am re-membering the brilliance, the luster,
The radiance of the diamond that we create together
I am learning how to open
To the full brilliance of that which we are
I know that in this and every moment
You are speaking to me and
Through me and through us All
Together we are unfolding a great, great story
Its full expression is a mystery to me
And that is why I must listen in each moment
As you inform me about what is needed—Now
We humans are blessed that among your creatures
We alone can look forward into future time
A gift we have as the Universe's collaborators
Calling the future into being
Dreams come true when we adventure together
Partners revealing the greatest story of All
Spiraling through infinite space and no time
We play our part, might as well play it well

As this Earth is our craft on which we ride
Let us care for her as if our survival depended
On her well being and happiness
To that end may I learn to be present and brave
For it is only in the present that the truth can be known
Let me be clear, connected, bright, and available
So that I may hear her Gaia-Dance
My part is to engage my influence wisely
Together, every thought matters, yours and mine
Synergistic worlds moving as One
Now is the time to move as one wise people
The people of this planet, One with All beings
Listening to the whisper of the Universe's song
The resonating wisdom field guides and waits
For our intention to activate the energetic response
And it caresses us with compassion and healing
If only we would receive, we are always held
A song sung through all God's creatures
Respond to her call as the Old Ones knew how
Let this prayer carry my breath, my words, my actions
In Beauty with Life-Giving intention for All,
I serve you, The Divine, now, and always!

—Patrick Ryan

INTRODUCTION
A Life Well-Lived

*I*magine a life through which you managed to rise above the fears and concerns that always linger faithfully in the background, haunting us with their song of intended safety, always with the purpose of keeping the status quo. Imagine a life without those messages you tell your Self about what you can't do, or those messages that diminish the brilliance of who you are in any way. You know the voice I mean.

Imagine that you integrated those voices in such a way that they no longer gripped you, but rather informed you about interesting and relevant conditions to pay attention to.

And now, as you are no longer held in false constraints, you are free. Free to listen and respond to the wisdom of the moment. Free to wonder what is possible in creating more beauty and dreams. Free to respond to the yearning of your heart that knows that more is possible.

This is the wisdom that informs you through every beat of your heart, through every thought of inspiration, and through your body that responds to the world around you as a drum responds to the vibration of the room while resting, waiting for the drummer to pick it up and bring its beat to life.

To have all this, you must be willing to respond.

You must be willing to risk shaking up your world and the world of those around you for the sake of something greater than your Self.

You must be willing to risk losing that which seems precious to you. Holding on to anything is futile. If it is still right for you, it will stay; and if it is no longer serving you, holding it will only delay the inevitable. And worry not, because you were never in control of those things anyway.

Allowing good things to pass through your life keeps the possibilities open for other good things to come in—and come in they will, if there is space, an opening.

You must be willing to engage in the dance of life with flexibility and compassion, and as you move you may dance in-joy. Stay in the game and turn it over at the same time. Turn it over to this great Universe that we live in. Invite it in and listen to the call. Like the call and response of a great drum circle. This is the call that informs you that now is the time to move, now is the time for you to commit to one more step towards that dream that is relentlessly calling you into it.

And why not? Did you think it could wait for another day?

How to Use this Book

This book is intended to be a guide to being an awakened human. In the Buddhist tradition, the diamond represents the hidden potential within. In order to bring the diamond to its full brilliance, it must be shaped, cut, and polished. That is what the journey of this life does for us. It provides us the opportunities to develop our Selves. To reclaim the brilliance that already is within us. We are born complete and whole, and we must learn how to be all that we already are.

The path of awakening is a journey through self-development and conscious daily living. I suggest that you read this book through at least once from cover to cover, so that you have a sense of the wholeness of its content. After that, you can use Part Two; Eight States of an Awakened Life, as an assessment tool and guide to determine where there are opportunities for Self-development. The Buddha taught that the most challenging thing to change is your Self.

To change your Self you must first know your Self. Be honest with your Self as you engage with the ideas of this book. Every one of us has much work to do in developing our Self to higher and higher states of being. Yes, it takes effort. I can assure you it is worth it.

Enter the Dream

I am inviting you into a dream. I do know that it is both my dream and the Universe's dream working on and through me. It is exciting that both are often true at the same time. It is a dream that I know a lot of you share with me. I know that because many of you have told me so. When a dream is shared and held dearly by so many, it becomes more like a prophesy than a dream.

Perhaps a prophesy is a dream that is being called in with the conviction and daring of the dreamer who says, "It will be so!"

It is a dream that has been informed by the collective wisdom that is offered to us all through the Wisdom Field, which I write about later in this book.

This is a dream that I have committed the entirety of my life to. It has stirred in me for years, and in retrospect I can see how my journey of the last few decades has prepared me so that I can serve this dream fully.

Let me share a bit about my journey, so that you have a sense of the perspective from which I write. When I was a teenager, I was called and compelled to walk far down into a dark and troubled valley. As I traveled down through the spiral, I knew at one level it was of my own making, and at the same time, from a higher place, that I was being mysteriously guided and called down a path of initiation. It was a path that took me directly to my own death, literally.

In the experience of that death, which I write more about later on, I was given a transmission of love so great and deep that I have never known the likes of it in any other experience in this life. It was the love of the Divine. The love that holds us all in every moment. The love that just is, and that we humans have to learn how to find our way back to our full and open relationship with. In that experience of dying, I got to know that part of me that is my Soul, distinct from the other aspects of my being that are of the body and mind and heart. I knew that experience would alter the course of my life forever. It did.

After that I found my Self on a path of healing—healing myself and, when I was ready, healing others.

As I moved forward from the death experience, I resolved my Self to follow a turn in the path. I had followed the shadow side as far as I could go and it was now clear to me that I had a lot to learn about walking a path of light.

To make my way in the world, I embraced the way of an entrepreneur and I created several different businesses. Through each one, regardless of the trade it was in, I was most interested in learning about how to be human. I sought out courses and teachers while I my Self stumbled and flew through daily adventures. Understanding the link between humanness and spirit was paramount to me.

One day I was sitting in my office (at that time I was happily running a successful real estate business) when I felt a calling from within. I knew it was important, so I left the business and the life that I had created around it and off I went—to where, I knew not.

The calling led me into the gates of a monastery in Burma (Myanmar), and though I expected to come and go after a few days of meditation, I ended up becoming a Buddhist monk at the invitation of an enlightened master who headed that particular monastery. I knew him respectfully as Sayadaw, a term given to the head of a monastery. He became a powerful influence on the course of my life.

After a year of immersion in an experience that grew more incredible with each passing day, Sayadaw and I both felt it was time for me to move out into the world. One day Sayadaw called me into a meeting to discuss what would be next. He suggested I go out to any place on the planet according to my choosing and that he would support me in creating a monastic center through which, he suggested, I could pass on the teachings with which I had been blessed.

I considered his generous offer. It seemed surreal to even imagine such a path. After a time of contemplating this opportunity, I felt I had to respectfully decline. I felt my path was to walk more as a human, as a layperson, as one who had to find his way through this life in the small "r" real world. I felt very resonantly that I could be of greater service walking a more ordinary walk. Sayadaw respected my choice and then sent me off, back into the regular world.

I eventually found my way back to North America after a time in Nepal and India. One thing led to another and I became a life coach and then a trainer of coaches worldwide, a leadership developer, an author, a husband, and a householder.

I love the life I am living and I feel blessed every day with the challenges of daily life. I have committed my path to serving the awakening of all humans. We each have a part to play in this awakening. I do not claim any particular level of achievement in this. I continue to make mistakes, to sometimes say the wrong thing, or occasionally hurt people in unintended ways. One thing I can claim is to be a hungry learner, and as such I know that my path today is one that reflects the integration of a life of lessons learned.

Over the years, even long before I became a monk, strangers would wander into my stores and businesses and ask me if I would support their healing. I never claimed any particular skill in that area, nor did I ever represent my Self as a healer, and yet people kept coming in off the street and asking nonetheless. So, as is part of the message of this book, I finally gave up my resistance to the calling.

My specialty is healing hearts—and there are more than a few broken hearts out there. Our hearts get broken when we are young, when we are taking the first steps of being human, when we are open and vulnerable. Our hearts still get broken when we are old. There are many different types of breaking. Most of the wounding results from our first relationships with well-meaning people—parents, family, others who are around us in that precious time—who become agents of the Universe in this service. They play their part in this, usually with good intention, and still the breaking of hearts happens, wounding happens. And then, in order to avoid being hurt or disappointed again, we create behaviors based on the illusions of what is needed to protect our Selves and to survive. We simply want to ensure that we won't get hurt again. Ironically, those very survival strategies separate us from fully experiencing life.

I do know that there is a purpose to this life. I know that ultimately that purpose is a great mystery. I know that there are some experiences that are shared by most humans everywhere. And so, as much as part of me would like to spare everyone from those woundings of childhood, I also believe that those experiences are part of why we are here in this human journey.

We are born as spirit entering into an animal body, flesh and blood, and the result is human.

It has always struck me as important to notice that regardless of how many generations of humans have gone before us, each new one of us has to learn how to be human. We each have to go through the journey.

WHAT IS IT TO BE HUMAN?

Author and mythologist Joseph Campbell talked about how, in the journey of a human, the first part of life is about the ego forming itself, having its worldly experiences, collecting its resources and skills; then, at some point in the journey, the Soul reveals itself more fully to the ego and asks it to align itself to the service of the Soul.

This book is intended to support all humans along that journey. No matter where you are now. Nothing can save you from the necessary bumps, falls, victories, and wins of your journey. You will have to find your own way through.

As you move through this life you will be engaging in the development of your Soul and that leads us back to the mystery. The ultimate point of it all.

I know from my own direct experience of dying that the point of this life is not for the sake of just this life, but for the sake of something beyond it. I cannot prove this and yet I know it. Most of you know it as well.

I hope that the offering of this book will support you in being human. It provides some context for parts of the experience that we all share. I have been privileged and gifted with the opportunities to receive from great teachers all over this world—from the prairies of Canada to the monasteries of Burma (Myanmar) and other parts of Asia to wise people in North Africa, the Middle East, Europe, and Central and North America. My journey has taken me far out so that I could find my way home. Home to the heart.

I am deeply called to being in service to the Great Awakening that I believe is already happening on this planet. As Winston Churchill said, "The night is darkest just before the dawn." We are very near the dawn.

I feel it and so do a great many others.

There is a way to walk on this planet. It is the walk of an Awakened One. It is the walk of one who is aware of our interrelatedness, who is present, who is willing to look out beyond themselves and to ask, "What is needed?"

There are many humans who are asking that question right now. They are courageously changing their lives in response to the wisdom that they receive as they dare to look out and ask.

THIS IS THE WAY OF AN AWAKENED ONE

Over these last years I have sat in hundreds of circles that have held many thousands of these people. These circles have taken place in small villages and big cities, in Eastern monasteries and Western training rooms, in small businesses and large organizations, and everywhere in between. Humans everywhere are asking each other, "What is going on? What can we do? Who do we need to be now, in this moment?" These are great questions. They will lead us somewhere.

A great awakening is upon us, it is happening, and it is good.

As for why I choose to write this book, I can only tell you that it was as though this book dance-hammered its way through me. It insisted on being written, and I have to the best of my ability listened and responded according to how I believe this story wants to be told. It is my hope that it becomes a useful offering that supports the unfolding of our collective journey.

That journey is a day-to-day, moment-by-moment walk. I am inviting you not to consider this walk as something you do, but rather as something you give your Self over to—that you become the walk, be in each experience, each idea, each feeling—and through that, that you encounter every aspect of your being, so that in the presence of each moment you fall in love with all the many facets of the diamond that you are. In the native traditions, the word *medicine* refers to our wholeness. As humans, we are on the quest of reclaiming the wholeness of who we are. In order to do that, we must come to love all aspects of our Selves. So perhaps it might be said that the point of this book is to serve as a guide back to love. It is the brilliance of love that heals. It is the brilliance of our wholeness that, after all is said and done, is all that matters.

Having said all that, as my Burmese teacher, the Venerable Sayadaw Thin Bury, once told me, "Take what works and leave the rest here."

WHAT IS AN AWAKENED LIFE?

"An Awakened Life is one in which you are present to the joy and possibility that each moment holds. You are the author of your life. You are actively engaged in creating and manifesting the people, relationships, purpose, resources, and quality of life that you desire according to your highest wisdom.

In an Awakened Life you are open and present to the interrelatedness of All. You are the Oneness. You therefore create through intention that is in alignment with the greatest good for All.

In an Awakened Life you understand that you are able to respond in a good way to what happens in all aspects of your life. You are in a moment-by-moment dance with the Universe around you.

In an Awakened Life you understand that living from the wisdom and energy of your Divine Essence is a choice. When you make a choice from your Divine Essence, it will be a choice made with gratitude and appreciation for all that is present in your life, including the challenging stuff.

In an Awakened Life you actively create beauty through each and every thought, word, and action."

—*www.AwakenedWisdom.com*

The Journey

I should warn you at this time that to read any further is to pass the point of no return. To look any deeper into the mystery of who you are as a human in relationship to this Universe is to assume your role and responsibility in the ever-unfolding story of this Universe.

I invite you into the opportunity of co-creating your journey. You and the Universe, which is the creation of the Divine, are in a dance together. Who you are and how you show up as the dancer has a profound effect on what gets created from each and every step.

Look around at the life you are living. I hope that much of it is good and according to your dreams. For some of you, that may not be the case. While some of you are pinching your Self about how well it is all going, others woke up one day and looked around and wondered how you got to where you are. Either way, there is much to learn about how to create the path ahead according to your highest wisdom. The life you are living today is the result of seeds you planted in the past, and so it goes that in this moment, today, you are seeding the future according to your intentions, words, and actions. Understanding the blessing of this, rather than getting too significant about it all, will allow you to accept this idea with grace, ease, and delight.

We are all on a journey. The only destination is to the heart. The heart beats in the present moment of now, and in this moment all our hearts touch the Divine as One. Now is home, our heart is home, connection with each other is home. It is only in the Now that we can rest freed from the struggle of illusion and the illusion of struggle.

To walk the walk of an awakened human is to live your life according to the wisdom of your heart, your body, and your mind. The path of heart is one of openness, courage, and facing into the experience of the present. The heart is the portal of connection to all beings. It is through the heart that we know we are all One. In our heart we know that kindness is a natural state of being. Any form of meanness requires a closing off of the heart, a shutting down of connection. It is only when we think we are separate or different from each other that we can do harm. When our heart is open and we are present in the moment, we experience the beauty of knowing each other as One. We are all journeying along a path of development. As we do, we are learning how to be human, and as humans we are remembering how to be Divine.

The mind in the moment of now is presence. In a state of presence, the mind is freed from distracting concerns and it can rest in quiet appreciation. A worried mind is not present to now; it is instead preoccupied with past and future events that have been imagined or remembered. In presence, the mind knows the difference between what truly needs its attention versus what is distraction. The mind is like a wild animal that runs around afraid to sit still for fear of imagined threats. It is only through practice, gentleness, and compassion that the mind learns that it is okay to be still. With practice we can learn how to be of still mind in an engaged way.

A way that is fully connected to the moment-by-moment journey with appreciation and life-giving intention.

Learning how to tame the mind is a good practice, and it is not for the sake of the practice itself but rather for the sake of connection to the Divine and all the beauty that is around us in each moment. It is for the sake of freeing our Selves from illusions and to become present to what is before us, in connection, right now and now and now.

Our body exists in the moment of now. Our muscles, bones, joints, and organs respond in each moment according to what is needed. Our body is always present to us even if we are not always present to it. Our body holds an amazing intelligence that informs us moment-by-moment to what is here now. It is a precious gift of human life that we have a body. It is through our body that we can know pleasure, and also pain.

For many of us, being aware and connected to our body is not so easily done, and so we must learn how to attune to its language. With effort we can learn how to respond to our body's signals. Our body is the carriage temple that carries us through this life and allows us to have the experience of being human. Our bodies are animal nature and our Souls are Divine nature. It is through our bodies that animal meets Divine and we have the unique experience of being human. In return we have the responsibility to care for our bodies; if we ignore this, it is to our peril. As a source of wisdom, we must all learn to open up more and more to what our bodies are telling us in each moment.

These three aspects of who we are—our hearts, our minds, and our bodies—combine to make up the human side of this great journey. Together they provide us the opportunity to develop our Souls and to grow according to the nature of our experience. It may be that the essential purpose of this life is in service of our Soul's development.

The Soul's development requires that we humans have the full range of experiences, from the anguish of deep valleys to the triumph of brilliant moments. It is the moment-by-moment unfolding of our journey that develops our Soul. Our journey is affected by the choices we make in response to the opportunities and challenges that the Universe presents.

Being an awakened human offers us the opportunity to be in choice as we move through our journey each day. Part of what we will be looking at in this book is how to discern different aspects of our consciousness—our Divine Essence and our Distorted Self—and to make choices according to our own greatest wisdom.

Together, in this exact moment, we are experiencing the unfolding story of this Universe. Together we spiral through the cosmos on the great planet Earth. We are being asked by the Universe to be conscious of the role we play in creating the day-to-day story of our journey together. As humans, we are privileged to have this life, and at the same time we have a responsibility that goes beyond that of other beings, such as other animals. This is because we are capable of a level of consciousness that has us be aware of the world we are in and the life we are living, and then to make choices that affect all beings. It is through us humans that spirit meets animal. It is the consciousness that is created from the merging of Soul and flesh that provides us with such a vibrant experience of mind, body, and heart. It is through this awareness that we are capable of experiencing joy or love, which may ultimately be the reason we are here. Joy is present in every moment regardless of the situation. Joy is experiencing the presence of our Soul through each of life's moments, even the tragic ones.

When we touch into the joy that is in each moment, we shine our light and become beacons of the Universe's light, healing energy, and wisdom.

To walk the walk of an awakened human requires a direct experience of life. We make mistakes, we learn. We are brilliant, we learn. We succeed, we learn. We fail, we learn. We humans are learning beings in every aspect of our experience.

The Greek word *gnosis* means to know through direct experience. Gnosis is a kind of knowing that cannot be taught or learned by reading a book or by being told something by somebody else. It is the result of living and experiencing and asking your Self what is here for you to know, through direct experience, in this moment.

The point of knowing is not just for the sake of knowing. The point of experience is not just for the sake of the experience. The point is for us to become that which we know and experience.

When I speak of knowing and experience, I mean to know the real truth rather than the illusions. The real knowing is to know our Oneness. The real experience is to experience Oneness. To know and experience Oneness is to become One. As we become One, we draw as close as is humanly possible to the Divine.

TO BECOME THAT WHICH WE EXPERIENCE IS TO BECOME ONE

The journey is for us to approach the Divine, to come to the One, to be a point of light that is of the source—not separate from, but rather as one aspect of the Universe. We are the embodiment of spirit and much of our journey here in this life is about returning to the Divine.

Despite what some of us believe about our lives, the future is not yet written for any of us. We are required to live out our lives, make our choices, have our experiences, and put effort into awakening our Selves.

It is through the struggle and the joy of life that we transform our Selves into brilliant points of light and heart energy.

Over the course of our lives, we learn how to live more and more fully as Divine beings. As we do, we learn to adjust our behavior to be congruent with our Divine Essence's wisdom. This is a path of opening—to love, to joy, to trust, to each other, to our Self.

In this book, we will explore the three primary forms of human intelligence—heart intelligence, mind intelligence, and body intelligence—that we have the most direct access to.

The heart intelligence knows through connection and relationship. That is connection to Self, others, and the world around us—or through the lack of those. Our heart intelligence is affected by the stories we create through our mind intelligence, as well as the memories stored in our body intelligence.

While the heart opens to allow the experience of Oneness, the mind uses the concept of Self as a way to orient, to have a reference point, to be able to observe. It is a real paradox that we are One, yet we mostly experience this life journey as a Self that is moving through it.

The mind intelligence uses the perspective of Self as a way of understanding, and in doing so creates stories that it tells through us. These stories often create the illusion of separation from the Universe and from each other. The illusion of separation leads to much of our suffering. When we are aware of our Oneness with Source, with God, there is no suffering.

The body intelligence holds physical memory and has the capacity to sense into the present moment for what is true now. The memory that is stored in our bodies is held in our body water like an energy charge. Our bodies store muscle memory as well as emotional memory. It is through the water system of our body that our emotional memory energy is conducted from cell to cell.

All three of these centers of intelligence affect each other, so that we relive the stories of the past, mixed in with this moment of now, we shape our present experience.

Living through life's illusions is the way many of us experience our day-to-day world—until finally, in our own time, we reach a point, usually quite unexpectedly, where we are open to the idea of transcending all the stored learning along with the cares and concerns of the mind, heart, and body intelligences.

*Transcendence allows us to peek through the mist and realize
that any sense of separation is an illusion.*

Transcendence is not as elusive as it might seem. It is, in fact, a state of profound joy that lives in the center of each moment—and is always available. It happens in any moment when the mind discovers what the heart knew all along and the body says, "Thanks for finally getting the obvious"—that there is no you and me, no them and us, no otherness at all. It is in any moment when the body lets go of holding the old stuff, when the pathway of the mind is freed from the stories, and when all is connected through the portal of the heart into the Universal Oneness.

What a moment of joy it is when we have a direct experience of the Divine Oneness! We have all known this connection before. We knew this joy before we were given the mission to be humans in service to our Soul's development and to the unfolding story of this Universe. It is the joy that a baby knows when it enters this world. It is the joy that a wise elder knows when death is near, when they're ready to cross back over, to be reunited, in-joy, again.

WHO ARE WE ANYWAY?

We humans are complex beings. We are biological in our physical structure. As such have to care for our bodies. Our physical bodies permit a direct sensory experience of our walk in this life. Our bodies experience pleasant events as well as unpleasant ones. Our bodies are the vehicle that carries us through each moment. All of this develops a body intelligence that informs us about our life and what is needed.

The processor of our mind intelligence is our brain. We are gifted with a brain that enables us to learn. We develop mind intelligence. Out of our daily life experiences we develop our stories and behaviors, and shape our life experience accordingly. When we use our minds for creating good and beauty in the world, it is an amazing use of our genius. Oftentimes, however, we use our minds to create separation and suffering for others and our Selves. When we do, we are sadly missing the truth of this life.

We are born with a heart wisdom that, along with our body and mind wisdom, connects us to Universal wisdom. As we go through life, each experience provides an emotional record of what it is to be human. When we are emotionally injured, we learn to protect our Selves. We do this by closing off our hearts and avoiding situations that might lead to discomfort. As a result, we often end up cutting our Selves off from one another. We then have to learn how to reopen the heart connection to that lost wisdom. As we learn to live, in trust and love, we open our hearts, experiencing the connection to All more and more.

As emotional beings, we are capable of great compassion, empathy, and communion with other beings. We are also capable of living in anger and rage. As awakened beings, we become able to choose about fully experiencing and influencing our emotional experience.

All of these aspects—the heart intelligence, mind intelligence, and body intelligence—combine to create a field of energy around us. That field holds a tremendous amount of information about who and how we are.

We are embodied spirit, universal consciousness, and we are having a direct experience of this. We are individuals, we are community members, we are diverse, and we are all One. Any sense we hold—of separateness, aloneness, or isolation—is an illusion—one that we must learn to dispel in order to know the joy that is available in each moment.

Let's align around some concepts about who we are and how we operate as humans before going any further. It would be useful to have some common jargon, words that clarify what we are speaking about. It is also necessary to create some context for the Universe we live in. Beginner's mind is useful here so that we might proceed with an open heart, mind, and body and be available to an even deeper knowing of these ideas than we already have.

THE DIVINE

When I refer to Divine, I am referring to the highest on high. To God. The Divine is that amazing Essence that we humans do not have the capacity to fully comprehend. All we can do is to approach the Divine as closely as possible.

> *We will never fully know or understand what the Divine truly or wholly is.*

In Hinduism there is a teaching that points us to understanding that knowing the Divine precisely is not possible for our human capacity, so the closest we can come to the Divine is through knowing what it is not. The practice is called Neti Neti, meaning "it is not this, it is not that." We can point to anything in our human experience and ask, "Is that the Divine?" The answer will be, "No, not that."

Throughout this book, I refer to the Divine. I also refer to the Divine Essence—that aspect within us, from the human side of experience, that approaches the Divine and yet will always be something different—no, not that.

THE UNIVERSE

The Universe is the manifested creation of the Divine. The Uni–Verse. *Uni* meaning "one" and *verse* meaning "to turn into." *To turn into one.* The Universe is not the Divine, it is the expression of the Divine. It is the creation of the Divine and we humans are part of the Universe. The Universe includes all that we humans can comprehend in whatever way we can. Anything that we can be or experience through our hearts, minds, or bodies is of the Universe. The stars, the galaxies, beings of every kind, the ideas of past, present and future, and all energy—all are aspects of the Universe.

We experience the Divine through the Universe in which we live.

FROM STARDUST TO HUMAN— HOW THE UNIVERSE CREATES THROUGH US

Let's take a meta-view of who or what we are, how we got here, and what is possible in our Universe. The creation of this Universe came first. Creation progressed and the Universe expanded out as stars, planets, and other phenomena. Things were created, destroyed, and created again. As this process continued, the ingredients of those stars and planets were recycled over and over subjected to intense forces. These ingredients were shaped and reshaped into new iterations of celestial forms, eventually leading to the creation of planet Earth herself. This is the alchemy of the Universe at work.

On this Earth, as the planet coalesced, the simplest life forms developed. Over a great period of time a variety of life forms came and went. Evolution and extinctions happened, and every form of life that was created came from the very same materials that initially formed the stars and planets themselves. From the dust, the minerals, and the elements evolved the building blocks of form that became the crucibles for life. This alchemical nature of the Universe used energy and base materials to ultimately create life forms.

Now, just for fun, and because it is true, let's call those building materials stardust.

Somehow, and exactly how still remains a mystery, we humans showed up. Stardust turned into organs and bones, and a human form came about.

We became one of the current expressions of the consciousness of the Universe. Over tens of thousands of years, we've continued developing our personal and collective consciousnesses to where we are now.

So here we are—humans made of stardust formed into human bodies, and consciousness—the spirit of the Universe embodied. It is through us that the Universe expresses itself. The Universe's desires and dreams are being actuated through us humans. Can you consider that we are being dreamed up by the Universe to unfold its ongoing story, carrying its destiny forward? We are called and moved through the expression of our life purpose to create—and what we create is on behalf of the Universe's dream.

As is true of other forces in the Universe, we embody both the greatest capacity for creating beauty, and we can be the source of the most outrageous violence. While other aspects of the Universe appear to be guided more strictly by laws of physics and science, we humans witness, learn, and come to have an understanding of the process of the creation of the stars, planets, and galaxies. We are the Universe observing and experiencing itself through our human and collective consciousness.

One thing that distinguishes us from other creations is the fact that we have the capacity to consciously choose between creating beauty or violence. We are more than a force of nature at the mercy of the laws of physics. We are sentient beings. We are choosers.

As the human species has developed itself as a collective, it has also developed a shared field of consciousness—one that knows we are all contributors to, members of, and completely one with everything else. This shared field of consciousness is the greater expression of humans and the Universe. As we are the expression of the Universe, it follows that the collective field of consciousness is holding the Universal wisdom.

We have an opportunity now, different from any time that has come before, to be more and more present to this Wisdom Field of consciousness. Through that connection, we are and will be informed about what is trying to happen in the Universe. We can choose to follow the field of Universal wisdom according to what is revealed through our own individual connection to that field. That is, we can tap into this Wisdom Field if we listen and open our Selves to this most amazing resource of intelligence.

Follow the trend of celestial formation—from star formation to earliest life creation to the eventual development of humans. Here we are now.

Here we are, not only with our capacity to create beauty, but to be awed by our creation—to be stunned by it, to be caught and held by it. We can give our Selves over to the open-hearted wide-eyed gaze of a child, or we can be awed by the delicate weaving of the petals of a mountain flower. Understand that all passage of time, from the very beginning of the creation of the Universe, leads to this particular moment before you. In this one moment, you may choose to express love and appreciation for another.

Or perhaps you will go for a walk and delight in a moment of awe as you witness something beautiful and fleeting. That is what I mean by the trend of the Universe being towards beauty. Yes, some of us are still given to violence, but this is not the trend. As we choose to move towards beauty, those who would still choose violence will be the last holdouts of something that is passing. We humans can choose to be the creators of beauty rather than the creators of destruction.

It is a choice we must make every day—the choice to be the source of beauty in every moment. Whether it's the beauty of a simple smile to a stranger, or a calling to create the next Taj Mahal. Simple or complex is not the point. Creating beauty is.

The Wisdom Field

Each of us creates a field of energy that emanates from us. Our brain contributes its own field, our heart another. In fact, every organ of the body has an energy field. The cells of our body and our emotional system also create energy fields. We are able to read and measure many of these fields with modern technology. Some people are even able to visually see these fields as auras under the right conditions.

All of these smaller fields combine to create a system of energy around each of us. Every being—whatever human, plant, animal, fish, insect, mineral—has a field. There is very little understood about this field, however. Some speculate that even our memories exist in the field, rather than contained somewhere in our brains.

When I was a monk, I experienced some incredible field-related events that I cannot prove or explain. At times, after prolonged meditation experiences, I was opened to sensory awareness of the field. I could see it and feel it in and around other people, plants, and animals.

I have led many intense group processes over the years. There I witnessed and was part of healings and other breakthroughs among the participants and my Self. Many of those events can only be explained in the context of a field that connected us all.

As of now I am left to imagine, to trust my intuition, and to notice my direct experiences with the field, as I attempt to understand how it works.

As our fields connect, they create a system together. This is a larger Wisdom Field that is contributed to and shared by us all.

In a hologram, each part holds the whole image. In the same way, we each hold the entire structure of the Universe within us, within our DNA. We are the Universe. We are also all part of an interrelated field of energy, wisdom, and information which we are each contributing to and drawing from. The aggregate of all the fields is the Wisdom Field, that connects us all.

In this very moment, you are immersed in a wide variety of fields of collective information and consciousness. These fields are repositories of developing information, dreams, and collective wisdom.

There is a blend that happens between the information that is available in the field and our readiness and ability to access and understand it. Certain people are better positioned to pick up on different offerings contained within the field by virtue of their professional training, openness, and the relevance to the path they are on. Oftentimes many people pick up on something that is in the field, but only a few are positioned to leverage what's available to be received.

For example, if there is a new technology that is emerging, the wisdom of that technology is likely held in the Wisdom Field. Although we are all in the field, we are not all able to comprehend the information that is available. Among those who can receive and comprehend the information, there may be only a small group that has the resources and opportunity to do anything with the information.

That is the synchronicity between the path of the human who is best positioned to follow through on the opportunities, and what the Universe is wanting to have happen at any given time.

As a group, all beings create these fields. There is a field of wisdom among your family, your community, your workplace, your city, country, and the planet as whole. There are fields of wisdom that are shared and contributed to by forests, wildlife, fish groups, plants, and more. There are contributions to the fields of intelligence that are more Universal in their nature, as well.

Animals are open and connected to these fields. I am sure you have witnessed flocks of birds or schools of fish or herds of animals that move and respond to something all in the same instant. This is an example of the way their field informs them. Animals have been known to become restless before an event such as an earthquake, or even to grow their winter fur according to an inner sense of their surroundings. This information all lives in the Wisdom Field.

These fields are shared by all beings that are on resonant frequencies. The members are able to contribute to and listen to their respective fields, as well as any other fields they can attune to. We humans may develop the ability and capacity to tune in to these fields more fully as well.

All beings contribute to the Wisdom Field.

You move through and with all these fields in every moment of your life. They hold important information about what is going on right now, as well as about what is trying to happen. We must learn to listen to the information of these fields. We humans can experience them through each of our intelligences. These fields inform our own wisdom.

Some of them are the aggregate of the voices of fear, while others are the collective of people's prayers. Still others are the whisperings of new ideas that want to be realized.

These fields, tuned to different frequencies, are present in every moment according to how they are being fed into by all beings—certainly not just humans.

Imagine them like the ultimate wireless hook up. We are sending thoughts, ideas, emotions and more into the field in every moment. We have the ability to receive the information contained in these fields through each of our three intelligences. Everyone has a greater or lesser ability to receive the information in the Wisdom Fields according to their willingness and their practice.

Each of us has stronger access to one of our three intelligences and its connection to the field than we do to the other two. Everyone of us, however, can learn to maximize all three. All three intelligences are discussed in greater detail later. For now, let's just touch upon each of them briefly, as they relate to the Wisdom Field.

THE WISDOM FIELD AND HEART INTELLIGENCE: INTUITION

Our heart intelligence is one way for us to access the Wisdom Field. This is what we know as intuition. Our heart intelligence receives impressions of other beings and people, the environment we are in, the state of being of those around us, as well as many other types of wisdom that are held in the Wisdom Field.

When we are in a Good State of Being (discussed in Part Two) and our heart is open, we are better able to receive and process this intuitive information.

THE WISDOM FIELD AND MIND INTELLIGENCE: PERCEPTION

When we receive information from the Wisdom Field through

our mind intelligence, we perceive what is available to be known. Our mind is a great observer of what is. Through our mind we read into situations and combine our perceptions with information that is gleaned from the Wisdom Field.

THE WISDOM FIELD AND BODY INTELLIGENCE: SENSING

We also receive information from the Wisdom Field through our bodies. When we receive through our bodies, we are sensing the surrounding information. When we are aware of the state of our bodies, we are better able to realize the wisdom that is coming through. In order to do this at a high level, it helps to maintain healthy body awareness.

WISDOM FIELD CHANNELS

While there are many different channels of information available in any given moment, we do not have the capacity to take them in all at once. It is much like your TV, in that it works best when it selects a channel and tunes into it. Over time we develop the ability and capacity to tune in and tune out according to what is needed.

We can learn to tap into the Divine Wisdom Field, or we can tap into the Distorted Wisdom Field. Everything is vibration and we are no exception.

According to a variety of factors, such as our body health, our emotional well-being, how rested we are, and our diet, we can shift the frequency at which we personally vibrate.

The biggest influence on this has to do with whether we choose to be in our Divine Essence and to live in a Good State of Being, rather than to live according to the whims of our Distorted Selves. (The difference between these two states will also be covered later.) This can cause an instantaneous shift in our frequency and attunement.

We are like tuning forks in that we resonate with others who are operating at the same frequency as we are. At different stages of our life we tend to inhabit certain frequency ranges, which puts us into closer attunement to some channels as opposed to others. If you put a group of tuning forks into a room together, the ones that are most closely matched will resonate with and activate each other.

For example, someone who is mostly run by their Distorted Self is in a dissonant frequency range. They may be preoccupied with fear. Fear is at a lower frequency than hope. People who live from a distorted place of fear attune themselves to the collective fears of the world. They are tapping into the collective field of frequency that is of fear-like energies. That person is not only receiving that lower frequency field, but they are also transmitting it, adding to the overall amplitude of that field.

Similarly, people who are living from their Divine Essence will resonate off one another. Only they will attract other Divine Essence beings and together they will add to each other's ability to sustain the presence of Divine Essence and its resonant fields.

The more people resonating with a certain field, the stronger that field becomes. In turn, the stronger that field, more people will tune into it.

We have all experienced what it is like when an entire nation is washed over with a field of fear. It feeds itself and draws more and more people and energy into it.

In those times, it takes more will and connection to Divine Essence to not be affected and to stay in the place of Divine Essence.

PRAYER FILLS THE WISDOM FIELD WITH INTENTION

There are countless stories of how people who are prayed for by others experienced spontaneous healing. It does happen.

When I was a monk in Burma, I would go into a meditative state with the intention of traveling around the world to visit people, as they occurred to me. Very often it was my family and friends, and sometimes it was people I had no memory of meeting. When I was with people in this way, I would call in healing energy for their bodies and hearts. As part of each session, I would create the intention of good will. Then I would invite in any and all connections to people that would occur to me, rather than directing my attention to specific people. I trusted that the healing meditation was useful to those who appeared in these sessions, that I was guided by the Wisdom Field to perform such meditations.

As well, along with all the monks in the monastery, I was part of long ceremonies of chanting over food. While we chanted, we held the intention that the food would be imbued with healing energy for those who ate it. Afterwards, the ceremonial food would then be distributed to people who were sick at a nearby hospital. The hospital staff had many stories about healings they had observed after the patients ate this food.

I believe that it was the Wisdom Field that connected the chanting and intentions to the food and then to the patients.

There is a growing body of studies that are showing very clearly that we share a connection, a field, between us all, and that we can add our intention, as we do when we pray or meditate, to the field in order to influence an event such as healing or crime reduction.

One documented example of this happened in 1993. A study reported by the Institute of Science, Technology, and Public Policy in Washington, DC, measured the effect of a large group of participants meditating on the crime rate of the DC area. It was found that the more meditators who participated, the greater the reduction in violent crimes during the time of the study.

When we create intentions, we are connected to the object of those intentions through the Wisdom Field. When you pray for someone your prayer is carried through the Wisdom Field. The Universe then aligns itself according to many known and unknown factors to manifest what is being intended.

HOW DID WE GET SEPARATED FROM THE WISDOM FIELD?

I believe there was time when tuning in and listening to the Wisdom Field was a natural part of daily living, though for most people it was an unconscious process most of the time.

About three to four hundred years ago, the knowledge base of the world shifted when so-called "modern" scientific principles were adopted. One of the biggest shifts was the way we began to view the world as the sum of its parts, and to view the parts as though they could be understood on their own, independent of one another. Everything was taken out of relationship out of its interrelatedness, seen only as a mechanical item that could be understood by cutting it up and then adding up the parts. In our quest for understanding, we abandoned some of what was intuitive and imaginative.

I do not need to know everything about how a car works to become a great driver, though the more I understand about the car, the more I can take the best advantage of all it has to offer.

One example of this is the wisdom versus the science around understanding intention. Every old and great religion, the repositories of ancient teachings, is filled with stories of creation that all start with intention and the spoken word. In fact, those teachings are so clear about the power of intention and words, that they are filled with dire warnings of what could happen if these principles are misused.

The effect of intention has been observable forever, yet science cannot prove nor disprove its power.

So all I am saying is that we ought to embrace our own personal wisdom on all of these ideas, and move forward in a good way. We will all benefit when most of the mysteries of the Universe have been proven. Until then, let's carry on with our own great experiment and learn more about how to stay open to and to harness our wisdom for good purposes.

We Are One

We are all One. So it follows that there are ways that we are bound together that defy explanation and proof. It is beyond the capacity of humans to fully understand the nature of the Universe, because that would entail fully understanding the nature of the Divine. We are lucky to have the opportunity of this life to eventually peek through the veils of illusion and come to know Oneness.

You only exist in the context of interrelatedness.

If there is no other, then it follows that there is no you. And, we humans still need the concept of Self to explain our Self to ourselves. We identify and explain our existence in terms of being and function: I am . . . I do . . . .

You are a part of the whole. You cannot be known out of the context of the whole, as there would be no you to know. It is only in the wholeness that you exist, and you seek to identify your Self in relation to where you are in the interrelatedness of all things.

Let's embrace the paradox of Oneness and Self to examine some of the aspects that make up who we are.

DIVINE ESSENCE

As the Divine is God, the Divine Essence is the closest we humans can aspire to in terms of getting close to God while living through our human experience. We can awaken to higher and higher levels, in approaching the Divine. But no matter what we think or feel the Divine is, however close we think we are coming to being like the Divine, the answer can only be: No, not quite that. The Divine is beyond that which we can fully know.

That is why I use the term Divine Essence to name the state of being that approximates the Divine. We aspire to emulate the essence of the Divine as best a human can. It is a great intention for how to take on the walk of Divine Essence. It will inform you about how to be in each moment of your journey. It will inform the many choices you must make in each day.

While you may know this aspect that resides in each of us as Higher Self, or some similar term, I am choosing not to use a name that has the concept of Self in it. As we get more fully into the state of Divine Essence, there is less and less Self in it. At some point, as we embody Divine Essence more and more, we come to know the Oneness of All. Then we are fully being our Divine Essence. That is as close to the Divine as is humanly possible to achieve while still in this life.

We are human, on our journey home, back to the Divine. The best we can work towards is an experience of the Divine, and attempt to emulate the Divine.

All of us have had moments in our lives when we've felt clear and connected to our Selves, those around us, and to our wisdom. If you recognize having had one of those moments, then you were most likely connected to your Divine Essence.

Divine Essence is that aspect of us that is clear, connected, open, resourceful, compassionate, wise, and joyful.

The Divine Essence is free from irrational fears, attachments, and aversions.

The Divine Essence is connected to, and one with, Universal

wisdom. The Divine Essence provides clarity and is connected to the "truth" of what is. We are talking about the real truth, not that which is imagined, illusionary, fabricated, or distorted.

The Divine Essence is not preoccupied with principles, egoist points, or being right, better than, less than, or anything that creates separation between beings.

The Divine Essence is connection, beauty, resonance, and congruence with the whole. The Divine Essence is in the present moment. Divine Essence is courageous, compassionate, generous, loving, and forgiving. Divine Essence experiences stillness.

The Divine Essence is our connection to the highest wisdom that is available in any given moment. As the Divine Essence is connected to Oneness, it is also able to recognize synchronicities (discussed in detail later on in this section)—coded messages and opportunities that the Universe is always sending to us.

Divine Essence is also willing to take risks. Therefore it moves and guides us through life in a way that supports us in having a full life experience. The Universe is always available to connection, as One with us, and the Divine Essence is the portal to connection with the Divine.

The full experience of Divine Essence is the closest we can reach as humans to the Divine.

DISTORTED SELF

Just as you've recognized the experience of moments when you've been in touch with Divine Essence, you will surely also be familiar with those moments when you've felt disconnected, angry, judgmental, confused, or victimized in relation to others or things that have happened to you.

We have all had those moments. They are indications that our Distorted Self has been activated. The use of the word Self here is accurate. The more we slip into a distorted state, the more we isolate into our Self. We create a chasm of separation between us and everyone and everything that could otherwise help us out of this state. The world becomes I versus you, we versus they. In a state of Distorted Self, we become victim or oppressor, superior or inferior, kinetic or comatose, distracted or afraid, unconscious or hyper-vigilant.

Distorted Self is an aspect of us that is commonly referred to as the inner critic, the committee, the saboteur, or the super ego. I will refer to it here as Distorted, or Distorted Self.

Have you ever looked into a mirror that's been bent and shaped to create a distorted reflection? Perhaps the mirror was curved to make you look very tall, or tilted in such a way as to make you look short or skinny or fat. You probably laughed when you saw your Self this way because you knew it wasn't an accurate depiction of who you are. That is what Distorted does.

It takes what is happening and changes it into something different. It creates a distorted view of what is. Distorted Self, therefore, uses misinformation to create paralysis, fear, shame, guilt, paranoia, and anger. The challenge for us is to recognize when Distorted is at work within us. Otherwise we believe its messages and take them as truth.

Distorted will twist things to keep us in a box or prevent us from taking risks.

DISTORTED'S MOTIVATION

Distorted's intention is to keep us safe, but its methods are ultimately not life-giving, and do not create beauty or resonance. When you were young, you likely encountered a variety of experiences that made you feel unsafe, hurt, or rejected in some way. Each time you experienced something unpleasant, your Distorted Self made a note of the situation and created a strategy that it hoped would spare you from ever experiencing that unpleasantness again.

It has a good intention, but not a very effective program,

because as you grew older, you no longer needed this same kind of protection. But Distorted is still on the job, as though you were going to be seven years old forever.

As you go through life and get hurt again, Distorted takes each situation as more evidence of why it needs to be on the job. If left unchecked, Distorted will eventually have you missing out on life itself because there is at least the possibility of getting hurt anywhere, anytime.

Only as Distorted learns that you are capable of taking care of your Self as the wise adult you are, does it then relax and back off from its hyper-vigilance.

Distorted can even become a useful ally, as it has such a great radar for danger. It can be useful to pay attention to what activates it, once you can look more deeply into the truth or the lie of the danger, rather than having Distorted run on automatic.

Distorted is highly invested in maintaining the status quo.

In any moment when change seems imminent, Distorted will rise up like a wave of negative energy and attempt to shrink us back. Distorted believes that no matter how bad things might seem, the status quo is better than risking a change and inviting in the unknown.

In contrast to the stillness that Divine Essence knows, Distorted Self will create stuckness that is absent of resourcefulness.

Distorted will try to control the world through you, and its tactics are tricky and effective. That is, until you're onto it and step up to stop allowing its influence over you.

Distorted will almost always include ideas that create separation between you and the people around you, or between you and your Divine Essence and the Divine.

Distorted will use a variety of approaches to hold you back, such as negative emotions or a sense of separateness through the heart intelligence, misleading thoughts through the mind intelligence, or pain or numbness, or wrong action or wrong inaction through the body intelligence.

The experiences of the Distorted Self are those of judgment, superiority, victimization, emotional overwhelm, sleepiness, or the distraction of busyness—all to keep you disconnected from the present moment.

DIVINE ESSENCE VERSUS DISTORTED SELF

The trick is to know, in any given moment, whether you are operating from Divine Essence or from Distorted Self. There is often no clear line that indicates one or the other. There is a lot of opportunity for shades of both to be present in any given situation. What we are talking about here are the degrees to which each may or may not be influencing you in the situation you are in.

To begin building a model of how all this works so that we may understand this better, imagine a sliding scale of polarity between Divine Essence and Distorted Self as such:

Figure 1: The Distorted Self—Divine Essence Polarity

Distorted Self		Divine Essence
10	0	10

In this scale, being at a 10 on the Divine Essence end would mean obtaining the closest possible attainment that a human can achieve in touching the Divine. Historically, only an extremely small number of people have ever attained this ultimate state, or managed to live from it on a continuous basis. In the course of a lifetime, most of us can only touch this state at times in our lives. Living a 10 in every moment is a great aspiration—it would be approaching the state of being attained by Jesus or the Buddha, for example.

A 10 in Distorted, on the other hand, is an extreme that few humans will ever fall to. A relatively recent example of someone who lived at this end of the scale may have been Hitler. Serial killers are also examples of people living on the extreme edge of Distorted.

In each moment of our lives, our challenge is to live more and more from the state of Divine Essence and less and less from Distorted. Being a human means living on a slippery slope where we manage to get closer and closer, until something happens and we slide back. With constant effort we do make our way up, however, and over time, even when we slide backwards, it is not as far back each time. We learn how to be of Divine Essence and we practice, practice, practice.

Now let's add more to the model.

When we are living more on the Distorted side of the model, we tend to experience the world around us as objects. Even other people are objects to us. When we see someone as a "boss" or as an "employee" first, rather than as a human who has a job to do called *boss* or *employee*, we are seeing these people as objects.

When we are on the Distorted side of the scale, we not only see individuals as objects, we also experience the world as an object system. When we view the world in this way, we also see the beings in the world as resources and commodities, which are there for us to use with little regard for them or their place in the Oneness.

For example, if we think that a forest is just a place where lumber is and that it only exists for our benefit, then of course it is easy to plow through the forest and gather all the parts of it and create piles of wood. Or if we see a village where people are willing to work for fifty cents a day to make shirts for the rest of the world, it is easy to work them until they drop and then to just replace them with another willing villager. From the place of Distortion, this is a practical approach to solving a problem.

From the place of Divine Essence, each person is a human first. Now you are in relationship with them and you are honoring them and your Self in that relationship. Now the forest is a living system. It is not okay to go in and rape it. Now you are in relationship with the forest and you understand that it is a living system, not an object system. With this understanding, you may still take lumber from it, but only if and when you have taken the time to listen to the forest and to ask it if it is willing to share its Self with you. If it is, you can then ask it how you can proceed in a good way that honors it and provides for its well-being.

Now when you go into that village, you see it as a living system of humans. Maybe you learn that they really want to make those shirts—only now you ask them what they need and you co-design the program with them as you support them with your own wisdom and good intention.

As you move further along towards the Divine, you get to a place where the humans and the living systems are no longer separate from you in any way.

You enter a state of realization in which every human, every being, and every living system is an aspect of you and you of it.

It is like the cells of your body, in that each cell has a life purpose that is in support of the wholeness of your body. You are made up of the cells and they are of you.

In Distorted, the experience for all beings is one of dissonance, as there is a lack of harmony and alignment. As you and those around you move more and more to Divine Essence, there arises a state of resonance. In resonance, all is in alignment. The resulting state is supportive.

In a hologram, every part contains an image of the whole similar to the way that even the smallest part of you, a sliver of skin, for example, contains in its DNA an image or a map of the wholeness of who you are. And in your DNA, within you, there is a hologram or a map of the entire Universe.

In this state of Divine Essence you have reached as far as you can towards the Divine while still being human. Knowing this is good. Experiencing this is better. Being this Is.

Now let's add these ideas about moving towards the realization and being of Oneness to the model:

Figure 2: The Divine Essence/Distorted Model

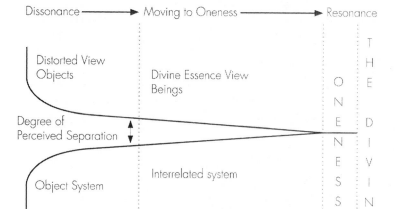

As you can see, the movement from Distortion to Divine Essence is a journey of degrees. There is no hard line that says now you are in Divine Essence and now you are not. It is more a question of how fully open you are to Divine Essence or how far away from it have you moved.

The gray vertical lines represent the zones of Distorted or Divine and the ultimate stage of Divine, which is the zone on the right called *Oneness*. That is the direction towards which we must keep moving.

GETTING TO KNOW
THE ONE IN ME THAT REACTS

One day I was walking along a crowded street in India. It was my first time there and I was shocked by much of what I was seeing. It all seemed so chaotic and the condition of some of the people was disturbing to that part of me that wants everyone to be fine.

I was getting hooked by it all; my defenses were closing me down. When those particular defenses go down, I get tunnel heart. I see it all and I don't allow it to impact me. I don't allow it to get in. It is a defense for a very sensitive, empathic heart.

As I noticed my reaction to the experience of walking through this sea of humanity, I wanted to learn how to walk with an open heart. How could I allow all this to touch me and still survive?

I chose a perspective that went like this: Imagine that every person here represents an aspect of who I am. Notice who and what is hard to look at. Notice what hurts. Notice who or what causes me to get angry or sad or happy. First, just notice.

This exercise opened me up and I saw five thousand faces of my Self. Every one of them became a part of me and I of them.

And I then allowed each person I was noticing to represent a part of me. The beggar allowed me to face the beggar in me. The Sadhu became the Sadhu in me, the taxi driver the same—and even the policeman, and on and on for each one who came to my attention.

As I experienced each person, I also got to experience that part of me that reacted to the sights, sounds, smells, and sensations.

When we say, "I am uncomfortable/angry/happy here," we are not being accurate. It is more accurate to say that an aspect of us is uncomfortable/angry/happy.

Then it is possible to get the paradox of the moment—that one part of you may be angry, another part of you sad, and yet another joyful about any given situation.

The more we can learn about these aspects of us, the more we can heal and integrate them into the wholeness of who we are.

The next step is to be curious about the one in you that is reacting. For example, when a beggar approached me and I felt uncomfortable, I became curious about the one in me that was uncomfortable.

I would ask that part of me:

- What is it about this beggar that makes you uncomfortable?
- What is it that you are afraid of?
- What is needed to stay open here?

Pay attention to any thoughts that occur during this process.

This is helpful any day. Perhaps someone at work pushes your buttons. It is not really about them—those are your buttons getting pushed, not theirs or your neighbors.

Instead of making them wrong for pushing your buttons, try this. Bless them first with loving-kindness. Open to that person and to the one in you that got triggered. And ask your Self:

- What is it that bothers me here?
- How am I creating this reaction?
- What does this part of me need in order for it to be healed?

Any time someone triggers us, it is never about them. In my mind I say to them, "Thank you for triggering my anger/sadness/frustration and for showing me where my work is."

Next ask your Self, "What is it time for me to heal/let go of/forgive?"

Being human provides us with endless opportunities to grow our Selves.

HOW TO MOVE TOWARDS DIVINE ESSENCE

It is one thing to understand that you want to do something. It is quite another to actually know how. You are the only one who can really know and understand what is truly needed in order for you to be able to experience less and less time in Distorted. Thankfully, there are some ideas that do work for most people. Hopefully these ideas will support you.

There are a variety of ways to move out of Distorted's grasp, and for the most part the first step always requires that you at least recognize when Distorted has moved in.

Distorted will attempt to use any and all of your three intelligences to accomplish its mission of protection and preserving the status quo.

Through the mind, Distorted will attempt to overwhelm us with confusion, stories of danger, or stories that involve shaming and blaming others or our Selves. Distorted will forecast possibilities and make up worst-case scenarios using the history of what has already happened as evidence that danger lies ahead. Distorted may use fear to keep us from a particular path or distraction, luring us off the trail. Distorted will twist any angle it can.

Emotionally, Distorted will activate a range of emotions associated with fear, anger, shame, or blame. When you follow the emotion back to its cause, however, you will discover that it was based on a lie. Even a slight twist of the truth is a lie. In other words, Distorted will make stuff up so that negative emotions arise. We become paralyzed in them. Distorted uses lies all the time to keep us stuck and "safe."

Through our body, Distorted works to disconnect us from our physical senses, or it heightens them in a way that exaggerates them. Distorted will use procrastination, sleepiness, or hurriedness and haste to distract from what it fears. Our action and moving forward is part of the body intelligence. Distorted will use illness and create stress so that we can avoid the parts of life that it believes are dangerous or bad for us.

Again, the intention is to distract or dissuade us from carrying on along a path of change.

As far as Distorted is concerned, the way you live your life now may not be great, but at least it is familiar. It is the unknown risk that scares and activates Distorted.

Distorted will create a world based on illusion or imagined and false ideas in order to keep us from being present.

In Part Two, I will suggest some exercises you can do to reduce the time you spend in Distorted energy, with the end result being the increase of your ability to access your Divine Essence.

THE OBSERVER

One of the first steps in developing the ability to know whether you are in a Distorted state or a Divine state is to develop the ability to spot the Distorted states as soon as possible. In order to do this, you must learn to activate an aspect of your Self known as the Observer. The Observer is that one in us who can provide a clean and clear report about what is going on, both within us and around us.

The Observer is essential as we move forward in life so that we can gather reliable reports about what is happening. With those Observer Reports, we are better able to make wise choices about what is needed in any situation we find our Selves in.

There are two aspects of the Observer that we can learn to access. One is the Subjective Observer and the other is the Interrelated Observer. As you move more fully into Divine Essence, you will have more and more access to the Interrelated Observer. In the meantime, any access to either Subjective or Interrelated Observer is good. With practice their accessibility will increase.

SUBJECTIVE OBSERVER

The art of developing a reliable Subjective Observer requires willingness to collect information that is as objective as possible. That is right, the Subjective Observer is providing objective reports. Objectivity is when your Observer is providing a report of facts of a situation that is not tinted with your feelings or biases about what is being reported on, at least to the extent that this is possible.

For example, if the Observer is reporting that there is a green chair in the room, that information does not need to be affected by your personal like or dislike about the color or style of the chair. It is simply reporting what is. There is a green chair in the room and the person sitting in the chair is smiling.

The Observer reports an observation of data points.

It can be argued that there is no such thing as objectivity. Herein lies another great paradox. It is true that as we observe anything, we are affecting it. Therefore what we are reporting on is influenced by us. At the same time, however, there is a level of factuality that is available to be noticed and reported. That is what I mean by objective. As the report is coming through an aspect of you, the Observer, it is more accurate to acknowledge that it is a subjective report, hence the Subjective Observer.

The information from the Subjective Observer is always filtered through our ability and skillfulness to perceive what is present in the moment. As long as we are willing to develop a reliable Observer, the skillfulness can be developed through practice. I will offer some methods of practice later on. For now, let's assume you have access to your Observer.

There are two areas to check in with when gathering a report from the Observer. One field of experience is the external world, the world outside of you. The other is the internal world, the world within your Self. That internal world includes your body intelligence, your heart intelligence, and your mind intelligence.

THE EXTERNAL REPORT

Let's start with the external field. Your Subjective Observer uses your body intelligence through the five physical senses of taste, sight, smell, hearing, and touch to gather information about the world around you. The Subjective Observer's job is to report what is present in a very factual way. Any judgment or opinion, such as liking or disliking what is being reported, is not the job of the Subjective Observer. The Observer is simply reporting the facts as they are.

Along with the body intelligence's report through the five physical senses, you will also learn to pick up information through your heart intelligence. For example, you may start to observe the emotional state of the people you are with. Separating out your own emotional experience from those around you is a tricky but useful skill to develop.

THE INTERNAL REPORT

In your internal world, your Subjective Observer may gather information using the body and its senses to report on any physical experiences, such as tension, pain, hunger, or relaxed areas of the body. Any report on the state of your body is useful information.

The Observer may also report on your heart intelligence, which could include your emotional state, your degree of openness, or your sense of connection. Once again, it is important to not make a judgment about liking or disliking what is going on. The Observer is simply gathering the facts.

Your Subjective Observer may report on what thoughts are on your mind, along with what it perceives your state of mind to be. For example, you may be confused, in which case the Subjective Observer reports to you that you are in a state of confusion. Being able to take in this information will bring you into relationship with the mind intelligence.

WHO GETS THE REPORT?

The information the Observer collects and reports is available to both Divine Essence and to Distorted Self. Each of these two aspects of our Selves receives the information from the Observer, and each makes a different assessment, and makes decisions and recommendations from it.

The report from the Observer may result in the arising of an intuitive idea about a situation that is happening. Be clear about the difference, though. The report is a gathering of information and an intuitive hit results from that. The intuition is not the work of the Observer. It may be a great intuitive insight, but it is not part of the Subjective Observer's report unless it is a fact. There is a fine line between reporting what is observed and making something up about it. The Observer reports the facts. The aspect of you that receives the report, Divine Essence or Distorted Self, creates the judgments, assessments, and recommendations about it.

THE INTERRELATED OBSERVER

As we move further along the path to a fuller experience of Divine Essence, we start to develop some more advanced capacities to extend the range and reliability of our Observers. This happens when we start to experience the Interrelated Observer. Through the Interrelated Observer you are now able to put your Self into the experience of some other person, being, or thing around you to get a reliable report of the situation you are in, as if it were being offered by that other one directly.

This is still information gathering of what is present in a given moment or situation. You have probably heard the expression about putting your Self into another person's shoes. This is a similar idea and it expands to any other being, including plants, animals, insects, and all that is available to you in any given moment or situation.

For example, you are sitting in a park and you notice a nearby tree. You might have a question that you are pondering, or it may be that you are just curious about the tree.

Allow your Self to get quiet. Feel your feet connect to the earth and the ground around you. As you relax into the connection to the park, allow your Self to be present only to what is here now. Stop thinking about any concerns, planning, or anything aside from what is here now.

When you know that you have become quiet and connected to the moment, allow your Self to imagine that you are in connection with the tree and ask it if it will allow you to enter into its inner space. If the answer is yes, then you may do so with respect and good intention. Now imagine that you are the tree. Imagine what it is experiencing. Imagine how the sounds of the park are hitting it. How the sun is warming it, how the nearby surroundings are affecting it.

Now really imagine that you are that tree and everything you are observing is from the point of view of the tree.

After you have gathered your report, imagine your Self returning to your own body, heart, and mind. From the place of your own Self, look back over at the tree and thank it for being of service and for its generosity in supporting you and all those who pass by.

The more you practice this, the better you will get at it.

Trust the information you gathered and remember it is just information. Allow it to inform you about the question you are holding, and put this report together with any other wisdom you have collected.

Your Divine Essence will know what is useful to take from this experience.

Practicing with nature will help you develop the capacity to access your Interrelated Observer more and more easily.

A word of caution. If you try this with other people, it can provide some interesting information about the situation that you are in with them, but be careful about what you make up based on your Observer Reports. It would be incorrect to think you actually know what another person is thinking, feeling, or experiencing. Whatever you imagine is just that: imagined. For example, you may observe that another person is sitting, smiling, and reading. They may be sitting, but they may or may not be comfortable. They may be smiling, but they may or may not be happy. They may be looking at a book, but they may or may not be reading.

Remember, using the Interrelated Observer should only be done with the greatest of love, good intention, and respect. And take the report with a grain of salt. Use the information to inform you about possibilities of what might be true for another. Avoid the temptation to think that your report is the truth for someone else. It may not be, according to what their own Observer would report. Use it only to inform your curiosity rather than to draw conclusions.

STAGES OF OBSERVER DEVELOPMENT

When we are caught deep in Distortion, we lose our ability to activate a reliable Observer. Distorted will tell us what it needs us to believe so that we can be tricked into believing its lies.

As we move more and more over to Divine Essence, we are opening our Self up to a more reliable Observer, one that is able to gather helpful data. You should be able to crosscheck your Observer Reports with other people and get a reasonably close agreement on what is being reported. Of course, if the people you are crosschecking with are caught in their distortions, it is possible that you are all agreeing to believe a distorted lie. That is why it is so important to activate your Divine Essence first.

Figure 3: Stages of Observer Development

Distorted Self			Divine Essence
10	0		10

No access to a reliable observer	Access to an increasingly reliable Subjective Observer	Beginning of access to the Interrelated Observer	Full access to the Interrelated Observer

SELF-AWARENESS

Once the Observer has reported, what then? As human beings, we have the capacity to be self-aware. That is the ability to know in each moment what aspect of us is out in front. This self-awareness can be cultivated to the degree that you know, at any given moment, whether you are more in a state of Divine Essence or Distorted Self. It is through self-awareness that we can activate the willingness to call Divine Essence forward.

It is easy to believe that we are self-aware, but the truth is that most of us would be shocked to find out how infrequently we are actually self-aware in our lives. We must learn to develop the capacity to stay self-aware through practice.

From the place of self-awareness, we get to choose which aspect of our Self we are going to put in charge of the decision department. We always have this fundamental choice available to us: whether or not to allow our Observer Reports to be received clearly, and which aspect of our being—Divine Essence or Distorted—we will listen to and follow.

It is worth repeating, we must choose whom to put in front of the decision department: Divine Essence or Distorted Self.

We must be present to be in a state of self-awareness. We are then conscious of which aspect of our Self is out in front. Once we become present and activate our self-awareness, we have the responsibility to choose. We must learn to choose well and to then follow through with that choice.

Figure 4: Self-Awareness—Who's in Front?

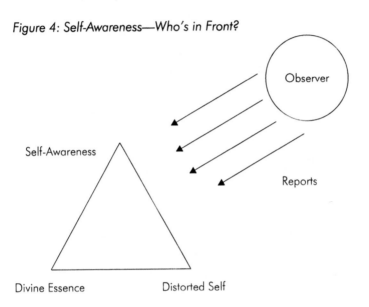

THE SOUL AND THE HUMAN

We humans are on quite a journey, or perhaps it is more accurate to suggest that the Soul we are—our Essence—is on the journey. Imagine that the ultimate experience of this life is for the sake of our Soul in its journey of forming, developing, and ultimately transcending into an enlightened essence. Imagine that if well- developed enough in this lifetime, it will go on long after our human life has completed. Imagine that every moment of this life is in service to the Soul and its development, and that that development is facilitated through the quality of our walk as humans during this life.

There is a sublime connection between human and Soul. It's one that we cannot comprehend or touch through our limited human faculties. Our Soul is that aspect of us that is of the Divine and of Universal consciousness, of the One. The Soul is an aspect of the Divine that is embodied in our human lives. It is connected to our Divine Essence, and must be formed and developed throughout this life, so that it can take its place in the Universe as one of the enlightened forms of consciousness.

The Soul uses our human body much like a carriage, being carried along through the human part of our journey. This human carriage is pulled along by two horses, one of which is Divine Essence and the other Distorted. The reins of the carriage are in the hands of our self-awareness. It is through the journey that our Soul is developed.

Herein lies one of the great paradoxes of spirituality. That on one hand here we are in a human experience, absolutely moving through this world with an egoist sense of Self. We have a viewpoint, as humans, that we are experiencing a life that is quite centered around us, with our body as the reference point for where we are in the world. On the other hand, we are of Soul, and as such we are One with all.

Your Soul is on a journey of development. As you journey through this human adventure, your Soul accumulates karmic fruit according to how you respond to what life puts into each moment.

Divine Essence understands that being in service to the Soul is beneficial to the human, while Distorted Self is afraid of the consequences of this idea. Distorted Self believes that our very existence depends on the illusions of separateness as a means of existing and, therefore, surviving.

THE DREAM OF SOUL AND LIFE PURPOSE

Joseph Campbell wisely pointed out that for the first half of a human's life, the ego runs ahead in search of experience and wealth. During this time, the Soul takes a back seat, patiently waiting for the ego to do its thing and to gather in what it needs. The Soul serves the ego by letting it run much like a wild hungry dog in search of adventure and wealth of whatever the ego is collecting. It could be money, other resources, or experiences.

Then there comes a time when the Soul turns its gaze onto the ego and says, "Thank you for forging ahead and for having the experiences you have had. There is a greater meaning to all of this and it is time that you, ego, sit back and serve me, the Soul, as I fulfill my bargain with the Universe and express my life purpose."

The Soul works us from within, so there comes a time in our human adventure when it activates and demands that we follow its yearning. For some, this time occurs at a young age. We recognize these people as "old Souls." When we are around them, we feel a deeper, fuller connection to the Universe.

Others may not have this experience until the last few short moments of their physical lives on Earth, when suddenly at the end of it all, they awaken and realize something important is being realized.

Still others experience this time at midlife, and it is often manifested in what we call midlife crises. I prefer to call these midlife awakenings. This is a time when, under the pressure of the Soul, many people start to ask questions about what this life is really all about. It is a time when people look at the houses, cars, boats, and shoe collections and realize that as nice as those things are, they aren't providing much meaning to their human existence.

If we are lucky, we are willing and still able to respond to the call when it comes. If we do, we let go of the attachment to the ego's treasures—which often confuses our families and friends—and we allow our Selves to respond to the call, to seek out some meaning in our otherwise productive lives. The Soul is grateful to the ego for amassing the resources, and assures the ego that these things will be put to good use.

The yearning of the Soul to be out in front at this stage becomes a major influence on our life's dreams. Many of the things that used to seem important suddenly fall away from our desires. The Soul has better and more important things in mind for you. The Soul works on us in mysterious ways that we often experience as a longing, a yearning that arises from deep within. This stirring causes us to be restless. It calls us out of our comfortable life. It beckons us, calls to us in our sleep. It shakes us in the waking sleepwalk of our regular life. It will haunt you, follow you, and pull away the illusions of your life that ego built. It will not allow you to sleep any longer. When it calls for you, you will at least know. Whether you answer or not is another question.

The Soul works on us with compassion and relentlessness for the sake of a destiny that demands to be answered. Yet it will be ignored if Distorted has its way.

The Soul will often seek its experience through a mission or a calling. It will call us out of our safe and sleepy existence by challenging us to step into an adventure of service for the sake of something that is beyond our personal aggrandizement and profit. It may be a calling that can be answered by going on a walkabout or a pilgrimage as an anonymous traveler wandering towards meaning. Or it may be calling you to take on the correcting of something that is not working well in society on behalf of other humans. The dream of the Soul, as expressed through life purpose, may be simple or it may be complex. It may align with the life you have created, or it may ask you to step away from it all and begin a new journey. It may be that the dream is to spread love or happiness in simple ways, or it may be that you are being called to express your Soul's purpose in much more tangible ways, such as cleaning up the local lake or revolutionizing the educational system.

Remember, the Soul wants to be developed through this human journey and it will challenge you. The dreams of the Soul are never convenient for the plans of the ego. They are almost always disruptive to an otherwise orderly life.

Sometimes the Soul will align with the established order and find ways of leveraging what has been created for more altruistic purposes. More often than not, though, the Soul will beckon you to abandon all that you have identified with, because it was your ego that identified with these roles and the stuff in the first place. The Soul never had any stock in it.

The Soul saves you by tearing you away from the fabric of illusion made up of fancy titles, cars, clothing, exaggerated stories, and a false sense of well-being and accomplishment. This tearing apart terrifies the ego. Given the chance, however, the ego comes to realize that by letting go of control, it will eventually have an easier time, even as Distorted is always standing by looking for any opportunity to attach itself to the next stable thing. After all, Distorted is a loyal friend to the end. But once the Soul has been released, it's not so easily put back in the box. Thank goodness—or is it thank Godness?

With that, the pace of life adjusts to the Soul's timing. More attention is given to the quality of each moment, to relationships, and possibly, though not necessarily, to making a difference to others. Some Souls want to enter into a quiet life that is fully engaged in each moment, though they may appear to be withdrawn from the world at large.

This can be a sweet time or a time that is filled with challenges. What is wanted is a surrender to the path of the Soul, as best as it can be understood through the wisdom of your Divine Essence.

For a while, the rational mind, that is ego mind, will still be freaked out by what it is being asked to do—or to not do. It will eventually calm down. The dream now is much more congruent with the Universe's desires, and as such with your life purpose.

And the ego, oh yes, the ego is still there, of course. Only now it serves the master, and the master is you, oh Soul, as known through Divine Essence.

MY OWN DESCENT INTO THE VALLEY OF DESPAIR

At some point in our journey, we—you and I—have all traveled into the valley of despair.

It is the adversity of such times that give you, as a human, something to respond to, and it is through that response that you find out who you are. During those troubling times you grow your Self, individually and as part of a collective, and through that experience you are doing your part in contributing to the unfolding dream of the Universe.

A profound growth experience happened for me when I had a death experience as a young and arguably troubled teenager. That experience opened me up to the depth of this life in a way that an easy or protected path never could have. I have written the full story of this event, along with many others, in my book, *The Eagle's Call,* so I will offer the bottom-line version here.

As a teenager I was called to walk on the dark side of life and death. My Soul took me on a journey that wound me down and down, using whatever mechanisms it could to facilitate the descent. One of those devices was drugs. I eventually found my Self at the bottom of the proverbial valley with a needle in hand, literally. Immediately after injecting my Self with the drug, I slumped to the floor, my heart no longer beating, my body no longer breathing or functioning. I had never intended to lose my life.

It seemed to me then, and as I look back on it now, that I had been guided along that path for the sake of my Soul's journey and development.

As my body slid off the kitchen chair onto the floor, my Soul lifted out of it and seemed to float above, though really there is no above or below in this state. My Soul was observing the chaos in the room as one person ran away and another rushed in to offer CPR to my suddenly lifeless form. As this was going on, I realized that I was being held by the Divine. I was with God. I found my Self held in a field of sublime love. It was a quality of love that surpasses anything that I had known up to that time and have not quite known since.

At the same time, it seemed that I was aware of the state of being of everyone in the world, whether I had personally known them or not. Images of people came to me. Some I knew, like family and friends, and many I did not. It seemed that all time existed as the present moment. The past and the future were somehow intertwined. I was in connection with all, One with it all.

As I experienced this, I became aware of the presence of the Divine. I don't mean Divine Essence. This was the Divine, the Big D. I was experiencing Divine love and joy, and a profound feeling of being love itself.

It was not experiencing love as though there were a me to have an experience, but rather I was experiencing being love, the essence. It was as if this field of love essence was everywhere, as if it were a form of consciousness, and I was a part of it. I came to understand in that moment that we are always held in this field of the Divine, and all that's required is our willingness to trust it in order to connect. Conversely, all that's required is our unwillingness to open to it in order to separate us from it. In other words, it is our choice that determines how fully we become One with the Divine in any given moment of our human life.

There was no regret, no recrimination for killing my Self with the drugs. There was just this amazing love and light that surrounded me. I could now understand through the images I was witnessing, like a holographic movie that I was also a part of, how that love and light surrounded everyone, and yet most people were not allowing themselves to receive it. It seemed that they had cut themselves off from it.

In my limited human capacity to understand what was going on, I could only interpret the experience. I knew that to fully comprehend the depth of what I was experiencing would be beyond the capacity of my mind. I was it without being able, or even without needing, to understand it—and the "it" was the Divine.

It seemed that I was being spoken to by the Divine. It was not as though the voice came from any particular source or direction, as much as it was that the words of the Divine were being revealed to me. I came to understand that the opportunity for my Soul to use this life to develop itself had not yet been completely fulfilled. Because of this awareness, and because my body was able to take me back, thanks to the efforts of the person performing CPR on me, I could choose whether or not to return to the living. I understood that if I chose not to return that I would have to circle back at some point to have this human experience again, and so I was fortunate that I could choose. Wow, free will even here in the presence of the Divine. I was faced with a choice that would have consequences in ways that that I will never fully understand.

I chose to return, as you can guess by the fact that I am here to write this now. In the instant of choosing to return to this life, I was quickly returned to my body.

Once that portal of connection has been opened, it can never be fully closed back up again. Having peeked through the curtain, I was forever changed.

The sudden awakening that occurred in that moment was one

of the most profound experiences of my life. As one who has seen into the deep mystery, I only know enough to be able to say that the veils of separation are thin. It is possible to peek through. On the other side of this human experience there is a wisdom so vast and deep that it cannot be contained in the consciousness of a human mind. Thankfully, it is known deeply through the infinite wisdom of the opened human heart.

Since that experience I have known great moments of the deepest connection to the Divine and, perhaps more importantly, I have still felt far from being able to fully allow my Self to surrender from ego and to be in that level of connection which I know is possible. I must continue to work every day to stay that open. Sometimes I can get there, but very often I get tangled up in the challenges of everyday life.

As the Soul develops itself throughout this life, the journey does get easier. We discover that it requires us to be present in every moment with compassion and loving-kindness for our Selves and for each other. I am still finding my way into living this life as fully as I know is possible. We are on the road together—I need you to lean into and I need you to remind me when I forget—and I am here to remind you as well.

OUR OPPORTUNITY

It seems that each person, generation after generation, is born into his or her life and must then learn how to awaken to the fullness of what is possible as a human. With very few exceptions, no one is given a free pass, no one is born fully aware and enlightened. We have the possibility of learning how to live more and more fully from Divine Essence and less and less through Distorted. It exists only as a possibility because of the fact that we can choose to push the opportunity away. We can ignore the call to live as Divine Essence and we can live asleep, not ever engaging in the work of awakening.

We can curl up with our Distorted Self and allow its twisted messages to cast a spell on us for a lifetime, if we choose to. That would be easy. All you have to do is nothing. That looks like holding the illusion of your smallness or aggrandizement, holding onto your victimhood, carrying grudges, or engaging in battles and old stories of how you have been misunderstood, overlooked, wronged, or mistreated, or born into a bad set of circumstances. It can look like holding onto differences between you and others, and using them as weapons—as though there were some honor in being hardened by life. There is not.

If we choose to engage in the path, to let go, to do our work, to consciously unfold our awakening, we will find a way to a walk that involves living more moments in-joy and less and less in fear, anger, or shame, or any other state of disconnection from Divine Essence.

In order for us to do this, we must first be willing to put in the necessary effort. I once had the opportunity to meet an extraordinary man who was a monk at the time of our meeting. He radiated a most vibrant light, appearing to be well along the path of awakening. In my conversation with him, he shared that every day he is still engaged in the moment-to-moment work of living from his Divine Essence. I was struck by his admission. He was so far along the path, yet he still puts in the effort every day to stay on it. After talking with him, I felt oddly assured by the idea that this work is never over. Each day we may take a few steps forward and/or a few steps back. Such is the walk of being human.

Being Human

Before I awoke in the infancy of this human journey
Before there was an I with the coordinates of a human existence
The Soul of I existed in a most mysterious way
One with the Divine and still something was needed
As such I traveled far across the eons of endless time
Except there was no time, there was no time; and certainly no I
Soul is born into this human experience; it came to be formed
The shock of separation roils through Soul's new human body
The ocean of blissful connection now left so far behind
Human comes in with innocence to a world of suffering
And meets human body with a cry; the shock wave sounds
The veils of the worlds are thin; human still knows of the
    other side
Entering in to this human presence; Soul has arrived
Beauty, wholeness, magnificence, and brilliance known before
And upon arriving now quickly forgotten; as human being begins
It's a strange thing to become human
Soul just is, One, joy, Love; as essence there is promise here
Energy is everywhere, a sea of pulsing pregnant possibility
No purpose yet except to be, and even Soul needs existence
Opportunity to realize its Self for the sake of serving the Divine
This human has just begun to feel the loss of Divine connection
Human begins as a seed and a spark of ignition to form flesh
    and skin

The Soul's journey as human begins; and ego starts to walk
The promise of life to carry on, a journey to unfold
The journey of this one does begin; a partnership of flesh and spirit
The latest turnings on the Universe's spin; blue consciousness sparks
A dream is cast and the Divine smiles a patient, knowing, smile
The mystery deepens, human is charged with the spirit's higher
    purpose.
The Soul settles in to this human form as the child runs ahead
Through adventurous days the little one plays as the world casts
    its spell
Child knows of the Soul and plays; and begins to record the lessons
The games of child and Soul are one; and the human being
    takes form
Growing older by the day the quickly fading memory of the One
Child human learns to be more separate to protect the space within,
An illusion that caught the older humans who guided the young
    ones way
Separated forgotten radiance with each passing day
The distance grows further and further till it becomes a fable in
A book of faded memories passed on for thousands of years
One day a yearning stirring; the compass takes a spin
It pointed to the Universe; a calling from deep within
It burned ever so faintly; a flicker on a candle's wick
Whisping smoke as human form; whispering God's love song
The cake of human life crusting; starting to crack and fall away
Deep inside a sacred memory; finding its way to the light of day
Soul waits patiently for the human to remember; adulthood
    moves on
Innocence left behind the human keeps moving; though it's time
    to return
To the Soulful journey, the yearning cries; competing for
    human time

But the world has demands and exchanges for favor
Houses to build and roads to walk, a family to come to
The pressure to buy stuff human doesn't need; the media shouts
relentless
Distractions of acquisitions, dream building, and
commercialization
Human dreams to amass good fortune; the family smiles
And Soul waits for the human to remember
Hypnotized by the messages; going faster for more and more.
The pace quickens, human is running, the game is on, the stakes
soar
The Soul cries out as the human stumbles along the chalky path
Weaving skills and knowledge, it's time now; for a different
kind of plan
The aging human cracks apart; as the lightening is overwhelming
Soul smiles through as the human starts to remember the
beginning
No one knows the way back for sure; the light of One a distant
flicker
It guides human into the heart; fleeting moments of lucid
presence
Soul is stirred in a sleepless night of tossing dreams and reckless
flight
Soul cries out its remembering song; and the human starts to
move
Towards the light that is now burning bright; fueled by presence
and joy
Human and Soul now aligned in purpose; and Universe is now
served

—Patrick Ryan

The Ring of Power

hankfully, there are a number of teachings that have been handed down through time that can inform us about how to be human in better ways. Remember that although we are born human, we still need to learn how to be in the best way possible.

Following is one such teaching. It comes from a tradition known as the Delicate Lodge, an oral tradition that is held primarily by three wisdom keepers: Rainbow Hawk, Wind Eagle, and White Eagle.

It is known as the Ring of Power. It is both simple and powerful in its effect on those who live it.

Figure 5: The Ring of Power

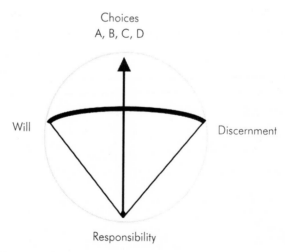

This teaching is organized as a wheel (see "Figure 5: The Ring of Power"). I have modified it slightly by showing the letters ABCD to represent the idea of creating a variety of options.

I have found different ways and opportunities to use this powerful and elegant teaching in my own life, and have introduced it to many others. Following is one scenario that incorporates the concepts of Divine Essence versus Distorted Self. The ring can be used in many other ways.

Suppose that you have heard about a special project that is being set up where you work. It is an exciting and interesting project and you would like to be part of the team that will take it on.

You activate your Observer and you gather in the information. Your Observer reports the following:

The department you work in is short-staffed, as two people are on leave.

The project start date is the following Monday.

The project will require some travel.

You have an important report due next week. You are almost finished with it, but there is more work needed to finish it in a good way.

On your last job review, you received an overall good report with one competency area in need of improvement.

Internally you feel stressed about your general workload.

Your back is tense.

Your mind is telling you two stories—why you should get the job, as well as why you should not.

Your heart is having moments of open hopefulness and then closing down.

With this report, you activate your self-awareness and you recognize that both Distorted and Divine Essence want to be in charge of this process.

Now you make use of the Ring of Power.

You know that you have a choice about how to view this situation. You start with the bottom of the wheel: Responsibility.

Step 1

You accept the responsibility that you get to choose whom to put in charge of the experience of getting assigned to this project team: Distorted or Divine Essence.

Imagine that taking responsibility is like stepping up to the Ring of Power.

Step 2

Once you have stepped up to responsibility, you may then put your attention to the top of the Ring and create some choices or options about how to be in this situation. In this case, you keep it to two fundamental choices, though whenever possible a greater variety of choices can be helpful:

CHOICE A: To view and to engage this situation through
Divine Essence.

CHOICE B: To view and to engage this situation through
Distorted Self.

Step 3

You activate discernment to make this choice. Discernment in this case means to be able to look clearly and wisely into each of the choices or options that you have been able to identify, and to then use good judgment in order to see things for how they are, so that you can make a choice wisely.

In this case you know that the wise choice is to put Divine Essence in charge, even though a part of you may feel compelled to put Distorted Self in front. Sometimes Distorted seems like a safe choice. Distorted Self is an old familiar part of you that will show up at any time to keep you safe. It is a false sense of safety, however. One that does not serve you.

Thankfully, you notice this and realize that you do not have to give into Distorted Self this time.

You choose to be Divine Essence in this situation.

Step 4

You point the arrow at Choice A and activate your will to follow through on this decision from Divine Essence.

Having chosen Divine Essence, you know that a conversation with your boss is needed.

You hear the voice of Distorted who is resistant to this idea, telling you that you are setting your Self up for disappointment.

You notice this and you keep your will activated to keep Divine Essence out in front. You follow through with the idea to have a conversation with your boss.

You simply notice what is going on as you tell her how much it would mean to you to be on this team. After the conversation, you are aware of more internal voices giving you mixed messages about whether or not you will get the assignment.

One voice tells you that you are not liked or respected enough; the other says that you have been doing a good job and you deserve this chance. You note the rising and falling of hopefulness in your heart. All of this is disturbing and familiar.

The next day you come to work. Your boss calls you into her office and informs you that you did not get the assignment. You notice that you are disappointed and angry. You manage to contain this while with your boss, but once you retreat to your office, you are caught in the pull between Divine Essence and Distorted.

Distorted says, "I told you so!"

Divine Essence tells you that this is for the best, even though you do not yet understand why.

You remember your commitment to live through Divine Essence, so you put in the necessary effort to do that. This is continuing the activation of your will to stay in Divine Essence.

Divine Essence advises you to ask for a second conversation with your boss so that you can better understand why you did not get the assignment.

You do so, and in that conversation your boss explains that because the office is short-staffed, she felt you were the strongest candidate to keep things going through a difficult time. It turns out that you did not get the project because you are such a valuable employee.

She promises you there will be many more projects and you will get to participate in some of them. She thanks you sincerely for your understanding.

You walk away knowing that you have been seen and recognized. You are thankful that you followed the advice of Divine Essence rather than that of Distorted.

In this scenario, the Ring of Power offered a method for making a clear choice and for viewing this situation through the lens of Divine Essence. The Ring of Power can be used in many other ways as well. Any time you need to make a decision, try it out. It is a simple, powerful, and effective way of keeping your decisions wise. After all, life is a never-ending stream of decisions, conscious or not.

I find it very helpful to use the Ring of Power over and over again each day, even when my choices seem obvious. For example, it is obvious to me that staying in a state of Divine Essence is a great choice in every moment of my life. If this is so, why would I bother to use the Ring of Power so often?

I have found that the act of choosing Divine Essence keeps me awake to the moment-by-moment work of living from Divine Essence. It is easy to go to sleep and to drift in and out of Divine Essence. In fact, that is what most of us do. We drift from state to state. Actively choosing a state of being is a powerful activator of that state, and it anchors me to it.

After I have used the Ring of Power to choose my state of being, I can then put the question that I am asking my Self in front of me and use the Ring of Power to gather in a range of possibilities for that situation. For example, let's say that I am choosing how to use some money that I have managed to save up.

First, I use the Ring of Power to activate Divine Essence, which may only take a couple of seconds on some days. Now I am ready to ask the question: What is the best use of this money?

I take the responsibility of choosing a good use for this money. Next I create a range of possible ideas. I might consider taking a vacation, investing the money, giving some or all of it to a charity, paying down some debt, or buying my Self that car I've been wanting.

After identifying all these choices, I use discernment to look into each possibility. In this case, I decide that a combination of investing, donating, and taking a smaller holiday seems to be the best choice.

I activate my will and follow through on this decision.

I encourage you to play with the Ring of Power in your daily decisions. You can even use paper labels by putting them down on the floor, then walking around the wheel noticing what it is like to stand in each one of your options. Remember to check in with you body intelligence, heart intelligence, and mind intelligence while you stand in each possibility. Notice what the Observer reports, as a way of gathering in the wisdom.

The Three Intelligences

*L*et's look more closely at the three intelligences: heart intelligence, mind intelligence, and body intelligence.

We all have three primary sources of wisdom and feedback as part of our makeup. Each of these sources holds its own field of intelligence, and all of them are interrelated.

All three intelligences are operating simultaneously and are constantly exchanging information with each other. They are influencing each other with their respective messages, though each field of intelligence operates through a different language and operating system than the others.

The Observer can check in with each of the three intelligences and report on what is being observed.

Three people in the same experience are going to get three different stories about what happened. One person might be primarily impacted by the mind which tells a story about the experience that causes the body to tighten up and emotions to shift according to the story that is being told.

For the next person, the same experience will be more oriented to the impact on their body which, for example, might result in their body tensing up, which results in the mind making up a story about what might be happening as their emotional state shifts accordingly.

The third person's orientation is through their emotional

world, and so their emotional state might shift by what has happened. Their body then tenses up in anticipation of something, while the mind starts creating a story to explain what is going on.

As you can see, all three intelligences are creating their own story about what is happening. The story is then compared to old running scripts. The scripts are created by our past experiences and are written and interpreted by Divine Essence and Distorted together. Our job is to learn how to notice all three fields of intelligence and to be able to interact with all three, collecting the available information and wisdom.

Many of us have one field of intelligence that is more dominant than the others. It becomes our specialty and we get good at compensating for neglecting the other intelligence fields. We often cut our Selves off from one or two intelligence fields, at least partially, if not entirely.

Just because we can get through life favoring one or two of our intelligence fields does not mean it's a good idea to do so. We must develop our access to all three.

It is through practice that we can learn how to open up our intelligences so that we have access to them all. Each of the intelligences holds its own special wisdom and ability to read into what is going on around and within us. It is the heart that experiences the joy connection. It is the mind that bears witness. It is the body that carries us through this life and offers us a full sensory experience.

Each intelligence is not immune from its own particular challenges, however. The challenge of the heart intelligence is to stay open and in connection. The challenge of the mind intelligence is to stay present. The challenge of the body intelligence is to stay open and relaxed. Each intelligence has to let go of stored past experiences and to stay available to move into new experiences in a way that allows the past to inform us without closing us off.

As always, we must choose which aspect of our Selves, Divine Essence or Distorted, to put in charge of how to use that information. Let's look at each of the three intelligences more deeply.

HEART INTELLIGENCE

Heart intelligence includes emotional intelligence, but it's also so much more than that. Heart intelligence is also the field through which we can experience the interrelatedness of All. We can extend our heart out and connect, in relationship, with all beings. Through that connection we can have a direct experience of our Oneness. That is a beautiful state to be in. We will discuss this more in Part Two.

Much has been written about emotional intelligence, as it is one of the three important wisdom centers within the wholeness of us human beings. Emotional energy is like a wave of water that is moving along. Some people fall into the wave and get swirled, spun, and tumbled around by it. Others learn how to ride the wave until the wave itself runs its course and loses or changes its energy. Still others simply stay on the shore and don't get anywhere near the wave.

Those who fall into the wave get tumbled around by it. It can seem that they are drowning and out of control. The resulting overwhelm can be debilitating. They can get lost in it, and at times find that they are unable to just choose to pull out of it. The practice for these people is to learn to experience their emotions without being drowned by them.

Those who stay on the shore and declare that they are fine have disowned their emotional experience, which is a survival strategy. These people must learn to allow themselves to be in the experience of their emotions without being too distant. They must learn how to get into the water. The more they practice this the more they will discover that it is okay to do so. Once someone knows it is okay to experience their emotions, they will be more connected to the emotional experience of each moment and therefore be more fully engaged with life.

In this metaphor, the objective is to learn where you are and how to engage with the waves. How to fully experience them without getting overrun or detaching. Emotional energy is a powerful source of wisdom. As such it has its own language that we need to learn to access.

As we learn how to interact with the waves, we gain the facility to integrate and connect to the wholeness of who we are. It is only through this path of integration and experiencing that we can find our way to a life that is in-joy and vibrancy rather than a life of drama or detachment, both of which disconnect us from our wholeness and from experiencing the world around us.

The only way through it is through it. Avoiding emotional energy or being a drama queen is not a life-enhancing strategy.

Many of our western cultural messages are about not letting your emotions get in the way of the decision-making processes. Our business world even holds these messages up as a preferred way of operating. Emotions are often seen as a weak point in leadership. Nothing could be further from the truth.

We ignore our emotional wisdom at our own peril. Those organizations that run on emotionless processes do not operate in a bubble. The decisions they make spill into the communities they touch and onto the planet itself. The impact of decisions that don't consider heart wisdom is potentially destructive.

We must learn how to use our emotional wisdom wisely. We must learn that emotions are not only natural, they are important. They offer us a field of insight that is essential to whole, life-giving, and balanced decisions. Any decision that cannot stand the test of heart wisdom is not a good decision.

What is needed then is for us all to learn more about how to access this all-important heart wisdom, and to include it in our decision-making processes.

I often hear from busy people that they believe it takes too much time to consider the heart intelligence that is trying to come through. In fact, by considering heart intelligence more fully, you will ultimately make better decisions that will return dividends that are far more valuable than saving a few moments and over-running this wisdom. The big surprise for many people is that the process of working with emotional energy does not often require a lot of time. In fact, productivity goes up as a result.

When emotional energy is not worked with it, becomes contained inside you and the pressure builds. You may be able to shut it off or ignore it for a while, but eventually it will resurface. As it builds up inside, it eventually starts to leak out in the form of outbursts or other spontaneous reactions. The cost of leaking untouched emotional energy is far higher than the apparent cost of time to work with it.

In our culture it is okay to seek out advice and opinions from experts in the fields of management, finances, marketing, and so on. Yet seeking outside professional support for our emotional needs is usually only considered after it is long overdue, and even then it is often kept under the table.

It is important to remember that all three intelligences serve us. Decisions based exclusively on heart intelligence will often miss the mark. This is equally true for decisions that might be made exclusively from mind or body intelligence. We humans are blessed with the ability to access all three. To be living awake, we must.

HEART WISDOM CONNECTION
In addition to increased emotional awareness, heart wisdom allows us to experience connection, and through connection we experience love and joy.

For some, the ability to connect starts with connecting to Self first. This includes getting grounded and clear with Self and opening to all three intelligences through the Divine Essence. Only with the connection to Self is it possible to fully and openly connect to another person, and from that connection to fully open to the whole of the world around us.

The path through which you find connection might vary from person to person, but the objective stays the same. Being fully connected includes clear, bright, complete, and open connection to Self, others, and the world around you.

In order to create that level of openness, we must each do our personal work. When we are viewing the world through Divine Essence, we are able to recognize whether or not we are fully open and in connection.

Fear gets in the way of this level of connection. It blocks our heart intelligence and holds us back from fully opening up. We then walk with a guarded heart. You are not bad for having a closed heart. It just indicates that you have some work to do to clear out the blocks and to open up. It may be that you are carrying the memory of a hurtful experience. It is natural to be careful after having been hurt. But it is not wise to shut down and tolerate being closed off.

In order to reopen, you must first be willing to reopen. It may be that you are carrying anger or disappointment around with you as a way of protecting your Self from any future hurt. Again, you are not bad for doing so, but you must be willing to let go of that stick, to put it down, to forgive your Self and any other person who is a part of the story, so that you can heal and move on.

Attaching your Self to, and then retelling, an old story of how you were wronged or hurt by another only keeps recreating that hurt over and over.

Often the process of healing such wounds is better carried out with the help of someone who is gifted in some sort of healing process. Your part is to recognize that healing is needed and then to ask for help.

Help might come in the form of a friend or family member who holds a healing wisdom. It could be a coach or a counselor. It is someone who can support you to fully embrace the experience you are having, while simultaneously not rescuing you from it. Ideally it's someone who can help you fully access your feelings, at the same time challenging you to move past the event when it is time. You don't want to work with someone who enables you in behavior that keeps you caught in the old story, holding onto it longer than is needed.

Here are some signs that a heart healing is wanted:

- You are blaming your Self for something that happened.
- You are blaming someone else for something that happened.
- You are angry at your Self or another.
- You are sad about something that happened and the nature of that sadness is not shifting over time.
- You are numb about something that happened.
- You experience emotional floods that overwhelm you.
- You are emotionally detached.
- You are hurting your Self or another.

If any of the above symptoms have settled in as a long-term way of living, then it may be that Distorted has grabbed this event and is holding onto it as way of keeping you from moving forward towards healing.

When you are fully open to heart wisdom, you will recognize that there is always more work for you to do as far as healing your Self is concerned. We all have to heal at some level. Recognizing that healing is needed is not only wise, it is normal. Resisting or denying that healing is needed is also normal—it just is not wise.

A healing heart is an opening heart. We must learn to walk

with an open heart. Someone recently asked me how I could walk around the world as I do, being so open and trusting. I pointed out to him that I am in the habit of assessing if there is any real danger. If I am not aware of any real danger, then it's okay for me to be open. We all must learn to discern between when we are at risk of true danger and when we are just operating from the habit of being closed.

Divine Essence knows the difference. Divine Essence knows when to walk with your energy pulled in, perhaps helping you to become invisible or to move by unnoticed, because it understands that you are in a situation that is actually dangerous. Divine Essence does not put you into situations that are openly dangerous without at least recognizing the risk.

Distorted Self, however, takes every opportunity to create the illusion of danger in situations where the risk is minimal. Distorted Self would rather have you be closed all the time, just in case. Once bitten, twice shy is the credo of Distorted. Distorted says, "Do not take any chances of being rejected or misunderstood or hurt in any way."

Divine Essence does not seek out being hurt. Divine Essence will, however, risk being hurt, because it knows that it is better to be open and risk being hurt than to be shut down and miss out on a brilliant life. This is where discernment comes into play as the key to moving through life and making moment-by-moment choices according to your highest heart wisdom, rather that your lowest Distorted fears.

Heart wisdom is of truth, compassion, and abundance, for the heart claims ownership over nothing except the joy of the moment. And therefore it has nothing to defend, it does not suffer from fear of loss. It does not get angry from false causes nor does it use shame or blame over you or others as a weapon.

Heart wisdom is ancient and wise and of the present moment.

The Universe communicates through our Divine Essence. It will come through as intuition or divine inspiration. Because of this, the information that does come through is often inexplicable by our minds. It has come through us, rather than to us, from an outside source. The heart inherently receives and understands the wisdom of the Universe. It knows that the greatest experience a human can have is to be in-joy, in connection, and in One.

Our hearts are portals that connect us into the Universal wisdom.

Our heart wisdom will connect us through the Wisdom Field, if we allow that to happen. And allowing is all that is needed. It is like being in a warm pool of water, held safely. We could cut our Selves off from the experience, perhaps by worrying about drowning or worrying that it won't last, or any other of a thousand distractions. Yet doing so would take us away from the direct experience that all is well and good in the warm pool of water.

The heart has no need of possessing. It is the work of Distorted Self that has us believe it is so important to have accomplishments, titles, excess possessions, or any other accoutrement to bolster our Selves. Distorted does not trust that it is enough to just be. Our hearts, when open, are beyond fear. Our hearts know that there is no I or you, they or we, or any truth in separation. Our hearts thrive on interrelatedness.

THE YEARNING

Our heart holds a wisdom that is distinct from that of our minds. To our heart wisdom, individuality and separateness are just concepts that the mind has created in its need to give context to what is happening.

As the heart yearns, it speaks to us in the language of the heart. That language is beyond words. The heart moves us according to its wisdom. It moves us with a pull towards something, the yearning. We feel drawn towards. When experience the pull of the heart, our mind attempts to understand. The mind gets drawn into the aching and the pulling. It wants to understand. It is spun around in its attempt to interpret what will satisfy this yearning of the beating heart. That heart pounds out its life call as a drum beat, reminding us that something more is out there somewhere. Sometimes the mind will get it, but very often it will not.

It is important to notice what we are yearning for. The pull of the heart could be coming from the Universe calling you towards your life purpose, or it could be the voice of your Divine Essence, the source of wisdom within you, as it guides you along your journey. It may take you into perilous waters to fulfill some unwritten contract with the Universe that requires you to engage with the aching of your heart, or it may be an easy part of the path that is filled with lightness and fun. It is all important, and all part of heart wisdom.

The pull of the heart demands that you engage with the path, so that you can fully appreciate the beauty of full and open connection to your Self and the world around you. It may be that our ability to know joy is directly proportional to our willingness and ability to dive deep into the yearning for love and connection.

And, of course, we must also be aware of the tendency of Distorted Self to want to mess with our mind and heart, to distract us from our Soul's path. Distorted Self would have you believe that to know such a longing is ultimately not survivable, so you are better off disconnecting from the pain whether that's through keeping your Self overly busy, using drugs, or engaging in some other form of avoidance. After all, according to Distorted, any form of pain is to be avoided at all costs and cannot possibly be good for you. On the other side, Distorted might tell you that it is only through your attachment to pain that life can have meaning. Neither of these ideas comes from the wisdom of your Divine Essence.

It is the heart that yearns, letting us know that something more is possible. The mind responds to that yearning, seeking out an answer. Then the heart and the mind pull at the fabric of our body to create the tension of restlessness.

Perhaps every situation we encounter can be placed between two possibilities: One is to move towards the ecstatic joy of connection—fully open, heart connection to God, the Universe. The second is to know the pain of separation. In between those two absolute extremes is where most of us live our lives.

Our Divine Essence is that aspect of our Selves that is the portal to the Universe. It is the doorway between our life in this body and being the Light of the Divine. We came from the Oneness. That experience preceded this embodied life. We have this life to remember it.

OLD WISDOM

Heart wisdom understands connection and respects all the other beings in our Universe. The native traditions hold a remarkable and beautiful heart connection to the plants, animals, earth, and the solar system. They intimately know how important their experience of Oneness is to the survival of all.

Our native ancestors learned how to live from heart intelligence and to collaborate with other beings—our relations as they were called. They knew that we could live in abundance as long as our behavior and intentions respected the needs of all the other beings as well. They learned how to listen to the world around them and how to communicate to the Universe and all of her many aspects. They knew interrelatedness at the level of being.

Our ancestors knew that it would be wrong and perilous to take from other beings without the due regard that enabled them to enter into conversation with the world around them in the first place. In those conversations they would seek the wisdom that would inform their decisions and actions. They had a concept of abundance through which they asked for as much as they needed, as much as what was offered according to the greater good of all. And they received their blessings with respect and gratitude, rather than entitlement.

Those native ancestors suffered as much as we do today. But their suffering was on behalf of the community. They knew that suffering was a normal part of the cycle of life and death. They embraced this cycle as a natural gift, so just as suffering became part of their way, so too did joy. Rather than resist death, they embraced the truth of it. In so doing, they could transcend it. The gift of living this way was joy and a vibrant life.

In modern times, we have mostly become consumers of the world. We take the resources of other beings without regard for the well-being of the whole. We fight against the cycles of life and death. In doing so, we push death off to the side, so that we don't have to look at it. We make suffering wrong, so that we can develop mind/body/heart-numbing drugs that level out the dynamic vitality of life, rather than face it straight on. Having lived this way for so many hundreds of years, we are now being confronted with the effects of such disregard.

At the end of the day, the Earth reflects our actions back to us. The Earth will eventually heal itself. That the Earth will carry on is not the question. Whether we humans will be around as part of the story moving forward is the more pressing question.

When heart wisdom is applied, the question of sustainability arises naturally.

Our native ancestors practiced seven-generation thinking. When they considered the use of resources, they asked themselves what the impact would be seven generations out. Then they chose and acted accordingly.

Figure 6: Heart Wisdom Reporting

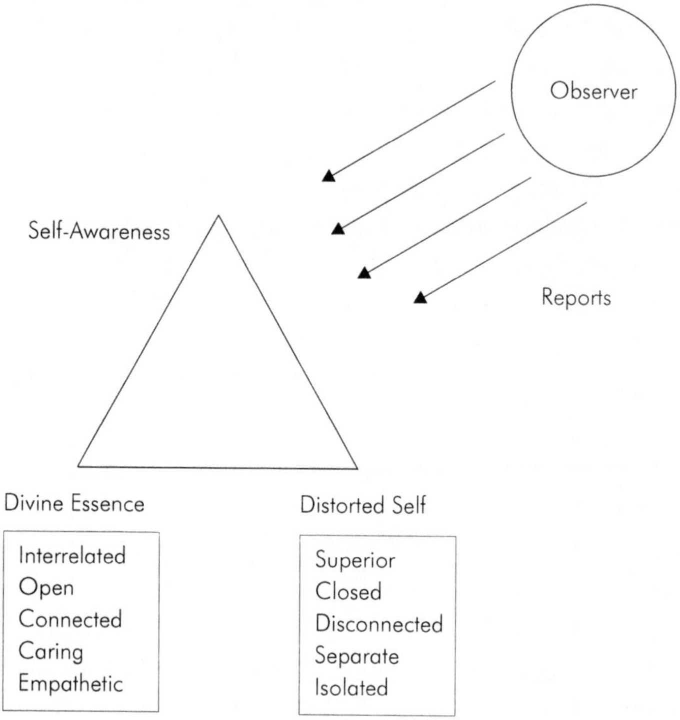

Self-Awareness

Observer

Reports

Divine Essence

Interrelated
Open
Connected
Caring
Empathetic

Distorted Self

Superior
Closed
Disconnected
Separate
Isolated

MIND INTELLIGENCE

Mind intelligence is constructed over the course of our lifetimes. The mind is beautiful and intellectual. It gathers facts, collects experiences, analyzes, and is wildly creative, when we allow it to be unleashed.

The mind is a crucial ally in the human journey, with two important directives guiding it simultaneously. The first is that it survive, and the second is that it learn and grow. These two driving forces are like two equally powerful departments—the department of survival and the department of learning—and they are often at odds with each other.

Distorted Self will collect data from life's experiences then use what it has learned from the past to keep you protected from it. It will build a box around you made up of rules, do's and don'ts that over time cut you off from a vibrant life. It will do everything it can to protect you from risking that which it fears the most. Examples of what Distorted Self might fear could be embarrassment, looking bad, failing, emotional hurt, and physical hurt.

What's wrong with that? you might ask. Well, the only way to avoid these things is to start avoiding situations in life in which you risk facing them. The more of life you avoid, the smaller your life gets. Eventually, you will be left with nowhere to go because the risk is anywhere.

We could cheer and applaud such brilliance, if it weren't so destructive.

Divine Essence has experienced the same life situations. But rather than collecting the stories to hold you back, Divine Essence learns what there is to learn from each experience, then uses the past to inform the present about what is the wise course. Divine Essence is willing to risk experiencing all that Distorted is afraid of, because Divine Essence is not invested from a place of ego. Divine Essence does not experience embarrassment or looking bad, as these are constructs of Distorted. From the perspective of Divine Essence, even being emotionally hurt is understood to be a part of a normal life. Divine Essence knows that you will survive such hurt, even thrive, as long as you remain willing to risk it.

Divine Essence uses the learning of the past to support you in moving forward through a rich and vibrant life that will be filled with challenges.

Distorted is invested in keeping you alive by imagining dangers and threats, and therefore causes reactions, even when there is no actual danger. Divine Essence is able to discern what are genuine dangers and threats. Divine Essence will assess a situation and know the difference between real and imagined.

Through curiosity and discernment, we learn to know the difference between Divine Essence and Distorted Self.

One of the greatest lies that Distorted will have us believe is that we are in any way separated from each other and everything. Distorted intends to create stories that lead to separation.

As has been said previously, Distorted will close the heart to protect it. Through the mind, Distorted will use thoughts of judgment to create separation. Distorted believes that if it can separate you, isolate you, and stop you from moving forward, it can then protect you.

Distorted thoughts will be some version of the following:

- They don't understand this situation or me.
- They don't get it.
- They don't like me.
- They can't be trusted.
- They are trying to trick me.
- They won't choose me because . . .
- There is not enough.
- I can't do it.
- I am not up to it.
- I don't know enough yet.
- I don't belong here.
- I am too busy.
- I should . . .
- I have no choice.

When we are receiving these types of messages, we are often experiencing confusion, stuckness, sleepiness, or panic. These are symptoms that manifest when messages from Distorted are running somewhere in the background, if not right at the forefront of our minds.

When Divine Essence is in front, we are creative, resourceful, able to consider options, willing to take risks, and clear—even if we don't know what the right choice is. In fact, Divine Essence understands that there often is no "right" choice and that there are often many feasible choices, even if none of them are perfect.

HOW DO WE GET PAST THESE DISTORTED MESSAGES?

Divine Essence knows the difference between something that is made up and something that is true. Distorted would have you believe that the statements listed above are true, but if you really examine each one, you will find that they can never absolutely be known to be true. There might be some small aspect of truth in them, but none of them are 100 percent true. Therefore, we have the opportunity to create some other possibilities.

Working in conjunction with our heart wisdom, we must first check in to see if we are open to the possibility that these ideas may not be true. If you are committed to any of those statements being true, then you are most likely in the grip of Distorted.

Divine Essence is not attached to any idea being true. Divine Essence is willing to explore and consider other possibilities. Divine Essence is willing to open up in order to discover what is really needed to move forward in a good way.

When Divine Essence is active, your thoughts are energizing. These are thoughts that allow openness to possibilities, to greater connection, to ideas that move you forward to the point where you can actually stop and be still in a clear and resonant way, yet still have momentum.

Divine Essence may not know exactly which path is best, because this life is full of mystery. We are finding our way, unfolding that mystery one step at a time. Divine Essence is, however, always willing to take the risks associated with moving forward.

Divine Essence knows that there are a variety of ways to accomplish things, not just one right way. Divine Essence knows that I can help you and you can help me. Neither of us needs to sacrifice each other or our Selves. Divine Essence knows that we can learn and understand as we move forward—we do not need to have it all figured out before we can take the first step.

Divine Essence knows that there is enough room for your beauty and brilliance, along with mine and everybody else's, and the more magic the better.

Divine Essence is unattached to power and control, because the shared road is more fulfilling than the controlled road.

Divine Essence knows that controlling the world is futile and exhausting. It is more about guiding it moment-by- moment, as in a dance with everyone at the same time. This can be fun, as well as effective.

When Divine Essence is in charge of the department of learning, it gathers in knowledge and experience as you move through life. Divine Essence will keep an accurate account of past experiences as a way of advising you in moving forward. Divine Essence will encourage you to take risks in order to create fulfillment and joy in the world. Divine Essence will use wisdom to support you, rather than to keep you overprotected. Divine Essence knows that sustained growth is a good thing and that attachment to things staying the way they are is not helpful.

So we are faced with the paradox that the journey of surviving and that of learning seem to be at odds with each other. Survival, according to Distorted, is about playing it safe, while the quest for learning is dangerous.

According to Divine Essence, we will not only survive, but it is a process of moving towards fulfillment. For Divine Essence, learning is an adventure of moving through life that sometimes requires that we go out into the world and play and experiment and risk failing.

So it follows, then, that life's experiences could lead to a lot of chatter and background noise in your mind. We must learn how to notice each message, then choose whether or not to give it any credibility or energy.

One simple and effective way to do this is to make note of a message when you hear it in your mind and to put the message in front of you by writing it down. Then compare the message with what you know is absolutely true—only what you can verify to be true is absolutely true. Anything else that has any room for any other possibility is not absolutely true and therefore should not be taken as a truth. It should be taken as just an idea, a possibility among many possibilities.

For example, suppose you are applying for a job. The chatter in your mind might say something like, "They probably won't hire me."

When you examine this thought, it is easy to see that it has no absolute truth in it. There is no basis in fact. It is simply a message that Distorted is telling you, likely in its effort to save you from experiencing disappointment. Upon acknowledging that this thought is not factual, you can practice releasing it.

In order to release it, try using a simple response. I like to silently say, "That is not true." I then offer another possibility to the situation. In this example, I would say something like, "I might be exactly who they are looking for, and there is no harm in trying." Or another favorite of mine that applies to lots of situation is, "Nothing ventured, nothing gained."

To create a physical experience of breaking the spell of Distorted's chatter, I will make a sharp movement with my hand as I say, "Nothing ventured, nothing gained." This practice integrates mind intelligence with body intelligence.

For the sake of our learning here, I am separating the three intelligences into sections, but in actual life they all live so closely together that they are in fact inseparable. Notice how when a thought occurs, your body responds. It may be a tightening of the stomach or the flinch of a hand. So when you create a mantra that helps you recover from Distorted to Divine Essence, you will likely also notice that a part of your body wants to move to support the shift.

As a way of knowing whether I am still holding onto the lie, I will check in with my heart intelligence to see how open it is to the idea of more possibilities. Remember, Divine Essence is not attached. So if you find you are committed to an idea being absolutely true, then that is likely a sign that Distorted is still in charge.

OH THE STORIES WE TELL

Things happen to us in our lives and we create stories. This is how we re-experience and share our lives—through the stories we tell about the events that happen to us. This is good when Divine Essence is in charge of the story department, but it can be destructive when Distorted is in charge.

When Distorted gets a hold of a story, it usually becomes a tale that lacks good intention in the telling of it. These are the stories that tend to depict versions of us against them; or how you won and they lost because you are superior; or perhaps how you were wronged and are a victim. Distorted is always happy to have one more story that makes someone in the world wrong, and it is a bonus if it makes you more of a victim.

Distorted takes any event and turns it into a tale that suits its mission. Then Distorted gets attached to the story, bringing it out over and over to drive the point home to you or to anyone who will listen.

One way to tell if Distorted is the storyteller is to look into the story and see if it creates a view that puts you or another down, or makes you or someone else wrong or better than. Distorted will twist the facts in subtle or not so subtle ways, because every tale can be turned and twisted according to the storyteller's motives.

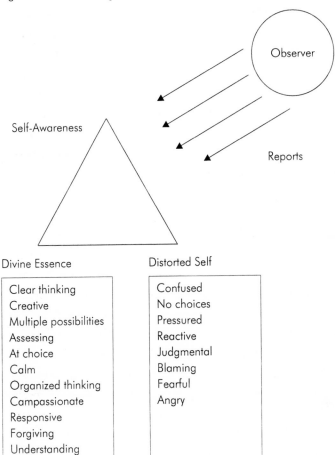

Figure 7: Mind Intelligence Reporting

Observer

Self-Awareness

Reports

Divine Essence	Distorted Self
Clear thinking	Confused
Creative	No choices
Multiple possibilities	Pressured
Assessing	Reactive
At choice	Judgmental
Calm	Blaming
Organized thinking	Fearful
Compassionate	Angry
Responsive	
Forgiving	
Understanding	

When Distorted is in charge, the story shows patterns of previous stories, pointing to Distorted's desire to remain stuck in a particular belief system. Or the story gets exaggerated and becomes worse and worse with each telling. Once Distorted gets a hold of a good story, it likes to keep it intact so that the power of the story stays strong.

When Divine Essence is the storyteller, the experience is one of truth and generosity. Divine Essence is conscious of the intention of telling the story. Divine Essence might tell a story to create a teaching or perhaps to create a healing. A healing story will shift with each telling, because as you heal the wound related to the story, the state of healing comes through and thereby shifts the story to reflect the healing process.

Divine Essence does not use stories as weapons over people, but rather as a way of sharing in a good way so that everyone may benefit from experiencing the telling of the story.

Divine Essence has a sense of humor, too. It will entertain with stories. As the storyteller, Divine Essence is telling the tale from a place of good intention. A story from Divine Essence will leave everyone feeling that they have been entertained—and that they have learned something in the process.

A STORY EXERCISE

Here is a great exercise to understand the difference between the stories as told from the point of view of the Observer, Distorted, and Divine Essence.

First, activate the Observer and choose three events from your life that have happened. Let the Observer report the facts of these events. This report should not have any judgment about whether the events were good or bad, or any assessment of what happened. Remember, the Observer is just reporting facts.

Now for version two of the story. Tell the story of the same events, only now, just for the sake of this exercise, let your Distorted Self really cut loose and have its own version. Distorted can exaggerate to make a point, blame people, or twist the story any way it wants. Have fun with it.

Now for version three. Activate your Divine Essence to tell the story of the same events. Divine Essence will not exaggerate, telling the story from a very clean point of view that will likely result in gathering in some learning.

Notice how different each version is. Notice that the Distorted version might have been entertaining in the context of this exercise, but imagine the impact of living a life where most of the storytelling being done is through Distorted's lens. That sounds like a life of victimhood or of superiority over others. It may satisfy Distorted, but it ultimately won't lead to any form of joy.

Divine stories tend to leave everyone who hears the story feeling touched and shifted. Divine stories tend to create learning for everyone who hears them, and they can still be very entertaining and funny when the story warrants it.

BODY INTELLIGENCE

Action, stillness, procrastination, and movement are all part of the realm of body intelligence.

When we are connected to Divine Essence, we are moving the action of our life forward in a good way. When we are being run by our Distorted view, we might find our Selves in procrastination, which is avoiding moving life forward, or we might be moving in haste, which is moving forward at a fast pace without the benefit of awareness in the moment.

Your body intelligence holds its own wisdom, and the more you learn how to read the language of your body, the more access you will have to that information.

Each event we experience in life has an impact on the body. This includes imagined events as much as it does real ones. As far as your body is concerned, an imagined event is just as real as one that you physically experience. That is why we can practice events over and over through visualization and get better at them for when we actually perform those activities.

Your body stores information commonly referred to as muscle memory, the memory of a particular movement of your body as it performs a task. The more you practice, the more your body can carry out that task. In some situations, the more your body is freed from your mind, the better the result of the activity. Athletes get into the zone when they are taken over by Divine Essence. Their bodies glide along, performing the event at a masterful level.

Bodies also hold emotional memory, which is stored in the water of our bodies. When we experience an emotion, our body water holds that emotion. If we keep re-experiencing the event, such as we often do through the memory of the mind, the body continually restores the emotional experience of that event, as if it were really happening over and over.

It's a good practice to learn how to scan your body and notice where you are holding tension. Where in your body are you relaxed? What emotion are you experiencing? What part of your body do you put forward and what part do you hold back? Knowing how to access the answers to these questions is a part of accessing body intelligence.

Your body is responding to the stories that your mind creates just as it responds to the real time, present moment and actual situations you are in.

That is why, as discussed earlier, it is essential that we notice what stories we are telling our Selves. Then choose whether or not to repeat them. Because every time we tell a story we are impacting our body by recreating both an emotional and a physical memory. Our body also activates its memory whenever a situation in the present moment reminds it of a past experience.

You might have found your Self in an apparently safe situation, only to notice your Self tensing up and panicking. The present moment is safe and yet something has activated an old memory that has been stored in your body.

Because the body is so impacted by all sorts of stored memories, it is easy to see how important it is to consciously interact with your body intelligence. Three of the most effective ways of doing this are by using scanning, movement, and breathing.

Scanning is when you choose to scan your body with your mind. This is an integration of mind intelligence to access body intelligence. You literally check in with each muscle group, organ, and part of your body to assess how it is. It is your Observer that does the scan and reports what is being noticed. The information is then passed on and, as you know by now, your job is to activate your Divine Essence. As a result, Divine Essence will likely recognize that something is needed to correct or improve the current situation.

Conscious movement is a good way to get past the hold that Distorted may have over you. This refers specifically to getting up and moving—getting your blood circulating, your muscles moving by exercising, walking, running, or swimming. It is challenging for Distorted to stay active when you move your body.

When in doubt, move!

Doubt is created in mind intelligence when Distorted is in charge. When you experience doubt, or any similar emotion like confusion, use the movement of your body to shift your state of mind. Give your Self permission to stand up at a meeting, or to pull back physically from a situation. Moving the energy through your body gives space for creativity and clarity to come back in.

Breathing is a powerful way to shift your state of being. Most people in western cultures tend to breathe in a shallow way. Notice when you are breathing shallowly. Then take a few long breaths deep into your belly. This will create a much-needed shift. Move your body at the same time and notice what changes in each of the three intelligences.

Get curious about what is going on in your body while you are in different experiences. You might start to notice things differently than before. For instance, as you go into a meeting, you check in on your body intelligence, you notice that your left shoulder is tense. Rather than dismissing it as you may be in the habit of doing, try getting curious with your left shoulder.

One good way to do this is to amplify the tension, making it bigger. As you do this, imagine that your left shoulder can speak for itself. Get curious about what concerns it is holding. Ask it what it wants you to know about the situation you're in. You might be amazed at some of the insights that can be revealed through the process of letting your body speak for itself.

Let's use public speaking as another example of a situation that might cause a reaction in your body. If public speaking is easy for you and does not give you anything to examine, then substitute an experience that does make you tense up as you read the following scenario.

Imagine that you have been invited to speak at a local community event and you're on in the next hour. As the idea of this sets in, notice what reaction your body has to this idea. You might be noticing a tightening in your stomach, or perhaps your arms want to fold up in front of you. Just notice whatever there is to notice.

Activate your Observer to report in on what is being noticed. Take a moment to collect the report.

Now, for the sake of the example, let's say your stomach has knotted up. Rather than trying to fight it, tighten the knot even more, exaggerate it, and get curious with the experience.

Imagine that your stomach can talk and that it has something to tell you.

Ask it what it is concerned about. What is it protecting you from? What is needed for it to let go and relax?

Gather in any ideas that occur to you during this process, no matter how unexpected or irrelevant they might seem.

Now get curious about each idea that has come to you. Follow them through with another round of questioning.

Curiosity is like gently pulling at the end of a ball of string that slowly unravels to reveal previously unknown wisdom.

Once you have addressed something, rather than ignoring it or pushing it away, you will have likely uncovered some simple and important wisdom.

When you listen to your body intelligence, your body learns that it's okay to relax as it hands its concerns over to Divine Essence. Once your body knows that Divine Essence is paying attention to its concerns, it knows that it no longer holds that responsibility.

As you get more skilled at this, you will start to notice waves of energy that move and shift through your body. You may start to notice that two different parts of your body will be having two very different reactions to the same situation. For example, your head and shoulders might be leaning forward as if to say, "Let's go!" while your hips might be pushing back trying to slow you down.

Remember that this should all be taken in for what it is: helpful information. What's important is the awareness of these messages. Chances are that you will not have to do anything about these physical signals; once they have been spotted, they have a way of taking care of themselves. So notice them, get curious, keep breathing, and move your body.

If you experience chronic pain conditions in your body, it is important to check in and find out what wisdom that aspect of your body is trying to get you to pay attention to. Ignoring something does not make it go away.

The only way through it is through it!

When I was living in Burma, I sat for hours in meditation poses that often created extreme levels of discomfort in my body. Each time that happened, I was amazed at how the pain would shift and become manageable once I placed my attention on it. We are often taught to look the other way when something hurts us. I suggest that you look right at it. You will learn that you are more powerful than anything that is troubling you and that the more willing you are to face into whatever is bothering you, the less power those things will have over you. Your body will be very grateful to you for listening to its intelligence.

Another aspect of the realm of body intelligence is action. If you are moving your life forward in a good, balanced, and steady way, then chances are that all is reasonably well.

If, however, you notice that you are not following through with ideas, either because you abandon them too quickly or because you procrastinate on them, then that's an indication that something is needed.

Distorted will have us turn away from our good ideas. This could be experienced through the body as getting sleepy every time you attempt to make progress on a goal or idea, or your body might start to hurt whenever you get to the time to follow through. Stuckness is created by Distorted.

Divine Essence will choose stillness only as often as it is wise to do so. Stillness has a very different resonance around it than stuckness does. Stillness will rest the body, open the heart, and free the mind. Stuckness will feel like persistent tiredness or sluggishness, and it will close the heart, shut down your creative energy, and dull the mind.

If you feel the stuckness of Distorted, it usually helps to get out for a walk, and it's even better if you call a friend to walk with you, so that they can support you in getting clear about what you might need to pay attention to.

The opposite of being stuck is to always be moving from thing to thing, never slowing down, never stopping to just sit and relax.

Some people are amazing in how much they are accomplishing in their lives. We look at them in wonder as they show up in the center of every event. They are getting so much done—yet often something is missing. If you notice your Self as one of these people, you might notice that being in constant action also means you are missing some things.

Action can be a convenient way to avoid facing directly into the emotional and relationship fields of what is going on. This is a tricky thing to navigate because these types of people are generally quite acknowledged for their high level of performance. This is especially true in western business culture where doing is prized over a good state of being.

Distorted will have these achiever types chasing after recognition, high performance evaluations, certificates, one more project after one more project. It's not uncommon for these doers to find themselves quite ill one day, as the body can ultimately no longer sustain such a pace. Or, they might find themselves alone, as their pace has kept them from developing any meaningful relationships.

If these doers stopped to ask Divine Essence what is needed in their lives, they would probably hear a message about slowing down. In order to follow that advice, they will need great courage, since it invariably means having to face into the parts of their life that they have been avoiding.

Each of these examples requires that we have the insight to learn what is needed to create more balanced lives—then the will to follow through on the wisdom that presents itself.

It is one thing to realize what is needed. It is something else again to correct the situation before a major life crisis forces the issue.

Figure 8: Body Intelligence Reporting

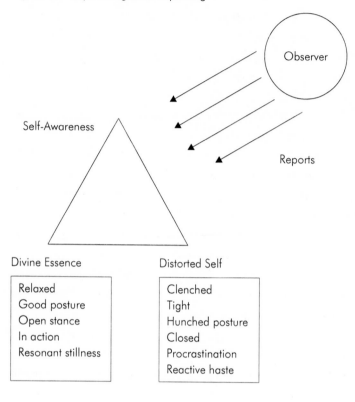

Dreaming and Life Purpose

As far as I know, we humans are the only beings that have the capacity to look out into the future, dream into it, and influence it by doing so. That leads to a very interesting question: Why us?

It seems that the Universe needs us to engage with it, using our dream capabilities, and in doing so we enter into an amazing partnership.

It is a partnership through which we get to have a strong and influential say about the way things will go. It also puts a lot of responsibility on us to be sure that we are dreaming from the wisdom of our Divine Essence.

When you dream, you aspire to be something, to create something, to have something. As you dream, you create a tension between the reality of your life as it is today and the way you would like it to look. That tension works like an elastic band that draws the dream in towards you. Therefore, when you dream you are in-tension, or intention.

When I use the word dream here I am not talking about the dreams you have when you sleep, though those types of dreams also inform and work on us and tell us a great deal about our life dreams. Instead, I am talking about the kind of dream in which you dream for something. Looking out into the future and daring to hope, ask, and act in accordance with your dream and the desire to have it come true.

Much of what each of us has in our lives today is likely the result of the things we dreamed about before today. The seeds we planted in the past are reflected in the life we are living today and the life we are living today is planting the seeds of tomorrow.

Of course, we are talking about the beauty of dreams from the wisdom of Divine. Distorted will also use the power of dreams against you. We will discuss this more fully later on, but for now, assume that we are talking about Divine dreams.

Beyond our own dreams, we are also impacted by the dreams of those around us whose lives are connected to ours. This is also true of the dreams of the communities we live in, our countries' dreams, and so on, all the way through to the dreams of the Universe—all of which affect our own dream walk.

WHOSE DREAM IS IT?

Let's take a step back and consider the sources of all the dreams that are pulling and calling you.

THE DREAMS OF THE HUMAN THAT YOU ARE

First there are the dreams of your Self. From the place of Divine Essence, there are many good dreams to be imagined. These are good and normal dreams, which may include the desire to have possessions, to be able to accomplish things, and to be in great relationships. They are dreams that are easy to understand. They are what they are, and it is good to have these dreams as long as your Divine Essence holds them.

YOUR FAMILY DREAMS

When you dream, you are dreaming on behalf of your family as well. As you imagine moving forward from today, you very likely will have some dreams that affect your family. They may be dreams for a nicer house or for other material things. It may be that you are dreaming for your kids to get a good education which you may have to pay for, and so you dream that you will have the money and resources for that. You may be dreaming of good health for your family. You may be dreaming of a promotion at work, or that your business takes off so that you can afford to provide the kind of life that you dream of for your family.

At the same time, your family has their own dreams. Many of those dreams will likely align with yours, and many may not. They may be dreams that compete with yours. It's possible that over time they can all fit together, but some may have to wait for others to go first.

CAREER DREAMS

How about where you work? You may be dreaming of a promotion into a job that you really want for a lot of different reasons. It may be more interesting, or pay better, or you may just want a change.

From the other side, your workplace may be dreaming of using you in a particular way that may or may not be aligned with your dreams. You are dreaming of one thing and your boss is dreaming of you being something quite different.

YOUR COMMUNITY DREAMS

You live in a community. It may be that you have a dream for your community. You might dream that it develops itself into a good community according to what your ideas of "good" are. Alongside your own dreams for the community are the dreams your community has for itself, and there is a part for you to play in that, too. What is your community's dream for you?

We can carry this process out further and further. Whatever group or system or anything that you are a part of—all of them play a role in dreaming into what is needed, and you have a part in that dream. It may be that your dreams are completely aligned with what's being dreamed up, or it may that that the dream you have and the dream that your community has for you are very different.

SPIRITUAL DREAMS

Next is the call of your Soul. Your Soul is on a journey and it also dreams. The Soul's dreams will have you look into the bigger questions of your life purpose and the impact that you are having on the world. Remember that we each have our own special genius that we carry, and your Soul dreams that your purpose will be expressed throughout your life.

WHAT IS THE UNIVERSE'S DREAM FOR YOU?

You have a part to play in the great unfolding dream of the Universe. As you live your life and carry your dreams, you are also being dreamed up by the Universe. The Universe is calling on you as the human you are to play your part. At the same time the Universe is very interested in the development of your Soul. Your Soul is what will live on after you have completed with this human life. It is that part of you that is not body, mind, or heart, but rather is of Divine Essence. Your Soul has an ongoing part to play in the Universe, so the Universe is dreaming, calling, and guiding you along your earthly path in a way that you will never fully understand in this lifetime.

A LOT OF DREAMERS

You can see that there are a lot of influences coming through you and from all around you that are all contributing to the life experience that you are living. Each dreamer is shaping your journey, and each dreamer has its own dream.

Dreams are guiding influences that inform our choices as we move through our daily lives. Sometimes they ask for changes that are of earthquake-like proportions whose momentum and direction has us completely turn our daily lives upside down. Other times they are subtle shifts and responses to simple wishes and prayers.

Dreams inspire us on good days, and they are things we aspire to. A spire is a structure that is usually found on top of something like a hill, or that points up towards the sky, as if to reach out more closely to God. When we aspire, we are reaching out to God, the Universe, with our human spirit as an internal spire that connects us to the Divine.

The art of dreaming is learning to hold the tension between being called forward to create something different than what is in our lives today, and at the same time to be present and to live in the moment of now.

We cast a wish, a prayer to the Universe, and then we move our lives according to Divine Essence's wisdom in order to realize those dreams.

All of the dreams are being held in the Wisdom Field. All the voices and prayers of all the dreamers are coming together and are having a strong influence on us as we are whispered to or shouted at from the Wisdom Field.

SYNCHRONICITY

There are no accidents. There is no such thing as coincidence. There is a beautiful, elegant, and powerful orchestration of emerging dreams that are interacting with each other, so that the intentions and visions of all those dreams may all be realized.

As you dream, you activate the Universe to meet you in that dream. As others dream, they are doing the same. As the family, organization, or community you belong to dreams, they are also activating the world we are all in to realign themselves in accordance with each dream. All of those dreams are playing out, including the dream of the Universe itself.

Now picture your own part of your dream—perhaps you dream of getting a new job that would offer you some new challenges and use you in a different way. As you hold that dream, the Universe is activating the world around according to your dream.

Now imagine that there is an organization out there, perhaps even your own organization, and that it, too, is dreaming. It is dreaming of a new department because it knows that it needs to adapt in order to survive. The Universe is also aligning with the organization's dream and things are starting to move around.

So there you are holding your dream, while the organization holds its dream—and both of you are moving along your path.

Then one day you see a posting describing exactly the kind of job that you were wishing for. You recognize immediately that this is the job, the dream, and how amazing that you heard about it just as you were dreaming for it.

This is synchronicity at work.

Synchronicity is when the trajectory of two or more things that are trying to happen meet and support each other towards the realization of their respective intentions.

Every time someone or something crosses your path, be curious about what is going on. You may not immediately recognize the connection, so you might have to look deeper. You might not understand how things are interrelated or moving you along until, in retrospect, you see that as soon as you said yes to one event, the river opened up and carried you far along towards your dream.

PLANS AND FLEXIBILITY

As we move through the world, we create a steady flow of ideas about where we are headed and how to get there. These are our plans. Plans are all well and good, as long as we are unattached to whatever our ideas might be.

The magic of an awakened life happens when we invite the Universe in to play and dance with us.

In order to do that, it is important to open up to the mystery of the unexpected. If we create a tight plan to move forward and lock into it, leaving no flexibility for the possibility of it working out differently, we will shut out the Universe from dancing with us.

In every moment of your life there is a certain amount going on that you are aware of. You can see it, plan it, imagine it, and move towards it. You are in fact only seeing the smallest portion of what is really happening. You are only seeing the tip of the iceberg. In each moment of every day, more of your path is being revealed to you. You must stay present and open to the emergence of the dream, both for your Self and for those around you. The mystery of the unfolding is beautiful when you get over the idea that you can control what is going on. You are safe in the hands of the Universe, so embrace not knowing how or where this life is leading you, and play your part in the great improvisation of life.

Learn that as long as you stay open and flexible to life as it dances with you, the path ahead will be alternately fun and challenging, easy and at times difficult, meaningful and sometimes questionable. Your part in the game is to follow the bouncing ball whenever you spot it crossing your path.

BELIEVE

Everything is happening wisely. The journey will test you. Remember that you are on a path of development. You are learning to be human, and every experience in your life is a teaching event. As you believe, it will be done. What is needed is for you to pass through the tests and challenges and to stay in believing.

You cannot control the Universe. You are the one who is creating the world experience that you are living. That is good news. Starting from believing and using intentions, words, and actions (all are discussed in Part Two), you are influencing the Universe towards aligning with your dream. What is needed from you is to stay connected to your Divine Essence. Then from the wisdom of Divine Essence to stay true to what you are dreaming in.

Staying true to the dream should not be confused with getting rigid or inflexible about how the dream might look or how it will come about.

I have had many dreams come true that at first I did not recognize because I was too distracted by my rigid picture, so I was not not seeing the dream even as it arrived at my door. Life happens while we're making our plans. Plans are useful up to a point, but as mentioned earlier, the Universe is bringing your dream to you—and it is infinitely wiser and more resourceful than you can possibly imagine. So it is most likely that the Universe knows how to deliver what you're dreaming to you better than you can plan it your Self.

The Universe is constantly speaking to you in ways that you, as a human, can understand only as long as you stay open to it. It will send people unexpectedly into your path with ideas and messages. It will bring books into your life that open you up to something new. It will send you confirmations and it will cause you to question. This is all part of the plan, for it is in the questions that the magic happens more often than in the answers.

The Universe will also shake you up when you are not paying attention. Imagine that everything that is in your moment right now might be telling you something—something important for you to pay attention to right now. The Universe is patient and persistent, and if we don't get it now, it will send us something else tomorrow.

As each day passes, the next step you thought you would be taking is likely changing, so you must remain open to new ideas while recognizing which ones to stay with until they blossom and provide the fruit they were intended to deliver.

You will make mistakes. You will miss turns. At times you might stay somewhere too long. That's okay!

In each moment you simply have to reconnect to your Divine Essence and ask, "What is needed now?"

Then you must listen to the wisdom that comes through. And then you must act on it.

WHO'S IN CHARGE
OF THE DREAM DEPARTMENT?

Divine Essence and Distorted Self have two very different ideas about what to dream for. As Divine Essence guides you farther along your amazing adventure, Distorted is most likely more invested in stopping you from taking risks, such as daring to want something. After all, Distorted might argue, if you allow your Self to really want it, then you might just end up being disappointed—and that can hurt. Better not to allow that. Distorted might have many different stories to tell you about how the world is against you or how you are not ready, or smart enough, or . . .

Recover to Divine Essence—that is your responsibility.

Distorted could also have us dream for things that are not really good for us, or that are not good for the world around us. Distorted's dreams do not consider the interrelatedness of All.

Distorted will often have us dream for too much of something good, because Distorted does not feel safe or trusting that all will be well.

Another trick of Distorted is to have us not be present in this moment, because we are lusting after our future.

Divine Essence knows how to hold the present moment while being in the amazing tension of a dream at the same time.

Distorted will often have us drift into dreaming as a way of taking us away from the present moment.

Divine Essence will create time and space for dreaming to happen in a good way.

Attachments and aversions are Distorted's way of holding our dreams against us.

Attachments and yearnings are the energies that often come over us as we move towards that which we aspire to, while aversions are those energies that have us push away from something, trying to avoid it. Both tend to be the nemesis for living an awakened life.

As humans, we have the capacity to want something, to imagine what the future could look like, and to then set about creating a series of events to make those dreams come true. Yet those very dreams can easily separate us from our wisdom, from walking the walk of an awakened human.

The key is to allow your Self to access the wisdom of Divine Essence and to get clear on what it is that you are dreaming in. Remember, as you dream anything in, you are creating a tension between you and the dream. Distorted may not like this tension.

The dream is drawn towards you as if you were a magnet. In

fact, you are. You create a magnetic field of attraction that pulls the dream in. At the same time you may be in action to create the dream. That might involve making calls, gathering resources, and moving through the plan of creation. This is all good.

Once Distorted gets a hold of the dream, it starts to break down. Distorted would have you believe that you are not okay unless the thing you are dreaming comes true. If you feel incomplete without it, or in any way unhappy or unable to be in-joy while you are holding the dream, then it might still be a good dream that originally came from Divine Essence. But it could be that Distorted has gotten a hold of it.

Distorted will likely either push you towards your dreams in a way that is not consistent with the Eight States of an Awakened Life (discussed in detail in Part Two), or it will interfere, distract, and delay you.

If you are experiencing a good sense of equanimity in relationship to your dream, then Divine Essence is likely guiding you.

That is when you are holding the dream in a way that has you believe that you are okay as you move towards it, or even if you end up without it. You are calm and balanced about it. You are able to be present to your moment-by-moment life while you and the dream approach each other.

Holding a dream from Divine Essence is to experience resonance in your life while you move and breathe your way forward. If Distorted has you, then you will be experiencing a lot of dissonance in life, especially with regards to the dream.

OWNING STUFF

There is nothing wrong with having stuff in your life. Material possessions can make life comfortable or fun or more fulfilled. It is important, though, to know what power we are giving over to our stuff. Happiness can only truly be found within. Learning to live a life of joy and happiness is important to living an awakened life. The idea that having that one more thing in order to be happy will never get you to know true happiness.

Many years ago, I owned a number of properties, cars, cameras, music, and entertainment equipment—all the stuff that seemed helpful in achieving a happy life. Indeed, to a certain extent I was happy and successful. And yet something stirred deep within me that drove me to look more deeply into the essence of life itself.

In answer to that urge, I decided to give up everything I owned and head off to a life of wandering. I packed a few things into boxes and gave a lot of stuff away to family, friends, and charities. I sold off my properties and my business, which helped me wipe the slate clean of old debt. Soon I owned nothing except what I could put in a backpack. Off I went on my great adventure. I bought a one-way ticket to Asia and committed my Self to following the wind and my intuition.

I felt the freedom of not having possessions, and I felt light and wondrous as I traveled around Asia living on a few dollars a day enjoying the mystery of what was to be.

Not too long into my travels, I came to find that even my backpack felt too heavy. It was a large backpack and in it I had everything that I thought I needed. Whenever I'd leave my backpack in whatever guest house I was staying in, I found my Self wondering if it would be okay. Was it safe from getting stolen? I had nothing of great value, and still I had attached my Self to these meager possessions as though my whole identity was tied up with them.

As I traveled, I acquired a souvenir here and there and my backpack started to swell with its growing load. Soon I started to give things away to local people in exchange for services like taxi rides and the backpack started to get lighter again.

Still, my stuff held a mysterious power over me that caused me to worry about its well-being.

Eventually, through a magical and synchronistic turn of events (which I have written about in much greater detail in my earlier book, *The Eagle's Call*), I found my way to an old monastery in Burma. It was there that I met the single most influential teacher of my life.

I stayed in the monastery as a guest until one day my teacher invited me to ordain and to join him in the Sangha of Buddhist monks. I agreed, continued to study with him until he felt it was time for me to enter the monkhood.

In order for a man to become a monk, he needs a sponsor, someone who will donate to him his robes, meditation beads, a straight razor, and a bowl. As a monk, I was only to have what had been donated to me and nothing more. So I handed my backpack over to the monastery. I released it with no expectation that I would ever get it back.

I felt freed from the weight of that backpack, both physically and emotionally. I had no idea what a psychic burden it had become until I no longer owned it. The impact of giving it up was as profound for me as having given up all my major possessions before leaving for Asia.

Some weeks passed, and I found my way into the life of a monk. I went out each day, as did all the monks, and collected alms, meaning that I left the monastery each day with my bowl and received donations of food from generous villagers. That is to say, each day I went begging.

We always had enough—some days more, others less. Living as a monk was an experience that taught me, along with many other lessons, about the excesses of our western ways.

One day I was asked to visit some villages in a remote part of

Burma. The trip would be fraught with peril, but I knew it would be important for me.

On that first morning of the journey, I woke up in a strange village along with the other monks at 4:00 AM to go out for the collecting of alms. The night before I had placed my bowl against the wall of the room where we were sleeping, but when I woke up it was gone.

There was nobody around who spoke English and I could not speak the local language. I couldn't ask for what I needed— my bowl.

I noticed that the other monks were going into a nearby room and emerging with bowls, so I walked over and entered.

Along the wall were stacked at least a hundred bowls, all identical, and all staring at me as if daring me to figure out which one was mine.

I noticed a voice inside my head that felt preoccupied with knowing which one was mine.

The voice was troubled as it shouted in my head, "Which bowl is mine?"

In that instant, I felt a shock wave roll over and through me. It was as if a lightning bolt were crashing through my body, my heart, and my mind, as if all my cells were being rearranged by this experience.

My whole body was recoiling in reaction as I thought to my Self with great shock, "Oh my gosh! I have identified my Self with a bowl."

The thought kept screaming out inside me. "I have identified my Self with a bowl. I have identified my Self with a bowl. I have given up all my worldly possessions and now I have attached my Self to a bowl!"

I was blown away by the absurdity of it all.

My ego was so clearly exposed before me. I witnessed it then in a way I never had before. As the wave of energy rolled through me, I felt as if I had been violently ejected out of a paradigm I had lived in my entire life. It was as if I were standing beside my old Self, seeing that part of me for the first time. That scared and fragile part of me that needed to identify with and attach itself to stuff so badly, just to know that it existed, just to know something about my Self.

As I stood there in shock, other monks passed by, moving in and out of the room, grabbing bowls to go out for the day. I grabbed the closest one to me and off I went into the rest of my life.

It is okay to own stuff as long as the stuff doesn't own you.

Today, I am blessed with an abundant life. I live well by world standards. I have a great partner, eat well, and I own things that make my life comfortable. But best of all, I have learned how to have things that make life fun and comfortable without those things owning me. I find my bliss and joy within, and as a result I am quite free.

HESITANCY AND COMMITMENT

Goethe said, "Until one is committed, there is hesitancy." And as long as you are in hesitancy, the Universe is willing to wait for you to decide.

It's normal to be uncertain about something, to want to wait until you know more, before deciding which way to go. But more often than not, we will never be certain, we will never be able to figure it all out in advance. A vibrant life is one in which we move through opening and closing doorways of chance and risk not knowing what will happen, unable to control the outcome.

The time of being called is an important time during which you have an opportunity to acknowledge that you don't know. This is when you are weighing your choices, deciding whether to stay the course or to try something new—perhaps in the hope that you will discover more about where you are headed. It is okay to seek to understand as much as you can. It is okay to weigh the costs and benefits, the pros and cons. It is good to sense into a situation and gather whatever insight is available. It is useful to notice what your body is telling you in the anticipation of something. That is all interesting information. But then the time comes, even if it still does not make sense, when you just know that it is time to leap. You may be scared or excited, yet off you go over the precipice of the known into the great dance of life's mysterious adventure.

There comes a time when you just have to commit to the leap. When we are committed to the path, the Universe knows how to meet us and support us. Just as the Universe wants us to support the unfolding of its path, it too is always supporting us in creating our dreams.

I am sure you have had the experience of choosing something, but soon after making the commitment, discovering that there are all kinds of choice doorways that have opened up for you that you did not see beforehand. This experience is the Universe responding to your commitment. This is synchronicity at work.

Most often, even if you don't know what it is you want, the best action is any action. It is amazing how getting moving on something can open up the blocks and reveal more information about which way to go. Even if it reveals that you stepped in what seems like the wrong direction, now at least you know with greater clarity. Had you not stepped, you never could have figured it out completely. This reveals another great paradox: that there never is a wrong direction—there are just directions that seem less direct. When you witness this, what you learn will help guide the next step.

Again, the walk of life is often like the Hindu practice of Neti Neti, no not that, no not that. When we think we know anything about what lies ahead, we are really only fooling our Selves in order to hold onto a false sense of courage from knowing. But this courage is based on the illusion of knowing.

The truth is we never really know.

We cannot understand what will be with 100 percent certainty. That opens up the game of trying things out. Like the childhood game of warmer warmer, colder colder, we go in one direction, but if that's not right, we try again until we get closer to what we're looking for. We keep assessing. Through this choice, am I getting warmer warmer, or colder colder? We then course—correct according to whatever wisdom we are accessing at the time.

WHEN LIFE IS MESSY SOMETHING GOOD IS TRYING TO HAPPEN

It always feels messy when things around us are falling apart or spinning in ways that seem out of control. The fact is that everything is out of your control. The idea that you ever control anything is an illusion—and not a particularly useful one at that.

Some among us thrive on mess. Those people might benefit from learning how to allow some smoothness into their lives. Most of us, though, want to keep things smooth, so we try to stamp out chaos whenever it spontaneously breaks out.

I was recently working with someone as their coach. Within the same week, he unexpectedly lost his job and his wife announced that their relationship wasn't working out. It threw my client into a turmoil of chaos that sent him spinning. At first there was too much for him to process and understand. He wanted to rush out and get the first job he could, and was completely at a loss about what to do with his relationship. His overwhelming desire was to grab anything to hold onto. In the chaos, this client realized that everything he had thought was "under control" was not. He was going into a distorted mode of panic.

Thankfully, he managed to find his way back to a centered position. From there he reconnected to his resourcefulness and creativity. Soon after that, he was offered a dream job that he hadn't even imagined was possible for him. He also went into counseling with his wife and they continue to work on their relationship. He was not aware of the good things that were trying to find their way to him.

It took the lightning bolt of sudden change to shake him enough to open up to new possibilities.

Einstein said that a problem cannot be solved from the same consciousness that created it. It sometimes takes a shockwave to wake us out of our sleep. That is the sleep of living a life of illusion through Distorted. The new consciousness is only available by moving further along towards a fuller expression of Divine Essence.

CHAOS COMES FROM ORDER AND FROM ORDER COMES CHAOS

What is confusing and disorderly is generally considered chaotic. Chaos is the state between the order that used to be and the next level of order. Chaos passes, and then order passes, and the cycle repeats itself.

Nothing ever stays the same, nothing.

The Buddha stated very clearly that all is impermanent. That is equally true for the good times as it is for the bad times. It seems clear then that the more we develop our capacity to dance with change, the better our experience will be.

Nothing stays the same—ever.

The more capacity we develop to be with both chaos and order, the more able we will be to stay present and resourceful in the day-to-day journey of creating an awakened life.

TO FULFILL ITS PURPOSE, THE EGG MUST BE BROKEN

Chaos and order will cycle in and out, back and forth, throughout our lives.

In order for something new to emerge, it often requires what already exists to be dismantled or even destroyed.

The more extensive the incoming new idea is (that is, the change), the greater the magnitude of chaos it will create.

If nothing stays the same, then it is our dreams that inform us about what is needed now—which way to move, or in what direction we should shift something that already exists.

Imagine the life of a bird. First the bird is brought into the world in the form of an egg. It is not for the sake of being an egg that the bird is born, but rather for the sake of something that lies beyond the stage of being an egg. In order for this bird to advance itself, the egg must be broken. Otherwise the bird does not fulfill its potential. When we create a comfortable life, it often becomes like that egg. We go to sleep in it, and we get attached to it until one day an event cracks the egg open, releasing us in a shocking kind of way.

The bird does not say, "On the other side of this egg shell is my destiny, but I must get there without breaking this egg."

We humans get very attached to our eggs. We hold onto them, hoard them, or pass them on to others, hoping that they won't break them or lose them—thereby burdening others with our attachment.

We must be willing to let go in order to be available for what is coming next. When the thing we are letting go of has become a part of our identity, letting go can be all the more challenging.

Take, for example, someone who has worked for years in an organization. They have created their identity according to their title, role, or even their paycheck.

This person has a dream to become an artist, but is conflicted by the perceived loss of the identity that they have attached themselves to. As long as the fear of losing that identity or paycheck is greater than their willingness to let go and become an artist, they will continue to hold on.

If they are lucky, something will happen—perhaps an economic shake up in the company that causes them to be let go. Their corporate identity will scream out at the injustice of it all. A wave of fear will roll through, even while the artist inside goes shopping for paintbrushes.

As the person starts to get curious about life as an artist, their Divine Essence will work out the details while their Distorted Self will use all manner of fear, anger, and victimhood to reconnect this person to another safe corporate identity as soon as possible.

The challenge for this person is to recover back to Divine Essence, as often as it takes, so that the new dream has a chance to emerge. It may be that being an artist becomes a way of life or a hobby, and that a new unforeseen career will present itself. What's important is that this person pay attention to the fact that something more honoring, which is a better use of their genius at this time in their life, is calling. This person's new potential can now be realized.

THE UNIVERSE'S DREAM EMERGING

At first the Universe's dream exists as energy that wants to emerge in response to the next thing or state that is trying to happen or to become. That is why it's not uncommon that when something is needed in the world, it gets invented by several people or groups in seemingly unrelated environments. The conditions in the world called for a new solution and the solution occurred to a few people at more or less the same time. To the Universe, this ensures that at least one of these people is going to be successful in advancing the idea through the dream stage into a tangible solution.

You've likely had the experience of hearing about the announcement of some great idea and realizing you had the same idea. That is the Universe being realized in dream, in thought. It is in the Wisdom Field that the ideas were waiting to be discovered.

When we realize that we have an idea, the idea itself has just revealed itself to us. The idea wants to come into realization.

It may not matter to the idea which human is successful in bringing it to fruition.

The idea just wants to be realized. All the time you are celebrating that it as "your" idea, you may in fact be missing the point that the idea was a gift, a seed that the Universe offered to you. Whether you follow through or not, someone will. We see this in nature all the time. For example, the dandelion flower scatters thousands of seeds into the world knowing that many of them will not catch. Only some will find the right conditions for thriving. That is why so many are scattered out.

So the idea starts as essence. It starts as a stirring within, perhaps an inspiration or a sensation of excitement in the body. As the essence reveals itself, it starts to take on more energy and a form. The form is how it is being realized. A dream can manifest in a number of different shapes and timings. The seed wants to grow, yet at the same time most dream seeds are very flexible with regard to how they will actually look.

As the seed takes hold, it takes on its own life force of attraction.

It creates an energy field of intention around itself and uses that energy to grow. As it grows, it attracts what it needs to thrive. It might need more people or resources, so it calls out to others and watches to see who is available to nurture it, shepherd it, give it what is needed.

This dream now has a life of its own. It doesn't belong to the dreamer anymore. It now asks the dreamer to serve it. If the dreamer is not available to serve it any further, it will ask the dreamer to get out of the way, because the dream wants to thrive, but is not attached to the person who originally dreamed it.

You have no doubt heard stories of identical scientific break-throughs that occurred in different labs in different parts of the world at more or less the same point in time. This is because the idea was a dream that was looking for someone to birth it. It didn't matter who it was, as long as it happened.

When you are called to a path, it is best to follow it. It may be that the path wants to be walked. If you won't do it, then someone else will.

I coached a scientist who worked in high-security labs under the greatest secrecy and security only to have the secrets they were working on be announced by a competing lab a week after they made the same discovery.

Maybe it's time that we stop taking our Selves so seriously, as if we were solving anything, and instead work to create a different kind of partnership with the Universe and the Wisdom Field that acknowledges the importance of the part we play without build-ing up our egos or taking our Selves too seriously.

What Meets Our Dream Energy?

*A*s we dream, our dreams are met by many forces in the Universe. Some of those forces seem to oppose us while others seem more supportive. Still others appear to be quite neutral in how they move in relation to our dream.

One of my teachers believes that praying is something best done very loudly. That is a point that varies among different traditions. When I asked him why, he laughed with his loud and resonant laugh and replied, "Well, imagine that you are the Divine and there are nearly seven billion humans all praying at once. You want to be sure that your voice is heard."

While I appreciate the idea of this, I believe the point is that the more we give our Selves over to the prayer, the stronger the energy around it will be. For some that may be through a loud cry, while for others it may be through a deeply quiet and resonant intention or request to the Divine.

Try on the idea that there are nearly seven billion human dreamers, not to mention all the other systems of beings. That is a lot of dreams to process at once. No wonder then that it takes some time for some of our dreams to be worked out.

LETTING GO AND HOMEOSTASIS

Imagine that you have your hands full, literally. You are in your busy life, moving fast to keep it together, and your hands are holding onto everything you have created. For the most part, you like your life. You probably would like to see a few things be different—perhaps you wish something really big and important in your life were different than it is, but either way you are busy holding that all together.

When you have a moment you might cast a wish out to the Universe: I wish that . . .

And your life quickly jerks you back to its persistent reality that demands your attention to keep it together.

Wow, that is busy work!

All the while, as you are running through each day, the very things you are wishing for may very well be trying to come through for you—and guess what? They can't get in because you are too busy grasping at the old things you wish deep down inside were different than they are now.

HOMEOSTASIS AT WORK

We humans are funny creatures. We get attached to things and conditions in our lives like sap to a tree. This is homeostasis at work. Homeostasis is a property of the Universe that supports systems to seek and maintain a stable condition. In other words, to keep things the same. Homeostasis is at work everywhere. Nature experiences homeostasis in order for systems and species to survive. We rely on it to maintain the world we live in, and it is a force that we must be aware of, if we desire to create a change in our life.

I hear from people all the time who have been trying to create something new in their lives. When it doesn't happen quickly enough, they get discouraged. In these situations, discouragement is homeostasis using your emotional system to keep you in line, to keep things the way they are.

Understand that to create a meaningful change in your life, you must influence the world around you. The world around you is organized to maintain its present order—and there you are daring to want something different. To the world around you—the people, circumstances, everything—the idea that you want to change things may not be welcome news. Imagine that all the elements of the life you are in are organized in a particular way that want to stay that way, and there you are in the middle of it all wishing, wanting, even doing things to make it change—yet it seems that everything is resisting what you want. That is not your imagination. That is the world around you doing its job. It is not that the world is against you. It is simply that there is an energetic field holding the orbits of the people and the circumstances together.

SNAP! IT'S ALL DIFFERENT

Then one day it all breaks free, sometimes in a shocking way. It might even feel violent in the apparent suddenness of how it all happens. Perhaps your job is yanked out from under your feet. When you look back at it after the initial shock has worn off, you realize that you saw it coming but you'd gotten attached and resisted responding to the early signs.

Oh, those early signs. All those times that the world whispered in your ear to look around and try something different. All those times you tolerated some part of your life that was not working well but were too busy or scared to address it. You kept looking the other way, hoping it would work itself out. All those times you told your Self I am too busy today so I will take care of that tomorrow, until one day it took care of you by jolting you out of an old reality that could hold no longer. When this kind of change happens, it is like being caught in an earthquake. All the stored energy is released in one big jolt. Everything around you that was not well secured is thrown around and broken free.

The world around us is beyond our control, so any energy put towards controlling is not the best use of you. Imagine that you are fully supported by the Universe. Imagine that there are new things that are constantly trying to come towards you and get you to pay attention to the messages they are giving you. Notice the wishes and wants you think of. Notice the comments that are spoken to you. Pay attention to what is trying to come in and to what is trying to be released.

The serenity prayer says it best:

God grant me the serenity
to accept the things I cannot change;
courage to change the things I can;
and wisdom to know the difference.

—Reinhold Niebuhr

WHAT CAN YOU DO?

- Look for what needs attention, and tend to it like an important garden in your life. Keep it vibrant by loving and nurturing it.
- Notice where the struggles are, and ask your Self: What is going on there?
- Is what you're doing a good use of your energy? If so, then keep working it. If not, then let it go cleanly and responsibly.
- When you want to create a change, look at the entire system of people and things around you, and address the system as a whole.
- Be persistent with what you truly want. It is coming to you

and it takes the time it takes. Not everything will move according to your schedule, tho many things will.

- Get help, get lots of help. Let people in, let the people around you know what you are trying to create, and allow them to help you. They will love you for that.
- Stay flexible and open about how it will look or how it will happen.
- Understand that interruptions and surprises are normal, and not personal. Nor are they signs from the Universe except, when they are. Sometimes an interrupted idea is just the Universe saying it needs a bit more time.
- Trust your heart, appreciate your mind, and nurture your body. You will need them all.

THE LAW OF SEVEN

The Law of Seven—and other similar laws—exists in many ancient traditions and mythologies. One line of the teaching was brought forward by Gurdjieff, a mystic and a spiritual teacher who lived from 1866 to 1949. He received many profound teachings while he traveled around Egypt and the surrounding areas.

In this section, we will be talking about the Law of Seven as a process that applies to the creation of our dreams.

The Law of Seven teaches that any process will experience periodic interruptions or shocks, and that nothing will continue forever, or in a straight line, without being interrupted. It states that energy is needed in response to those shocks, if that process is to continue. There are seven steps in each phase of a process, and the process will experience interruptions. If the energy that is applied in each shock is neutral, or without intention, the result will be that eventually the process will circle around and end where it began. As we put intentional energy into processes, we influence the events to move in a particular direction. And, we have to keep providing energy in order for the process to continue.

That is a mouthful, so let's break it down.

Notice that the creation story happened over the course of seven days; that there are seven levels in the periodic table of elements; seven notes in an octave—Do Re Mi Fa So La Ti. When you start to look, you will find sets of seven in all the great traditions.

Each time you move through an octave in your life, you advance up to the next higher octave. In order to jump up to the next level, a burst of energy is required. As we journey through life, we advance our Selves an octave at a time, and as you move forward through life you will experience interruptions and shocks. They are inevitable. They are a natural part of the way the Universe unfolds.

Every process will be interrupted, it is not personal.

Sometimes when people get interrupted in their journey, they think that it is personal and that it is a sign that it is not meant to be. That is most often not true. It is more likely to be just a normal interruption, a sign that new energy is required.

When you look at the branch of a growing plant, you will see that it goes straight for a period of time and then slightly or greatly changes direction. Even in plants that grow straight, like bamboo, you will notice periodic joints that break up an otherwise smooth pattern.

These points of interruption represent events that posed a shock, and so we can call them shock points. An example of a shock to a plant is the arrival of winter, which shocks the plant out of growing. This gives the plant a chance to rest so that in the spring it can resume its growth.

So what does that tell us about our dreams? That it is normal to have our journey interrupted or shocked. It tells us that interruptions are unavoidable, so we might as well embrace them and discover how to create from them.

Imagine that every time your journey to creating your dream is shocked or interrupted that you are being asked by the Universe:

"Are you sure this is what you want?"

"Are you sure it is in that direction?"

"What adjustment is needed to continue to have this path be good for you?"

"What new energy is needed to move to the next level?"

"What other dream might be more imperative at this point?"

"What is needed for you to stay on this course and follow through to the next shock point?"

During these times of shock, you are offered the chance to turn to a new path. It may be that you were never meant to finish a particular plan. Maybe the path you were on simply served the purpose of moving you forward to a place where something else could happen.

These are the times when you get to recommit. If it is still the right path, then are you being called to add new energy to it?

Every time you feel interrupted or knocked off the path, think of it as an opportunity to celebrate that you successfully arrived at a point of intersection. You had to be able to advance or shrink back to arrive at this point.

If you feel discouraged, then add some heart.

If you feel tired, then rest.

If you are unsure or confused about what is next, move to higher ground, look around, and ask, "What is needed?"

THE LAW OF THREE

Another important law to consider is the Law of Three. Three shows up in many teachings and it's often regarded as a highly spiritual number.

We humans experience the Law of Three in many ways. For example, when the desire for the dream itself is matched up against the cost of going for it, we are confronted by two forces that often cancel each other out. That is the telling moment that invites in a third influence—the deciding force that most often sets the direction for what will be.

For example, there you are sitting on the fence wondering whether or not quitting your job and setting off on that entrepreneurial adventure is the right move for you at this time. One part of you wants to go for it, and another part of you is against it. In that moment the phone rings.

It is a trusted friend. You think to your Self, "How amazing that they called at the perfect time." This may be synchronicity at work.

The first two influences are within you, to go or not. This friend is the third influence. They might suggest you go for it, or they might suggest you are crazy to give up your security—that you should stay and improve your current situation. This friend becomes the third force that propels your decision one way or the other. Your friend's comments might not make your decision easy, but you will certainly experience the power of their influence over you.

Those first two influences represent the desire to move forward and the fear that rallies against it. The third influence, something that pushes us one way or the other, often comes from the Universe.

No matter what the friend recommends, to go or to stay, the fact is that it results in the next part of the process happening. In other words, something different than the existing order will result. Thus forward progression will have been made.

This is an example of the Law of Three at work. The Law of Three tells us that a positive force will be met with an equal negative force, and that a third force will determine the direction of the next step of the process. That result will be higher or lower than what was.

SO MANY DREAMS, SO LITTLE TIME

Can we have all our dreams come true? I hope that you have so many dreams that you could never have them all come true because of the sheer abundance of them.

Each day we must activate Divine Essence and check in on what course is the best one as of this day. It's important to stay committed to our dreams when times are challenging, unless that dream no longer fits for you.

Sometimes we have to prioritize our dreams in terms of what is important today and what will wait for another time.

A classic example of this are the dreams that parents have for their children. It's one thing to have a dream for your children; it's another to stand in the way of what your children can pursue after they've grown up.

At times we might be rolling along on a dream path when the world interrupts with a shock. In these moments, we have to set aside our personal dream for a while, until the world dream has been satisfied or no longer needs us. Then, if that original dream still fits, we can get back to it.

An example of a dream interrupted is when someone is called to military service. The life they were dreaming is put on hold until their time has been served. The call to military service is answering the country's dream.

At other times a dream might need a lot of lead time for it to start getting traction. Imagine the Universe dancing with almost seven billion dreaming humans, moving energies around to meet everybody in their hopes. It might take a while to make all the necessary arrangements. That is why it is important to stay true to your dreams, since you never know how close they are to being realized. Too many people turn away just a moment before the dawn shines on what has been dreamed of for so long.

There are no easy answers here. At the end of the story it will always come back to you staying connected to Divine Essence and making the best choices you can, while being ready, willing, and able to dance with the call of many dreams from many sources.

GRACE AND AWAKENED LIVING

In this book I am talking a lot about how to engage with life in an intentional way. There is another great paradox at work here as well, and that's turning it all over to grace. In our lives, after we have done all we can do, there is a lot of wisdom in turning it all over to the Divine. Turning it over to grace.

In order for us to be in grace, we must be in relationship with the Universe. To be in grace, we must be open and engaged.

I have seen people fall into resignation, calling it grace. This is more of a Distorted state of having given up, let go, disengaged from being in relationship with the Divine. For some people, this seems to be what happens after they realize that they don't control anything. It is as if they are full on with control, then full off with resignation. That is not grace. For the people who fall into that state, it might be a step forward. Certainly letting go of the illusion of control is a helpful thing. What is needed from resignation, however, is to recover back to your Divine Essence and to then engage in a way that invites the Universe into the dance with you.

Grace happens when you are in the dance with the Divine.

You take your place at the side of the Divine. Through this relationship with the Divine, you move with ease and delight along your path. As you move, you are open to the interrelatedness of All. Now, when you dance with grace, everything that is around you is joining you, is dancing with you. Even obstacles that appeared to be in your way become teaching events to move through or around. In this way you move in-joy and everything is seen as a gift.

It is much more fulfilling to move through life in this connected way than to think that you are in charge, that all you have to do is push harder to get your way.

For many of us, grace does require surrender. From the place of your Divine Essence, you give your Self over to the Divine. That looks like letting go of outcomes.

The wisdom of the Divine is to know what is best is beyond our capacity to understand. Doesn't it seem wise to trust? Trust the Divine aspect of your Self, that things will come around, that the Universe is supporting you in ways that you both can and cannot know.

Gathering It In

As Gurdjieff tells us so clearly, we must learn to be human. The Buddha taught that the most challenging thing to change is your Self. That being so, it is a challenge that we must take on.

We are in a dance of interrelatedness with all that there is in this great and mysterious Universe. It is important to know whom we are putting onto the dance floor in each moment of our life. In the simplest terms, is it your Distorted Self or your Divine Essence?

The reason it is important to know what aspect of your Self is present, is because you are always creating your life from the seeds that you plant through every intention you hold and every word that you speak. When Divine Essence is out in front, then your words and intentions will be congruent with the Universe. That is because your Divine Essence is the most open to attuning to the highest frequencies of the Wisdom Field. Those are the frequencies of creating from joy, love, and life-giving energy for All.

Distorted is also a powerful creative force, but it only creates from fear and doubt. It will consume and use other beings in the Universe as though we had a "right" to do so.

We humans also have three primary aspects that we are experiencing life through: heart intelligence, mind intelligence, and body intelligence. These three intelligences form a system together. They operate together and they each have their own domain. We tend to have better access to one over the other two, but we must learn to draw on the wisdom of all three.

We humans are blessed in that we are active participants in how things are unfolding in the Universe. One of the most powerful ways that we are collaborating with the Universe is through our dreaming. It is through our dreams that we create the intentions that go on to create our realities. Who we put in charge of the dream department matters, and so again it is imperative that we put our Divine Essence out in front. Every thought, wish, or prayer we utter is a dream that is sent out to become creative energy. Remember, the life you are living today is a result of yesterday's dreams, and today's dreams are shaping the next moments to come.

We must learn how to approach everything in our Universe in a more holistic way that has us be in partnership rather than being consumers—because to consume is to destroy. Consider the example of how we can be in partnership with a forest. Divine Essence will be able to dream into the forest in a way that honors the living system that the forest is. Divine Essence will dream about how to be in collaboration with the forest so that we humans may still have the privilege of accessing the lumber and other things that the forest will offer to support our lives. We, in turn, must honor and respect the forest, engaging with it through the Divine Essence's intention of offering life-giving energy back to the forest. The forest will willingly support the needs of the humans, as the forest is completely attuned to the interrelatedness of all beings that depend on her generosity, including the humans.

In order to do this, we must be willing to listen deeply to what the forest wants and to then align with the forest's needs for well-being, rather than our old way of just taking by force.

As we learn to live in this way, we are also honoring the journey of our Soul. This is still the biggest mystery of all. Our Soul is that aspect of us that is most closely connected to the Divine. Perhaps we could say that just as the Universe is the manifestation of the Divine, the human is the manifestation of the Soul.

Every thought, word, and action we give energy to has a karmic impact on our Soul. Our Soul is on a journey and this human life is a developmental stage for the Soul. As we clear up the karma for our Soul, we free it to higher and higher levels of lightness. It is the Soul that will go on, past the time of our human lives. The choices you make today affect the well-being of the Soul you eventually send off onward into its journey.

We will be challenged in many ways during our human journey. Some of those challenges will take us down into our very own valley. It's often there where we meet our Selves. It is easy to be kind and generous when things are going well and easily. In the valley, however, we find out who we really are now. I say "now" because you get to form and reform who you are. That is the development journey that we are on. Some of us will meet our valley in the corporate boardrooms as we are faced with situations that will have us choose whether to engage from Divine Essence or Distorted. Others of us will meet our valley through our personal relationships, while still others will be in the day-to-day journey of finding our way back to the fullness of our Divine Essence. None of us are to be spared from the suffering and struggles that are so essential to our Soul's development.

Now that we have set the scene, the next part of the book is about how to move forward in a good way—a way that will enable you to sustain your connection to your Divine Essence.

For that, we will turn to the Eight States of an Awakened Life. As you live more and more fully into these states, you will find that the times of Divine Essence will become more, and more and the times of Distorted less and less.

THE DREAM SLEEP

I sleep, sort of, a restless case that pulls me out
Of the satisfaction of a deep sleep
Something is emerging, coming through,
My head is tormented by distraction
It is impacting my otherwise solid plan
This yearning in my heart doesn't make sense to my mind
And my body processes are disturbed
In a way that is quite, well, disturbing
I didn't ask for a new idea,
it all seemed quite fine at the time
So what is driving this and why me
I ask as if there was someone to listen
I lie here my skin being drummed upon from
inside and out writhing, not sleeping
oh my gosh what is it
I feel like going on a trip, I don't know
Why or for that matter why not
I feel like going on a trip
Some other voice inside points out,
This is a trip you are already on,
Where doesn't matter though it seems like
it must be East and to my mind it doesn't
make sense and there are so many difficulties
in going on a trip at such a time as this
and this seems to be the time anyway
Something is driving me, pulling me,
Making me a little crazy
and if I could just sleep
tomorrow is another day
though this all started long ago
perhaps I should listen

but what is the point it doesn't make sense
and my heart is yearning
and my skin is restless
and my legs want to move
and my body says go
and my head says no
and I don't know why
and the alarm goes off
saving me from this torment
and the phone is ringing
and who would be calling
at this early hour, what could the Universe want . . .

—*Patrick Ryan*

Figure 9: Dream Chart #1: The Circle of Dream and Creation

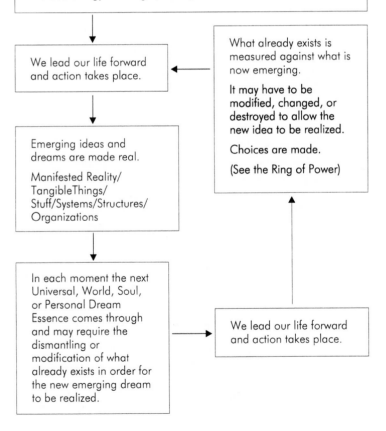

Through Divine Essence, Dream comes into awareness and potential is realized.

This Dream was held in the Wisdom Field and could be from:

- The Universe.
- The World we live in. Community, country, regional, and earthly needs and desires.
- Our Soul – the call to a life purpose.
- Our personal/family desires.

This dream becomes an idea, a yearning, or a feeling and wants to be turned into form and made real.

We add energy of thought, words, or actions.

We lead our life forward and action takes place.

What already exists is measured against what is now emerging.

It may have to be modified, changed, or destroyed to allow the new idea to be realized.

Choices are made.

(See the Ring of Power)

Emerging ideas and dreams are made real.

Manifested Reality/ TangibleThings/ Stuff/Systems/Structures/ Organizations

In each moment the next Universal, World, Soul, or Personal Dream Essence comes through and may require the dismantling or modification of what already exists in order for the new emerging dream to be realized.

We lead our life forward and action takes place.

Figure 10: Dream Chart #2: The Many Dreamers

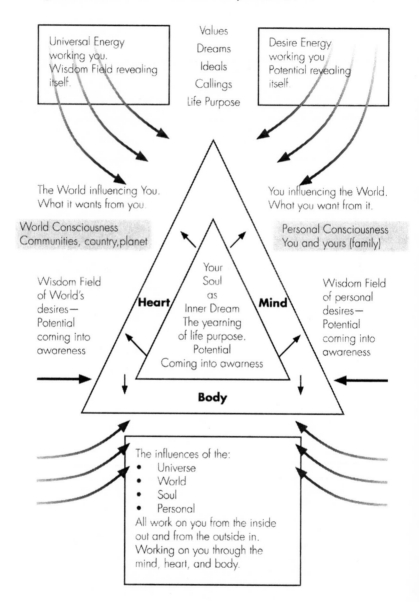

Values
Dreams
Ideals
Callings
Life Purpose

Universal Energy working you. Wisdom Field revealing itself.

Desire Energy working you Potential revealing itself.

The World influencing You. What it wants from you.

You influencing the World. What you want from it.

World Consciousness
Communities, country, planet

Personal Consciousness
You and yours (family)

Wisdom Field of World's desires— Potential coming into awareness

Wisdom Field of personal desires— Potential coming into awareness

Heart **Mind**

Your Soul as Inner Dream The yearning of life purpose. Potential Coming into awarness

Body

The influences of the:
- Universe
- World
- Soul
- Personal

All work on you from the inside out and from the outside in. Working on you through the mind, heart, and body.

PART TWO

The Eight States of an Awakened Life©

My Soul's Song to You

Hello Divine, Great Spirit
Hear this as my Soul's song to you
So that together we may create a good story
About the adventure that awaits in this day

Divine, I need your help to live fully
From the spirit of my own Divine Essence
That aspect of me that is closest to you
That expresses your dreams through my own

According to the guidance of your wisdom
Let me hold good intention for all
Beings of this Universe as we travel together
By your grace on the Spaceship Earth

My Divine intention informs my words
They are powerful when carried by my breath
Creating Our experience together in each moment
Let them be of beauty and life-giving to All

To the relationships that I foster
With All beings in this world
I intend that they will be clean and bright
Honoring and supporting the promise of Us

I will allow my Self to be well used each day
My purpose is, with humility, a simple offering
To bring out the brilliance of all your subjects
In service of Great Spirit's mysterious dream

I will move through each day of this life
With the effort of joyful ease and delight
Applying a good measure of strength and softness
Knowing when to lean heavy and when to be light

Each day, each week, each month I follow
My wisdom, my practice of Body, Heart, and Mind
Respecting the gift of this body so Human
As I choose to walk the walk of Divine

And my actions I take according to
What is needed to create our highest dreams
We move together, One people in a good way
Life-giving, creating beauty, discerning

And the measure of a good day is in touching
Into the Oneness of it All
Witnessing, creating, and writing
Our stories All woven together
For the Universe's dream song

—*Patrick Ryan*

The Inspiration

I have been blessed with some great teachers in my life. Some of them were strangers passing by, travelers on the trails, and some were more formally my teachers. Some held indigenous wisdom from the regions of Asia, Central, South, and North America, and others presented very modern teachings.

Over 2,500 years ago, the Buddha walked on this planet and offered us many amazing teachings to help guide and support us in walking our own awakened walk. One of those teachings is commonly known as the Eight Fold Path. When I encountered this teaching many years ago, it touched me deeply, for in it I found a simple and profound wisdom.

Around the same time I found this teaching, I was considering what I was learning from my experience of creating prosperity while being a contributing global citizen. I had read every book on New Age attraction principles, and my library was full of the latest self-help books. As useful as they were, I was still left wanting to understand deeper and deeper levels of human nature, consciousness, and spirituality.

It seemed that most of the teachings that attracted me were from teachers living "holy lives." That is, they were living as monks or priests, were in ashrams, or were living other unusual lifestyles that, while appealing to me at many levels, were also not what I was called to.

So I started getting curious about ways to apply these ideas to the ordinary life. That is, the life of one who lives as a householder in the everyday world. A person interested in contributing to the improvement and development of their community and to the planet as a whole. One who is also interested in a happy life with great relationships, wealth creation, prosperity, and a comfortable life with nice things and good people in it.

In this usage of the word "ordinary," I am referring to the life of someone—you, me, anyone—who is living out in the world, dealing with the day-to-day challenges of creating an amazing and ordinary life.

Ordinary here includes the rich and poor, the most famous people you know of, along with the people you never notice or hear about. It includes the low-, middle-, and upper-class families that are doing their best. Ordinary people, all of us, who are making it one day at a time—with all our dreams, hopes, goals, and desires, as well as our challenges. We each have a different hand dealt to us, and we all have to do and be the best we can, given all of the above.

We all have to make decisions and choices every day that will impact our lives and affect the outcome of our dreams. As you know, doing nothing or not choosing is a choice anyway, so there is no escape from some form of decision-making.

That is the proverbial good and bad news of our situation.

It makes sense, therefore, to have some guidelines and insight into ideas that can support us in making the wisest possible choices that enable us to walk our walk in the best way possible.

When I was contemplating my own life, I went to the Eight Fold Path as well as many other great indigenous teachings. I walked with them, sat with them, meditated and prayed with them, and committed my Self to learning everything I could about these teachings as a guide to living a most extraordinary and still ordinary life. A precious life.

After much play and work, I freed my Self from the original guidelines and reinterpreted them. I wanted an offering that would speak to me in a modern, relevant way, according to what I needed to create a happy and prosperous life now, in this day and age. I wanted it to free me up, not box me in. I wanted to be free to use my own wisdom day-to-day, rather than live by a strict set of rules.

I knew it had to honor the well-being of All—the environment, global communities, and family and local community. What I found I now offer to you with an open hand and heart. Use the teachings as they work for you and are congruent with your own wisdom. If something doesn't seem right, then leave it here and take what works.

What to Expect

*I*n Part Two, I present a wheel of teachings that I call the Eight States of an Awakened Life. Each section of the wheel represents one state of being that we can put our attention towards in order to live a more awakened life. Within each state, four different sections are explored: (1) A Personal Aspiration; (2) Description; (3) Collective Aspirations: A Note from the Future; and (4) Practices.

SECTION 1: A PERSONAL ASPIRATION

This section of each part of the wheel contains a personal aspiration, written from the point of view of the Self in the present moment. Use it as a benchmark for what is possible in attaining this state, or use it as an inspiration for you to write your own possibilities. Each time you read the personal aspiration, use it as a visualization, as though it is already true for you. As you imagine it, it is true. As you intend it, you move the world and your Self towards it.

An aspiration is just that: what we aspire to, what we grow towards, and what we hold as a desirable way to be. As we dream our Selves forward towards it, we adjust our Self and our life as needed, so that we become congruent with the aspiration.

If there is anything that is missing for you within any given personal aspirations, or if an idea doesn't resonate with you, then I encourage you to write your own.

Then read at least one, if not the entire set, every day. Amazing things will happen if you do.

SECTION 2: DESCRIPTION

Second, each state contains some brief context and description of that state which is intended to further deepen your understanding of it. As you have your own direct experience, you will no doubt come to understand each of the eight states in a more personal and intimate way.

The Buddha taught that there are three stages of development. The first is to know about something. As you read these descriptions, you will know something about each state.

The second stage is to experience something. As you move forward knowing about these eight states, you will have your own direct experiences with them in your life. This deepens your knowing and, at the same time, takes the ideas presented here and moves them into your being, resulting in your own wisdom around them.

The third stage is to be it, to become it. At this point you become the embodiment of this wisdom. You move and breathe according to your Good State of Being in relationship with this wisdom. This is the place of mastery. For most, it will take many years to attain such an integrated state. Remember that although this is a worthy state to aspire to, it is not a destination point after which you are done. It is in the breath, the heartbeat, and the walk where this wisdom will be revealed through you each day.

SECTION 3: COLLECTIVE ASPIRATIONS— A NOTE FROM THE FUTURE

Third, each section contains my dream for what is possible for us as a whole, as a collective. In these sections, a storyteller is telling us about what happened from the point of view of a person living at some date in the future. These are written as if they were a report or a journal entry from the future, at a time when we will have collectively attained the realization of these eight states.

Again, feel free to use this as a guide for visualizing, or you can write your own dream for what you would like to attract on behalf of us all.

SECTION 4: PRACTICES

In the fourth part of each section are practices that you can use to deepen your own understanding and direct experience with each state.

I encourage you to use these practice ideas as possibilities, and to then create your own additional practices that appeal more directly to you. These ideas are meant to inspire your own wisdom about living into the state more and more fully.

WHAT IS IN IT FOR YOU?

Learning to live through your Divine Essence is about releasing your Self from the prison of your habits and behaviors, and in so doing you are freeing your Self to the full range of responses available, according to your vision and your greatest wisdom and resourcefulness. This is in response to what life is putting out in front of you at any given moment, informed by your hopes and dreams.

It is from that place of divine and wise liberation that you are available to touch into your dream, and also into the Universe's dream for you. It is the Universe's dream for you that calls you to your life purpose and that promises to make the best use of you.

This is the way of the Eight States of an Awakened Life.

The Eight States of an Awakened Life Wheel

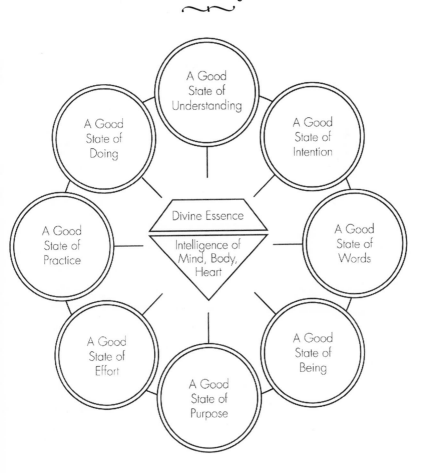

A GOOD STATE OF UNDERSTANDING

I Am in a Good State of Understanding.

- I understand that All and I are interrelated and as such we are One.

- I understand that we are all part of the Wisdom Field.

- I understand that my intention and words are powerful tools of creation.

- I understand that I am my own healer, and that the healing and balancing of my mind, body, and heart is a constant process.

- I understand that holding a question is more useful than holding an answer.

- I understand that what I believe to be absolutely true becomes true because I believe it.

- I understand that I am the self-authority of the whole of my life, and it is through my choices that I author the unfolding adventure.

- I understand that All is energy, that energy just is, and that energy is transformed according to the intentions of my thoughts, words, and actions.

- I understand that I create my own karma. Every intention, thought, word, or action has an impact, and every impact has a consequence for which I am responsible.

- I understand that like the four seasons there is a natural unfolding of events in this Universe, and as such All is subject to cycles and timing.

- I understand that all people, beings, things, and circumstances are impermanent, and thusly I understand the opportunity of each moment is to be present, for past and future live only as story or dream, and the moment of now is where all is One.

- I understand the Law of Attraction, which states that whatever I put my expectation and intention on is what I will create in my life. I understand that I am in a dance with the Universe, and therefore what I call in will be in accordance with the larger unfolding picture of All.

- I understand that this Universe is generous in its nature, abundant in its possibilities, and filled with all the resources that all beings and I need.

I Am in a Good State of Understanding.

A GOOD STATE OF UNDERSTANDING

Having a clear understanding of how the Universe works would be very helpful. The answer to what is the "truth" about this life, this Universe, varies widely depending on whom you ask and the lens through which we examine the question. At this time, most of what there is to know about the meaning and purpose of life, how the Universe works, and other such questions are a deep and profound mystery. As much as I love understanding things, I also really dig the mystery of it all.

WHOSE TRUTH IS IT?

For the last three to four hundred years there has been an unnatural split between organized religions and the scientific community. They have each taken a hold of their half of the story and spoken down to us, the people, from a pedestal of authority.

For the most part, they've been quite successful in separating us from our own wisdom. Too many people have been happy to give their responsibility to think for themselves over to these two groups.

If there is anything in this world that is truly dangerous, it is when we the people abandon our wisdom to a higher authority.

Religions tell us what to believe according to the doctrine of their particular faith. Faith is the key word here. Unfortunately, over the centuries, certain ethics such as thou shalt not kill became inconvenient, and exceptions were sometimes made in the name of the Church. There has been a long list of wars, crusades, murders, and robbery carried out in the name of religion. What is the truth in that?

The scientific community tells us what we should believe according to what has passed through the application of the scientific method. There is an assumption behind the scientific method that suggests there is such a thing as objectivity. Well, it seems that objectivity does not really exist. The very act of observing has an impact that changes the outcome. So there is more to understanding than what the scientific method can explain.

Of course, religions offer many great benefits to humanity, as do the contributions of science. Disregarding the wisdom of those communities would be just as foolhardy as giving all your power over to them.

As science moves on, it overturns old beliefs in favor of new ones. As religions move on, they adjust their teachings, however slowly, according to the latest wisdom.

Our part in all of this is to stay curious, to trust our own wisdom, and to allow the findings of science and the teachings of religions to inform us rather than control us.

WHAT IS THE TRUTH?

Truths or laws or paradigms, as we often call them, seem completely true until we discover that they are not. Then after that we are likely to rush out and get a new truth to replace the old one. We humans like having answers and certainty.

The trap of an answer is that we might stop asking the question. The problem with certainty is that we are in an uncertain Universe where anything is possible.

There are some phenomena that so far defy explanation, yet we know that they exist. For example, we know gravity to be a true force in the world. We can see its influence every day. Yet, as of the time of this writing, gravity itself has never been observed directly or proven in how it works. Scientists have studied, pondered, poked, and challenged it, and we wake up every day assuming that it will be there for us, yet we don't really know what it is or how it works. It's just that the evidence is so strong to suggest that it does exist, that we don't question it. In fact, we are so sure that it is there for us, that our beliefs around gravity are unshakable. It could therefore be argued that we are caught in the spell, the belief, so intensely, that we add power to gravity. We add gravity to gravity.

It is time for us to be willing to take back our power with regard to what we understand.

I understand that All and I are interrelated and as such we are One.

It is easy to see how we are all connected in terms of our relationships on Earth. The chain of life that links cells to insects to plants to animals and humans shows us that when a species is removed from existence, the ripples go out in all directions.

We live in a Universe, a system, that is always rebalancing itself and which thrives when all the members of the system are having their needs met and are doing well. As we add life-giving energy to all aspects of the Universe, we support the well-being of All, including our human Selves. When we take away from, destroy, or diminish other beings, then we are also doing that to our Selves.

One of the important lessons that we, as a human race, have yet to learn is that we are not the masters of it all, and that the Universe and all the creations in it are not here just for our consumption.

I understand that we are all part of the Wisdom Field.

As discussed in Part One, when we combine our collective fields of energy and consciousness together, we, along with all beings, create a Wisdom Field.

Have you ever thought of someone and they called just in that moment? As though they were hearing your thoughts?

Have you ever set out to find something unusual and you "stumble" right onto it and were amazed at your luck? It happens all the time.

Have you ever been in a meeting and you were about to say something when, at that very moment, someone else speaks the exact same idea? These are all examples of being tapped into a collective field of information and consciousness that we are all a part of. The Wisdom Field.

I understand that my intention and words are powerful tools of creation.

In the section a Good State of Intention, we will discuss this much more fully, but it must be mentioned here that intentions and words are fundamental aspects of having a Good State of Understanding.

Over the last four hundred years, the scientific community has applied a tremendous amount of research and thinking to seek out an understanding of gravity. What if we had been encouraged, with the same level of conviction, over the same period of hundreds of years, to understand the power of our intentions and words? In fact, both gravity and intention are attractive principles. Just as gravity attracts things together, intention also pulls things together.

Every ancient religion and teaching talks about the power of words, yet somehow the idea that intention and words can be used in such a direct way is still considered by many as a fringe, out there, concept. Intention is easily observable, and I do believe that if it had been studied as much as gravity has been over the last few hundred years, we would be much further along in our understanding and skillfulness in using it.

Intention is informed by our dreams and wishes. There was a time when people laughed at the idea of flying machines. Thankfully, believers and dreamers persevered. They intended to fly, pushing back against the mass misgivings and, of course, the rest is history.

I do expect that we will be presented in the near future with some very compelling evidence of how some of these forces are working. In the meantime, I encourage you to do your own experiments and observations, staying very curious about these ideas.

I understand that I am my own healer, and that the healing and balancing of my mind, body, and heart is a constant process.

Imagine if we had been brought up believing that we each have the power to heal our Selves. What if we had been taught to develop our Selves as our own healers, as a regular course in school?

I believe that the medical community is populated with many great people who completely get the connection between the patient as healer and the practitioner as a partner in creating healing. I also believe that the highly profitable big business machinery of the pharmaceutical world is more invested in disempowering us, so that we rely more on the buffet of chemicals that turn a profit for them and less on our own power as healers.

If intention could be bottled and made profitable by the pharmaceuticals, we would be inundated with all kinds of media bombardment on intention-based cures.

I am not saying that the contributions of drugs have not helped many people. Of course, there are lots of great products for certain situations. What I am wanting is for a more balanced approach where people are supported in a more holistic way, and that we slow down in the rush to treat symptoms by taking drugs.

The placebo effect refers to healing that results essentially from belief. It has been measured and proven to work. Yet it is held back from mainstream treatments. In fact, it is widely believed that the placebo effect aligns with and supports the effectiveness of drugs that also have an active healing role. Almost any doctor will tell you that even with the best medical treatments, the likelihood of the treatment being effective is greatly diminished if you don't believe in them. There have always been known cases of spontaneous healings. We'll discuss this more in "A Good State of Intention."

You are the healer of your body, heart, and mind. You and you alone hold the responsibility for your Good State of Being. Your mind, heart, and body are in a constant process of balancing and rebalancing. Healing is an ongoing process that will benefit from your wise guidance.

Of course, it is helpful to align with good professional medical support that does not take away from the idea that you are the one who is ultimately responsible to facilitate your healing.

I understand that holding a question is more useful than holding an answer.

Most of us as students were taught and rewarded for getting the "right answer." This is especially true in most western educational systems. In fact, getting to an answer is so highly prized that, in many classes, teaching the memorizing of answers is given priority over teaching how to think your way through to a possible solution.

It is much more powerful to hold the right question, however, than it is to close it off with an answer.

Every time you think you have answered a question that you were asking your Self, note the answer that occurred to you, then release it as just one possibility. Then go back to the question and ask again. This is especially important to do when you think you have arrived at the right answer. You will be amazed at where this process can take you.

I understand that what I believe to be absolutely true becomes true because I believe it.

It is fascinating how powerful belief is. A well-known example of pushing through a belief happened when Roger Bannister broke through the belief that no human could run a mile in under four minutes. Up until the point when he did it, it was widely believed this was an impossible feat. As soon as he did it, others quickly followed, and the four-minute mile went from being impossible to becoming a benchmark for competitive runners. The only thing that changed overnight was that the lie in the system of human beliefs was revealed.

We humans tend to form our Selves into groups around belief systems, and then combine our collective strength to hold each other in the system. What we usually have to give up, in order for this to work, is our curiosity.

When someone questions established beliefs, they are usually shunned or at least marginalized by the group. The group needs the existing beliefs to hold its identity together. It takes a lot of courage to think outside the box of groupthink and belief.

It starts when someone dares to imagine what else is possible and begin the process of dreaming themselves towards a different reality than the one that the group is caught in.

Shifts in belief are created first by imagining, What if . . . Then a new experience happens, the belief is changed, and the reality of the world follows.

Yes, you really are that powerful. Take a look at what you really believe. You will see that it keeps becoming true over and over. It makes sense then that we be careful about our core beliefs, and really question them. Are they true? Does believing what you

believe serve you? Is there any other possibility?
Remember the power of holding the question.

> *I understand that I am the self-authority of the whole of my life, and it is through my choices that I author the unfolding adventure.*

You have considerable influence on your moment-by-moment experiences and the world around you. You create and influence your life with every breath you take. Your responsibility is to keep returning to your Divine Essence and to live your life as a series of good choices and responses to what is needed moment-by-moment.

We are not the masters of the world, and we are not able to control what the Universe brings before us. But we sure do have a lot of influence over it. That influence is extremely powerful. So much so, that it can be said that we are creating the life we are living.

We create the experiences of our life through our intentions, our words, our actions.

> *I understand that All is energy, that energy just is, and that energy is transformed according to the intentions of my thoughts, words, and actions.*

Everything can be explained in terms of its energy. Items that seem solid are just energy held together to function in a particular way. Situations are the same. They are just fields of energy configured in a certain way and embodied in the form of people and other beings. Learn how to move the energy, and you become a masterful creator according to your own vision and wisdom.

I understand that I create my own karma. Every intention, thought, word, or action has an impact, and every impact has a consequence for which I am responsible.

Karma is our thoughts, words, and actions, and it is cumulative. That is to say that every thought, word, or action you have ever been a source of has a consequence. For the sake of this teaching, let's have the word action include everything from the subtlest thought or intention to words that are spoken and physical actions that are carried out.

The fruit of karma is like a weight or a lightness that becomes part of the energetic world that you live in. I like to imagine it as a backpack that either accumulates the weight of actions that results from bad karma or gets lighter and lighter as a result of good actions until it has no weight at all—and even becomes uplifting, as radiant light, in its effect on you.

The determination of good or bad is not as clear as we might like it to be. First of all, it goes according to your intention. In their simplest form, well-meaning actions result in lightness, and bad or ill-intended actions result in burden. Not knowing that an action could have a negative consequence does not save you from the karmic result of that action. We are expected to do our due diligence, to be as responsible as possible for our actions. Even if after due diligence, an action creates an unintended negative result, there will still be a karmic consequence.

There is no clever argument that you can use to get your Soul around your own karma.

I do believe that the amount of karmic weight we carry is determined by our awareness. So an action in which you were aware of what would happen will have a larger karmic effect than one in which you could not have foreseen the result.

This is true for lightening or positive actions, as much as it is for burdening or negative ones. So if you intend to do good, you will lighten your load more than when you do good as a happenchance event.

What is good, lightening, or positive, or what is bad, negative, or burdening, is not always a matter of simple judgment. At the end of the day, that is between you, your conscience, and the Divine. As it is simply a Universal law that responds to your actions, karma is not affected by whether or not you have been caught or found out in your actions. The Divine is always present to you, whether or not you are always present to the Divine.

You know the expression that what goes around comes around.

The Universe responds to every karmic event according to the intention and the resulting impact of the action.

Therefore, actions such as acts of kindness, thoughts that are life-giving to all beings, and those that create beauty will be met with a karmic response that is congruent with that energetic impact. They will lighten your karmic weight.

Anything of ill-intent or of a destructive or diminishing nature or consequence will add weight.

Karma is equally applicable to how you are towards your Self, as it is to your impact on others and the world in general. When you are self-deprecating, you add weight to your karmic back-pack, just as you are when you are putting someone else down through judgment or blame.

Karma is an aspect of the development of the Soul. Many

traditions teach that your karma will follow you past this lifetime. One confusion I often hear from people is that good things happen to "bad" people and bad things happen to "good" people. For example, there are many cases of people who have acquired great wealth through actions that are illegal, destructive, or unethical. Though it seems they are having a lot of success, the journey of their Soul will ultimately have to answer for the actions of this life.

This is equally true for good people who have tragic things happen to them. We live in a wild Universe in which many things happen that are not a direct consequence of our personal actions. I do not believe that we have personally attracted every grand scale event into our life. If a plane goes down with four hundred people on it, I do not think all those people deserved that fate. They were on the wrong plane at the wrong time.

If a government drops a bomb on someone's house by accident, or kills someone as a result of a case of mistaken identity, it does not mean that those people deserved that.

What does matter is what their karmic imprint was at the time of their passing. That is why we must live each moment as though it could be our last in this life. Most of us will never know when we will be crossing over.

Countries, communities, and organizations also have a karmic record. It is important for all members of a group to do everything they can to steer the group they are in according to their Divine Wisdom. If you know that your organization is creating wealth in destructive ways, then you are responsible for your contribution to that. It may be that you will have to leave your job if it comes down to that. You are the one who has to know. You must put your Divine Essence in charge of such decisions.

The good news, and perhaps the most important point of this, is that it is never too late to improve your karmic situation.

I understand that, like the four seasons, there is a natural unfold-ing of events in this Universe. As such, All is subject to cycles and timing.

Everything has a cycle and a timing. Everything has a begin-ning, a middle, and an end. Every journey will be interrupted at some point. This is all normal.

So if things are not going exactly as you would like, the clue as to what is needed may lie in this simple rule. It may be that you have the right idea and it is only your timing that is off.

I understand that all people, beings, things, and circumstances are impermanent, thus I understand the opportunity of each moment is to be present, for past and future live only as story or dream. The moment of now is where all is One.

Everything is impermanent, no exceptions. Even the cells of your body die off and get replaced with new ones. You are literally not in the same body that you occupied a couple of years ago. Some cells change more quickly than others, but ultimately they all die off and get replaced. That is true for every thing, every situation, and every being. Life is like a flame. Look at a flame. See how it continues from moment to moment. It seems to have a continuous existence, but in fact it is a different flame with each passing sec-ond. The source of energy of the flame in each moment is con-sumed, and new material is needed continually in order for the flame to continue.

We humans get so attached to stuff—like life, for example. Everything is going to pass by—and you and your stuff in this earthly form is no exception. When you really embrace this idea, the liberty of it is brilliant.

It means the good times come and go, the bad times come and

go. You get to release your Self from the effort of holding onto what you have. It takes a lot of work to hold on, to maintain the illusion that you can keep things as they are. It is a futile exercise.

It's a much better strategy to stay present and out in front of the inevitable changes by dreaming into the present moment and actively creating the life you want.

I understand the Law of Attraction, which states that whatever I put my expectation and attention on is what I will create in my life. I understand that I am in a dance with the Universe. Therefore what I call in will be in accordance with the larger unfolding picture of All.

So much has been written on this already, I just want to highlight the part that states that we are dancing with the Universe in all this. There is a bigger picture at play here, and thankfully you have a part to play in it. Sorry, it doesn't all revolve around your wishes and you don't actually "control" anything—and that is good news.

I understand that this Universe is generous in its nature, abundant in its possibilities, and filled with all the resources that all beings and I need.

There is so much energy in this Universe. All you need to learn how to do is to create an open and full relationship with the Universe from the wisdom of your Divine Essence. You and All will have everything you need for an amazing journey through this life.

Yes, it all comes back to you.

You Are in a Good State of Understanding.

COLLECTIVE ASPIRATIONS FROM A GOOD STATE OF UNDERSTANDING—A NOTE FROM THE FUTURE

We are now in harmony with the Universe and all the aspects of it. Once we really got that planet Earth was not here to serve us, but instead that we were here to serve her and the Universe as a whole, our lives really opened up for everyone.

Thank goodness the Earth was quite resilient and ultimately wanted to be well and in partnership with us in a good way.

After the Great Awakening, one big shift was that we stopped hoarding. We were so concerned about not having enough, that it used to drive us to wanting more than we needed in a distorted way. It was not sustainable.

Now we have found great peace in allowing abundance to flow through and around us. We know and trust that we will always be fine. Greed is no longer a strong force on us, and we no longer need to grasp at stuff. We learned to receive and to be generous with an open hand rather than a closed fist.

Learning how to activate our relationship with the Universe, to finally allow it to partner with us, was brilliant. It is funny now, when we look back on it, that we ever doubted.

Once we stopped destroying the land and instead started using the concept of creating beauty as our standard of good judgment, the air seemed to clean itself and new sustainable technologies emerged swiftly. As we learned to breathe, the planet breathed with us. That period of relying on fossil fuel worked for a while, and then it really didn't—we just had a hard time letting go of it.

We did have to go around and make reparations for the time before. We had to go and clean out our karmic backpacks. We started with our own families and local communities, then spread out from there. Once we stopped adding negative karmic weight to the backpack, life changed quickly. It wasn't that hard after all.

It helped to understand that each of us was the self-authority for the life we were living. Once we really got that, it was surprisingly easy to create meaningful shifts in our lives for the good of All.

As we started creating from the visions of Divine Essence rather than from our distortions, the Universe aligned with us. The breakthroughs were stunning and the joy factor on the planet has never been so high.

We still face challenges, only now we stay connected and resourceful in the face of them—and things turn out well. We work in partnership with the Universe now. Even young children are taught basic Divine Essence manifestation at a young age. They are also taught how to be resourceful, how to be the self-authority of their own experiences. They are taught how to think creatively and how to turn to each other and to the Wisdom Field for support.

It is now a core understanding for all that we are part of a Wisdom Field. That interface with the Universe enables us to be in communication with all aspects of her. Our direct knowing of interrelatedness is so profound now. As a result we are in the most exquisite dance with all the beings everywhere.

When something does not seem to be opening up, we know now to look deeper into what is really going on. The cycles and timing may be off, or perhaps we are not quite clear about what we are being asked to create. We learned that whatever is going on we can work it out as long as we stay resourceful, flexible, connected, and unattached.

Everything evolves, moves on, transforms, dies, and something new emerges. We just had to settle in with that idea and work with it, rather than resist the fundamental law of impermanence.

Learning how to interact with the Universe at the level of energy was so cool. We knew it was right in front and all around us all the time. It just took us a while to really embrace the idea and to then learn how to be masterful at it. Now we create by aligning with the energy fields of the Universe and it is all quite natural for us. It is good that we remembered what we used to know so long ago.

The Great Awakening was a shock to many at first. It required that we changed how we did almost everything, and now we are so much happier. It was worth it.

PRACTICES FOR A GOOD STATE
OF UNDERSTANDING

Practice Suggestion 1
Identify three people you know who seem to be creating life in a way that you resonate with. Arrange to meet with them (buy them lunch, if possible) and interview them about what they believe is true regarding their understanding of the nature and workings of the Universe.

Practice Suggestion 2
Given that holding a question is more useful than holding an answer, give your Self an open-ended question to carry with you each day throughout the day.

Practice Suggestion 3
Because you are the self-authority of the whole of your life, and it is through your choices that you are authoring your own great adventure, examine any situation in your life and ask whether you perceive it to be good or bad. Ask your Self how you managed to create it. Notice your contributions, then ask your Self:
1) What can I learn from this?
2) What is needed in this situation?

Practice Suggestion 4
In order to be able to move forward in your life in a good way, create the intention to clean up any entanglements of the past that are still lingering around you.

Think of an issue from the past that comes to your attention from time to time. Look for one that still seems to be unfinished for you.

Ask your Self the question, "What is needed to clean this up?"

Notice any ideas or information that come through, and follow through on them according to the guidance of your Divine Essence.

Practice Suggestion 5
Each day read one of the eight states as a visualization. Then ask your Self what is needed so that you may have this more fully in your life today.

A GOOD STATE OF INTENTION

I am in a Good State of Intention.

- From my Good State of Intention, my thoughts arise. A stream of consciousness, a stream that carries beauty and good intention along with life-giving energy out to all beings that are touched by her waters.

- I notice each thought as it arises and choose whether or not to encourage it, to feed it, to fan its embers. If through discernment I decide that thought does not add beauty or is not life-giving, then I choose to release it.

- My thoughts create beauty.

- I understand that it is my responsibility to discern which thoughts to give energy to. I am responsible for each thought that arises. I accept this responsibility with ease and delight.

- I know that as each thought arises, a proportionate consequence is created according to the underlying intention of that thought. Therefore, I choose to only give energy to intentions and thoughts that give life to and that respect all beings of any form, be they human, plant, animal, mineral, or spirit.

- My intentions burn bright with love and the willingness to be generous with my time, my effort, and my resources to all beings and my Self.

- I am tolerant and curious with those I do not understand.

- I am also compassionate with the negative and judgmental aspects of my own Self. I realize that any sense of other, or separation, is of my own making. Therefore I hold the intention and willingness to remove any veils of separation that exist and touch into the Oneness that we are all of.

I am in a Good State of Intention.

A GOOD STATE OF INTENTION

What intention do you hold for how you will speak or think to your Self? Have you ever told your Self that you are not good enough for something, or not deserving, or not adequate in some way? Have you ever doubted? Have you ever told your Self something that diminishes who you are or what you are capable of? Have you ever told your Self anything that was not absolutely true and in some way allowed that thought to keep you back? Well then, you know what it is to be a liar.

Most of us lie to our Selves very often.

We get so used to the critical voice, the self-judgment, the thoughts of negativity that we direct towards our Selves or towards others, that we start to accept them as facts and half-truths, though in fact they are lies.

If a friend or neighbor lied to us as much as we lie to our Selves, we would most likely not tolerate it. At some point we would stop listening to them, and we would most certainly not believe or give credibility to what they say. Yet we are not so vigilant with our own distorted inner voices that we hear and that are so quick to dampen our spirit and put us down in one way or another.

The lies that I am referring to here are the messages that come from the Distorted aspect of who we are. Any time we listen to or allow those messages to take hold, we are colluding with a lie.

The most effective strategy that Distorted uses over us is turning fact into fiction, or turning fear into fact. It is our job to know when this is happening and not to let these ideas take hold in any way whatsoever. This takes a constant state of attention and effort.

This starts with you creating the intention that you will only be loving and kind to your Self through your thoughts and words.

INTENTION, EXPECTATION, THOUGHTS

These are the energies that lie beneath our words and actions. These are the carrier waves that live between the words we speak and the actions we carry out. It is our intentions and expectations that guide our course in each moment of our journey.

Intentions and expectations are conscious or unconscious— that is, known or unknown—energy that is intended to create something. Many of our intentions and expectations are known to us, while others live beneath the surface, running as operating scripts that never get questioned—until they are revealed and brought into the light for examination as we further our journey of awakening.

When we talk about intentions and expectations, it is always good to be clear about whose intentions and expectations we are talking about. In this book, we have been talking about the two aspects of us that live within: Divine Essence and Distorted Self. Either of these two aspects of us could be in charge of the intention and expectation Department at any given time.

At the highest level, the intentions of Divine Essence are to experience life as fully connected to the Oneness of All as possible, as well as to create beauty, further the unfolding story of the Universe, and be in-joy.

The intentions of the Distorted Self will be more in the range of protecting you from perceived dangers and risks, which includes avoiding the risk of change. The main driver here is protection.

The intention of Distorted Self is not necessarily wrong, but its methods are ineffective and, ironically, eventually lead to the very thing that Distorted Self is trying to avoid—the total and complete diminishment of the human.

Our life experience is created largely through our thoughts, words, and actions. The intentions we hold as we think, speak, and act affect the impact that we have on our world, and in return affect what the world gives back.

When our expectations are congruent with what we are saying and doing, then we are sending a clear message to the world around us. The response back is reflective of that.

Sometimes our expectation is different than what we are saying and doing, the message we are putting out is therefore incongruent. We might say that we want to have a good day, while inside we are not expecting that. This can confuse the people around us. We might not even be aware that we are doing it.

The Universe is all too willing to comply with our wishes, so we had better be clear about what it is that we are asking for.

INTENTION AND ENERGY

The Universe is made up of energy that is available to be created from. That energy does not have an opinion of what is good for you or not, and it is available to become anything according to your wishes, hopes, prayers—and conversely according to your fears, concerns, and darkest expectations. As energy is available to be created from, it is up to us to use this truth in a responsible and powerful way. This energy is all around us all the time. It responds to our wishes and it responds to our fears.

We interact with this energy through the use of our imagination. As we imagine different scenarios, we are in fact influencing the energy around us to align with that intention. This process is working all the time, whether we are conscious of it or not.

WHO'S IN CHARGE?

It's important to be clear about what aspect of your being you are allowing to be heard. Your Divine Essence creates intentions that are in accordance with the greatest wisdom of the heart for creating Oneness, beauty, abundance, generosity, and life-giving energy.

Your Distorted Self will hold intentions that are meant to keep you safe, but it uses tactics like fear-mongering, judgment, criticism, and blame. Distorted Self will therefore be holding intentions that will sabotage you along the way, in its earnest desire to keep you protected from your Self.

Distorted Self knows that doubt and isolation are two powerful ways to ensure paralysis, resulting in everything staying the way it is. This distorted energy, if allowed, will wrap itself around and in between your words and actions, and will give you a bit of leash—but it won't quite let you reach your heart's desire. If you should create wealth or a great relationship on Distorted's watch, then Distorted Self will use the fear of loss, which looks like hoarding and jealousy and a gripping hand to hold on tight. Not pretty! Distorted's mission is to keep you safe, not happy—and certainly not fulfilled.

Divine Essence is of the heart. It understands that life is an unfolding adventure. It also knows that you are an amazing human being who is here to experience life, to know joy, and to be happy. Divine Essence will hold these intentions for you and, if allowed, will support you in opening to the abundance of the Universe.

INTENTION AND ABUNDANCE

Abundance is a word that is used a lot in the western cultures. I would like to put some context around it. First, let's open it up so that the concept can apply to anything from money to great relationships to family experiences and great adventures. All according to what your Divine Essence attracts in accordance to its wisdom.

Imagine that you put your Divine Essence in charge of your abundance department. What is different for you now?

Divine Essence welcomes in all the resources required for you to have a great life and then knows how to put those resources to good use on the planet. Divine Essence is not greedy, so it recognizes when enough is enough. If you have created a flow of resources that surpasses your personal needs, then Divine Essence is generous in its nature and will inform you on how to use those resources in a good way.

Distorted will operate from fear. From this place you can never have enough. No matter how much you have, Distorted will always be afraid that it won't be enough.

Divine Essence operates in trust, so has no need to hoard wealth or to be jealous in relationships. Divine Essence is open to the mystery of this life, facing each experience with an expansive heart and an open hand.

THE PRAYERS

We are in a dance with the Universe. There is a story that is unfolding—it's the Universe's story and we are playing our part in it. We are not in a vacuum, either. Look around at all the people, and imagine the cacophony of prayers, hopes, fears, dreams, and distractions. The Universe responds to all of it. It is an elaborate matrix of chaos mixed with intentionality that is playing out every nanosecond. The Universe is the orchestra and there are billions of conductors, each asking to hear a different song.

What must it take to satisfy all that is being prayed for and asked for, not to mention what the Universe itself might be up to?

Your energy is fuel for the Universe and your intention is how to direct the fuel.

The more you give your Self over fully to your prayers and dreams, the more the Universe is able to meet you in them.

Hesitancy creates hesitancy, commitment creates results.

WHAT KIND OF UNIVERSE IS IT?

Many people experience a kind and loving and generous Universe, while others experience the Universe as cruel, tumultuous, and violent. It seems that it is all available to us. As we move through the world, we are exposed to it all.

The Universe just is. It took violent explosions and unimaginable forces of pressure and heat and cold to eventually form our planet. Then one day, a beautiful and delicate flower arose. If the world were an ideal environment that was completely safe, organized, and guaranteed, then it would afford us no opportunity to grow our Selves, to learn.

As the world is chaotic and unpredictable, we have the possibility to develop into the full expression of our Divine Essence. That is the journey we are on.

INTENTIONS AND HEALING

When you really get how powerful the idea of healing through the power of your intentions is, you start to understand how fundamental it is to life itself. Imagine that you are able to influence your health and well-being from a Good State of Intention.

That means that you are the one who is responsible and respondable to what is going on with your health. You can learn to create an intention that will affect the condition of your body. There is a tremendous amount of research being developed at this time that supports this idea.

We have been hypnotized into believing that sickness is inevitable, or that healing comes in packages of drugs from doctors and pharmaceutical companies. The entire medical system depends on us believing that is true, so the system itself does not discourage such thinking.

Your body responds to your thoughts. This is easy to experience. Just imagine one of your favorite foods sitting in front of you right now. Chances are you will notice a shift in your body. Your mouth may begin to salivate, your stomach may be preparing to take in this food, and you may feel inspired to get it for real now. All of that just from a suggestion. That's an example of your body responding to all the thoughts and suggestions that you are putting into it. Meanwhile, doesn't it make sense that cultural messages telling us what is good for us and what is bad for us makes it true as soon as we believe it?

RECOVER TO DIVINE INTENTIONS

Key to the development of our being and to our ability to create supportive intentions is the ongoing practice of recovery to Divine Essence. To recover is to return to or to regain our connection to Divine Self. As long as we live from Divine Essence and keep recovering back when we slip away, then good things will happen.

Remember the oral tradition, the Delicate Lodge, that we talked about in Part One, and the teaching known as the Ring of Power?

What's important to remember from this teaching is that we each have a responsibility to our lives. We are the self-authors of our experience, so the story we are living is of our own making. We have the power to use the Ring of Power as a way to create intention according to the wisdom of our Divine Essence.

As we move through this powerful tool, we accept our personal responsibility, create and make a choice with discernment, and then activate our will to follow through. By activating our will, we are aligning our Selves with our intention and following through according to what is needed now.

This would be a good time to discern whether or not it is right for you to commit to living from the energy of Divine Essence. That is, to create the intention. In choosing to do so, you also commit to recovering each time you notice that you have slipped into the throes of Distorted Self.

With practice the moments of Divine Essence become more

and more, and the time of Distorted Self will become less and less. Of course, vigilance will always be needed.

DIVINE IMPECCABILITY

If you have committed to living fully from your Divine Essence, next comes the intention of holding to the course in a good way. It is normal for us humans to succeed often and to fail often. Both are part of a normal process of learning. The more willing we are to risk failing, the freer we are to stretch our Selves out for the sake of learning more, having more fun, and further awakening.

Divine impeccability sets the standard that you are striving for. Divine impeccability is the bar that you are establishing for your Self, regardless of what you are up to. It is how you know how well you are doing.

When Distorted Self holds the bar of impeccability, it is much less kind. The standard it sets might look like perfectionism that is unattainable or unsustainable—and when you slip and miss, Distorted may engage in berating and judging you or others around you.

Distorted Self sometimes goes the other way, too, convincing you that a low bar is safer, perhaps offering the idea that you can't do it well anyway, so why bother trying. You will just be disappointed, or it is too much work.

Distorted will have a dissonant energy that will be visceral in the heart and body intelligence and noisy in the mind intelligence.

In the hands of Divine Essence, impeccability is a high bar of attainment that honors what is possible for the extraordinary being that you are. Divine Essence holds the bar of impeccability to serve your development with a spirit of calling you forth to stretch your Self. Divine Essence holds this bar with loving-kindness for the human that you are and with compassion.

SUCCEEDING AND FAILING

Living a life from Divine Essence does not mean always being Pollyanna happy. Divine Essence will know the difference of a win or a miss, a blunder or brilliance, misfortune or good luck. With Divine Essence, the response to anything you take on will be resonance. Even when you experience disappointment, you know you are in Divine Essence when you are honoring and supporting of your Self and others involved, and when you are willing to get to the truth of what is available for you to learn.

Whether you succeed or fail, Divine Essence will always be compassionate and supportive in gathering in the learning. Divine Essence will always have the impact of resonance, which you can be more and more aware of as you continue to check in with your heart, body, and mind intelligences.

Again, as you learn to gather the information through the three intelligences, you will know when recovery to Divine Essence is needed. When you realize it is recovery time, you must activate your will according to your intention to live life from the energy of Divine Essence, then start the recovery process.

Remember that over time your relationship with Divine Essence will get stronger and stronger, and recovery will get easier and will be needed less often.

DIVINE ESSENCE INTENTIONS

Divine Essence will hold many intentions according to your own wisdom. Learning how to access and trust that wisdom is an important part of the process of living an awakened life.

Divine Essence is attuned to your heart intelligence and holds the intellect of your mind in a fair balance. Divine Essence is like a guide that will support you in navigating through life in a good way.

There are some high-level intentions that Divine Essence holds that are common to us all:

- Divine Essence is always of the Oneness. Any idea that we are separate is a Distorted illusion, so Divine Essence intentions are aligned to what is needed for the good of all.
- Divine Essence intends to create beauty. Beauty is created through our intentions, thoughts, words, and actions. If beauty is not honored or created in a decision process, then it is likely that Divine Essence is not being activated in finding the answer.
- Divine Essence intends that all energy will be infused with life-giving support. Therefore, as we create intentions through goals, visions, and actions, we transform energy from one state into something new according to the vision of that new intention. Divine Essence will ensure that every intention includes life-giving energy.
- Divine Essence will hold good will for all. Divine Essence is generous and compassionate and understands that there is enough for everyone and therefore withholds nothing.
- Divine Essence puts loving-kindness into every thought, word, and action. Divine Essence is understanding of the challenges of being a human, and so holds an open heart for us all as we find our way along the river of life.

COLLECTIVE ASPIRATIONS FROM A GOOD STATE OF INTENTION—A NOTE FROM THE FUTURE

People have learned how to intend and to live life fully from the energy of Divine Essence. We learned how important a Good State of Intentions is. Now we recover quickly and easily if we slip out of this state. It happens from time to time, only now we recognize it and we are all adept at helping each other get back to intentional resourcefulness.

Because of the infectiousness of Divine Essence, it's now easy and natural for everyone to sustain the way of good intention. Holding the good intention and understanding that in every moment we can create life-giving experiences has brought the entire world into a closer relationship, one that is founded on creating beauty as a guiding principle.

Fear has been recognized as a normal early-stage condition and is met with compassion rather than collusion. Judgment and projections are the energetic seeds of our past experience, so we learned how to use that power for good, which is the power of transmuting energy through good intention. For example, now we project about how wonderful we all are. As we've done that, people have started responding to each other accordingly.

The healthcare systems now embrace this concept fully. Clinics are filled with practitioners who are trained in the science of guided intentions. Doctors and nurses have returned to the ancient ways of supporting people in recovering their wholeness through an amazing series of developments and new procedures. Placebo clinics are now open and the results have been extraordinary. The overall well-being of everyone, including the practitioners, is at such a high level that the entire healthcare system is now aligned with this way of treating people.

The intention to create beauty is the new standard of quality and good decision-making. It is now considered a standard intention at every level of society—from that of the individual and family systems right on through to every branch of business and government.

Because we have learned to operate from the energy of Divine Essence, our intentions have shifted from the old ways. Archaic concepts like government defense departments became redundant and have since been replaced with more life-giving ideas from the department of loving-kindness.

Now we are all committed to living more fully according to the intentions we create, in alignment with the inspirations of Divine Essence. We create now in ways which we had previously never even imagined possible.

When it comes to how high we can fly, we still don't know what we don't know. We learned to stay open to the great mystery and the delightful unfolding of this beautiful story that we are all intending together. Now we intend to reveal new levels of beauty, brightness, and awakened wisdom and we do so in every moment.

PRACTICES FOR A GOOD STATE OF INTENTION

Practice Suggestion 1
Set a daily intention. Include setting the intention for your personal Good State of Being. For example, intend to be happy or grateful and set an intention around a result for something that you are doing. Remember that monk who intended to walk happily.

Practice Suggestion 2
Observe the underlying intention behind something you are doing each day. Watch for the mixed signals and get curious if you discover any. For example, you may be applying for a job. As you send your resume you notice that you expect to *not* get the job. Get curious about the negative expectation and choose something different.

Practice Suggestion 3
When you are doing something that involves other people, gather them for a discussion on your collective intentions for that project. Discuss the intentions even before you discuss how to do anything related to that project. Set the group's Good State of Being before you activate the Good State of Doing.

Practice Suggestion 4
Each day do a visualization that supports you in balancing your body systems and creating health and well-being for your Self and others around you. Hold the intention that amazing health is normal for you, and that you can interact with your body in a good way.

A GOOD STATE
OF WORDS

I am in a Good State of Words.

- My words are created from my Good State of Intention.

- My words create beauty and are life-giving.

- My words honor all those around me, including my Self.

- My words create positive impacts on those who hear them and those whom they are about.

- My words are chosen. I am responsible for their impact.

- I use discernment to choose my words according to my Good State of Intention.

- My words are not used as a weapon against others or my Self.

- My words evoke beauty, generosity, and appreciation.

- My words inspire creativity in others and my Self.

- My words carry my breath and they blow encouragement onto the embers of possibilities for others and my Self.

- My words give life to what wants to be born and give completion to what it is time to let go of.

- My words cast the dreams of my wisdom onto the ears of other Divine Ones.

- My words are truthful, kind, and needed.

- My words express the Universe's song of love and appreciation.

I am in a Good State of Words.

A GOOD STATE OF WORDS

You most likely know that your words matter, that they are powerful, that they affect your world. Yet even though you know this, it is likely that many of the words you speak are still working against you and those around you in some way. It is one thing to know that words matter, yet another to fully live into the practice of a Good State of Words.

If you truly embrace the idea that every word and every intention matters, I suspect that you would not speak much of what you presently speak.

When was the last time you uttered a complaint, expressed a judgment, or went along with another who was doing the same? It is truly a remarkable act to fully and completely clean up our use of words. It takes a tremendous effort and constant vigilance—and it is important that we do so.

You have no doubt had many experiences where something happened around you that turned out very close to the way you said it would. You probably thought, "Hey, I told you so!" If it was a good event, you might have noted to your Self how great it was that you forespoke that event, while if it was a negative event you might have cringed a little and wished you had predicted something different. Either way, the power of your words was at play.

It is not that we have absolute power over events just because we say that the outcome will be this or that. We are each powerful in our impact, but none of us controls the world around us. We are at best strong influencers of the unfolding of the Universe's story. When we speak to something, we send out an energetic force that moves and vibrates out sound waves in action, and those influence and change the course of what is to be.

Events have a trajectory as they unfold. That trajectory is created by the influences of what has already happened. Then our words interact with that trajectory and the path it is taking, influencing things according to the intention that carries those words. Your words add to, or take energy away from, what is happening.

LISTEN
First, let us listen. It is one thing to have something to say, it is something quite different to have something to hear. Very often when I am gathered with friends or colleagues, I notice that most of us are more invested in speaking rather than in listening. When that happens, the voices rise, the pace quickens, and the people are more present to their own words than to what is being said by others.

When you listen, listen to what is being said in between the words. Listen to the heart of what is being said. Listen to your body and to the energetic hum of the room you are in. Imagine that you are the room, listening to your conversation from the point of view of the room. Notice any impressions that occur to you and include the reporting of that to the people you are with. Allow the wisdom you are gathering to be shared and known by everyone so that together you will discover what is really being expressed.

When you do listen, do so with an open heart, mind, and body. Notice where you are defended and ask your Self what is needed to be able to listen openly.

Words are powerful and they want a place to land. Words want to be heard.

ANCIENT WISDOM
The Buddhist teaching of Right Speech asks us to consider four points before we say anything. They are:
- That the words are spoken with meaningful purpose. This also includes the idea of avoiding idle chatter that is distracting the mind from being truly present.

- That the words spoken are true. To not lie or withhold important information is an important aspect of Right Speech.
- That the words are spoken affectionately. Use words that speak to the heart rather than words that are of anger or are intended to hurt.
- That the words are spoken harmoniously, avoiding words that cause division and slander.

You can see in this list how a Good State of Intention can inform words as well as the one speaking them.

THE THREE GATES

There is another beautiful teaching from the Sufi tradition called the Three Gates.

It teaches that your words must pass through three gates before they are uttered.

- The first gate is to ask if what you are about to speak is true.
- The second gate asks if what you are about to speak is needed.
- The third gate asks if what you are about to speak is kind.

I appreciate the elegance of these simple and straight-forward teachings. They speak for themselves. The fact that all the great teachings have commentaries on the use of words is a strong indication of the importance of right words.

WORDS ARE LIKE PAINT ON AN ARTIST'S BRUSH

Words are used to create a picture according to the artist's skill and ability and underlying intentions. We use words so much during the course of each day of our lives that we often don't think about their real meaning and impact.

The good news is that we humans are creative beings. The good and bad news is that we are magicians in our ability to create according to our spoken word. We are always creating as we take in each breath, and we add to it our intention. Then we release that breath along with the intention in the form of words. Every single word you speak is a spell that is cast out into the Universe asking to be heard and manifested. Like drops of paint, they scatter out onto the Universal canvas. The life you are living is the colorful reflection, according to the images and pictures that you have spoken.

KARMA

Your karmic backpack is the weight of past actions along with your present and future intentions. Your karmic weight shifts according to how you show up in each moment of your life.

Each word you speak has a karmic influence. When you speak poorly of others, complain, or put your Self down with your words, you are adding weight to your karmic backpack.

When you speak well, tell the truth, speak words of beauty, and speak with good intention, you are lightening your karmic weight.

Most importantly, your words must be held and spoken with good intention.

YOUR STATE OF BEING

The words you speak now and the words that others speak while around you or about you have an impact on your state of being. That is your present condition in this moment. It includes the intentions you are operating from, the words you speak, and the actions you take. We will discuss this more in a Good State of Being. For now, be aware that your words go out like the beating of a drum and they vibrate through everything that they speak to and about. The quality of that vibration has a profound impact, not just on your Self, but on others as well.

The extent to which we are awake to our influence and own our responsibility—and to which we remain in choice as a creator according to our Divine Essence's wisdom in each moment—is the extent to which we are creating from awakened wisdom.

The only two other choices for us, aside from creating through our wisdom, are to create unconsciously or to create from the energy of our Distorted Self.

Creating unconsciously seldom works out. If we are not present in any particular moment, then we are not available to our Selves or to whomever is with us in that moment, nor are we open to the amazing magic of the Universe as it dances with us.

When we are present and living through our Divine Essence, then life will unfold quite magically. We then bring forward the best of who we are. That is our creative, resourceful, and magical essence.

When our Distorted Self speaks to things, we are unconsciously creating from fear and the myriad forms that fear takes on, such as anger, shame, or a mix of many other destructive energies. This energy spreads like a wildfire. From this place we are contributing to a world that is created from a distortion, and therefore takes on all the aspects of a distorted world. That is a world of separation, protectionism, greed, and destruction. It doesn't have to go that way.

THE ROLE WORDS PLAY

When your words come from your Divine Essence, they tend to create beauty when they are spoken. They will be words that are life-giving to the world around you. Words from Divine Essence honor the speaker and the one being spoken of, alike. Such words create a resonance around you when spoken, and it is that resonance that moves the Universe to respond accordingly.

Your words are like a song out to the Universe. The Universe responds according to the lyrics and the melody that is heard.

If your song is beautiful and life-giving, the Universe is willing to reflect that back to you. Conversely, if your words are distorted and filled with fear or negativity, the Universe is just as likely to mirror distortion back. Now imagine the chorus of people around you, and you start to see how important it is for us all to be discerning about the words we release.

CATCH OR RELEASE

In the chapter on A Good State of Intention, we discussed that you cannot control whether or not a thought occurs. You must be alert to notice each thought, then decide whether or not to give it energy.

Well words are different, in that you can catch your words before they are spoken. So you must start to be responsible for them before they are even uttered.

We are talking about a high bar of vigilance here. The possibility of living at the highest standard is a matter of practice.

As a group, we humans have some good word habits and some not so good word habits. Good word habits contribute to the resonance all around us. They tend to be those words of support, truth-telling, and acknowledgment. They create beauty and they come from a place of good intention.

Words on the opposite side of the spectrum are those that create dissonance, such as complaining, criticizing, making others wrong or less than, negative judging, lies, gossip, or spreading fear and negativity. These do not come from good intention.

We have all engaged in both good and bad use of words, as that is a part of growing as a human. Our job is to become conscious and responsible for the words that we do speak.

Living life as an awakened human is a moment-by-moment, day-to-day, process that requires the willingness to stay on the leading edge of the wave of your impact. To do that, you must first own your responsibility in the matter. In this case, we're talking about the words you choose to use.

No matter what you say, even if you are really angry or upset, you remain responsible. Your karmic backpack is a running account of how you are doing.

For some, this requires a lot more editing than it does for others. So be it!

The good news is that this is a learned process, and the more you practice the better you get at it. It is the process we must engage in. That means that when you speak words that do not meet the standard your Divine Essence recognizes as the bar, then you get to clean up after your Self and set things right. This might mean taking things back, apologizing, or setting the word right depending on the situation. Your Divine Essence will know.

The key to it all is to always hold good intention behind your words. If you mean to hurt through speaking judgment or blame or putting down, then there is no good intention there.

One aspect that is tricky for many people is what to do when someone in their life is doing wrong towards them. It is easy to go straight to complaining, gossiping, or making that person wrong in some way.

It is useful in these situations to create a distinction between the behaviors of that person versus the human being they are. As humans, we do things that don't work out, we make mistakes, we mess up. That is just part of the journey of this life.

When someone around you has this kind of an impact, it is important to talk to them about the behavior that impacted you negatively, not to make them wrong as a person.

Being curious with Distorted Self is a very effective management technique. Distorted Self will win just about any argument. But genuine open curiosity, without making Distorted wrong, is very disarming and informative.

How this applies to words is to notice the words the Distorted would have you speak, then ask your Divine Essence if the words can pass through the three gates. If not, then don't speak them.

This is one process through which you will be able to learn a lot about what makes you tick. The more you learn about your personal operating system, the more you will be able to live an awakened life.

Because our emotions often affect our choice of words, you may notice that angry people use shouting, or they whisper angry words. It is important to stay ahead of the wave and to remain resourceful and discerning.

GOSSIP

Gossip is another distorted word habit. Gossip is, simply put, talking about someone. It is not that you should never talk about someone; on the contrary, you could talk about people a lot. But it is the intention you hold as you speak your words that matters. The words you speak are born from the intention you hold.

If in talking about someone you are in any way complaining about them, putting them down, separating them from belonging, or anything close to these energies, then the talking is coming from a distorted place. Such talking does not create resonance. It is easy to find colluders in such talk, people who will gladly join in these conversations, because one person's Distorted Self will activate the Distorted Selves of anyone within listening distance.

Once again, ker ching, ker plunk, and the karmic backpack just received another distorted deposit.

The words of the Divine Essence are words that create beauty and are life-giving in their underlying intention.

Imagine gathering around the water cooler at the office and the only conversations you heard were those singing the praises of other people. Imagine the resonance of people gathering to speak words of appreciation. That is, creating beauty with your words and intention.

It takes willingness on your part to discern what conversations to participate in or not. If you have been a gossiper up until now, you keep good company. I suspect we have all participated in such conversations at some point. Now is the time to decide that you are no longer going to have those conversations from a distorted place. Instead, have them from the place of your Divine Essence.

Here is an acronym for gossip that I suggest you try out in the future:

G—Great

O—Observations

S—Sighting

S—Sensational

I—Inspiring

P—People

Ker ching—aaaaaaaahh, your karmic backpack just got lighter and brighter.

It may be that you are observing some behavior in another person that is not working well. Rather than turn to gossip as a way to deal with it, approach them with some feedback that could serve them in their own growth.

At the end of this chapter are some suggestions on how to offer feedback.

LEADING WITH WORDS

Words are powerful. They move people according to the message and the intention of the one speaking them. Words are one of the most effective resources a leader uses to shift the world according to their vision and agenda.

Words can unify people into an alignment of purpose that changes the shape and texture of the world we live in every day.

We all know what it feels like when a politician uses words of fear, warning, and the prophesy of doom. We know what it is like to have leaders who use these tactics to manipulate public opinion to suit their agenda.

Moving people using tactics of fear creates separation. Though sometimes effective, it is leading people from the Distorted Self of the leader, who is in turn activating the Distorted Selves of the people. This way of leading others is life-diminishing, not life-giving.

History remembers its leaders, though the way in which they are remembered often highlights abuse of power rather than enlightened leadership.

There have been those leaders who have known how to move people from the vision and resonance of their Divine Essences. The impact such leaders have is to create a sense of openness, optimism, and Oneness with all.

WORDS AND AGREEMENTS

Another way that words create spell-binding impacts is through the agreements we speak with others, as well as the words we speak to our Selves.

We will look into this more fully in the chapter on a Good State of Being. For now, it is enough to say that every spoken promise counts, and every unfulfilled agreement is a sticky string that will pull you back to it until it has been followed through on or released. This includes the light promise of phrases such as, "I'll call you," as much as it does the promises to Self and others that are not kept.

I had the experience once of walking along a street in Burma looking for an address. An English-speaking monk came along, and noticing that I appeared lost, he inquired as to whether or not I needed assistance. I explained that I was looking for a particular pagoda. He was not familiar with it, and still he offered to help me find it. I accepted his offer and off we went in search of it.

We wandered around for a while checking likely places and asking around, but we had no success in finding this small, relatively unknown pagoda. At one point in our walk, the monk turned to me and told me that he had an obligation to be somewhere else soon, but he also explained that he felt obligated to assist me according to our initial conversation.

I assured him that I would be okay on my own, that he could go on to his meeting. He then asked me if I would release him from his obligation to assist me. I agreed and told him that he was released from the promise to help me find that pagoda. He smiled and walked off.

As I watched him walk away, I was startled by what had just transpired. I felt a clean break of the energy between us.

When the monk first showed up, he'd said, "I will help you." And when I accepted his offer, an agreement was made. A cord of energy was connected between us.

When it was time to let go of the search, at his request I spoke the words, "I release you." With those words the cord of energy was severed.

The sensation in that moment was visceral. My body felt the release between the two of us. He was allowed to go to his meeting and I was free to continue my search.

Almost immediately after that I found the pagoda I was looking for. My intuition kicked in and took me right to it. I would never have been available to receive that support from the Universe if I had not released the monk from his obligation. In releasing him I not only freed both of us, but I opened the door for the Universe to speak to me through my intuition.

I am grateful to that monk for a very important teaching that has served me many times since.

I must admit that I sometimes get strange reactions from people when I respond to their offer of "Let's meet for lunch sometime," with the response, "Thank you for offering, but no thank you." I respond politely in these cases, but I do so because I know that the lunch is not likely to happen.

I would rather walk in the truth of that than walk away with a strand of energy that I have no intention of following through on.

Often when I meet people at workshops, for example, who I may never see again, I might say something like, "It would be good to see you again." Those words are the truth for me in that moment and do not create a string of agreement between my Self and the person I'm speaking to.

Living in a Good State of Words requires a constant level of consciousness. It requires looking not just into the words that are spoken but also into the intention beneath them. As with many of the ideas in this book, the biggest challenge for most of us is breaking the old patterns and learning new ones. One challenge in this is to stop colluding with cultural niceties that make easy moments of social politeness, but actually just lead to incongruity and create karmic weight.

One of the most important considerations behind every aspect of living an awakened life is to hold good intention and to be willing to walk the path according to your Divine Essence.

The choice will always come back to you. You might choose to live in a Good State of Words, or you might choose not to.

COLLECTIVE ASPIRATIONS FROM A GOOD STATE OF WORDS—A NOTE FROM THE FUTURE

Since the time of the Great Awakening, we have reached a place together where the power of our words is well-known. From that knowing we are all happily responsible and therefore speak in a good way, with loving-kindness. People gather now to discuss ideas and to share stories that tell of the adventures of the day.

When people talk now, they are grounded in the wisdom of their Divine Essence. They speak from the Good State of Intention that is behind and around their words.

The biggest shift is that we have learned to listen. We listen now with an open heart and a clear mind. In this listening we have learned to be patient, to allow some silence to be part of the process, to let go of the fear that used to shut down the space for listening.

Because of this there is now much more room for differing views and ideas. Now everyone is much more interested in discovering what is needed rather than being right.

We have learned how to support each other with our listening and our words. For example, when someone has had a negative experience, perhaps with another person, and they have a need to talk about it in order to get clear of the impact of the incident, we now know how to listen and support them. We listen in a way that gives that person the opportunity to speak so that they will find their way through to the other side of their anger and negativity. We guide them through this process with an open curiosity intended to reveal the learning that is available to us all. The one who is talking holds an intention to move past the event that angered them so that they are no longer invested in the stickiness of being right. We have learned how to be clear and open, instead of being right or winning points.

We no longer pass judgment on the one who is speaking about issues on which we differ. Instead, we listen fully, openly, bringing curiosity to the conversation in a way that serves the one who is talking as well as the listeners. The result of all of this is that people no longer need to hold onto their views. They can express all their related emotions such as anger, sadness, even their joy and happiness. We now move these energies through us in a good way. It is not that there are no longer any conflicts, as there will always be opposing views; it is that we now have the respect and space for all viewpoints.

Now, when we gather, we share the stories of how brilliant, beautiful, or fun our friends and coworkers are, and our words create even more beauty. This we know because we see it in each other's faces and we experience it in the open hearts that gather.

Each day now we speak words of our dreams, prayers, and visions openly. Those who listen add their good intention to our words. We recognize the power of combined intent and honor the various dreams that each of us holds.

We cast wishes about with great consciousness, and the Universe responds in a way that is more profound than ever before.

We also listen carefully to the Wisdom Field that speaks to us in its own way, using our words to give life and energy to what is trying to happen on behalf of the collective good of all.

PRACTICES FOR A GOOD STATE OF WORDS

Practice Suggestion 1

Actively stop your Self from speaking unkind words today. Instead, choose words of appreciation that add beauty to who or what they are about. This is an especially good practice when you are speaking about a person or situation with which you are unhappy.

Practice Suggestion 2

Pick three people each day to whom you will speak words of loving-kindness and appreciation. Think of a quality in each of these people that you like and tell them what it is. For example, they might be courageous. If so, tell them that.

Practice Suggestion 3

When you find your Self in a conversation with someone who is complaining respectfully and compassionately, turn it into a conversation that is creative and life-giving.

Practice Suggestion 4

Notice a speaking habit you have that is not honoring of your Self and replace it with one that creates more resourcefulness and beauty. For example, if you have a habit of using words that put your Self down, find something that is positive and speak that instead.

Practice Suggestion 5

Feedback Protocols

- First ask your Self if the issue you are concerned with is really about the other person, or whether it might have been created by you.
- Ask your Self what you are contributing to the situation and adjust as needed.

- If it is still necessary to speak about this issue with the other person, then set a Good State of Intention for the conversation.
- Ask the person it is about if they are willing to listen to some feedback.
- Let them know that you care and are holding good intention for them.
- Describe the specific behavior they do that is not working for you.
- Offer a tip to improve.
- Be sensitive to how well this information is coming across and offer support if needed.

A GOOD STATE OF BEING

I am in a Good State of Being.

- I am living as One with all.

- I am in right relationship with the three intelligences of body, heart, and mind.

- Because I am in a Good State of Being, my spirit is bright and joyous.

- I am in right relationship with my body intelligence and therefore I care for my body with kindness, good food, exercise, and care.

- I am in right relationship with my heart intelligence and therefore I check in often with my emotions. I activate my heart wisdom.

- I am in right relationship with my mind intelligence and therefore practice discernment of words and thought always.

- When I am experiencing discordance with the wisdom of my Divine Essence, I look into the cause and ask what is needed. I then respond and follow through.

- I am in right relationship with God, the Great Spirit, the Universe, which holds me.

- I am in right relationship with all and therefore I keep all my relationships clean and bright.

- I am in right relationship with the Earth and all the beings, including the plants, animals, minerals, soil, waters, and every aspect that is of the earth and the surrounding Universe.

- I am in right relationship with the Wisdom Field and therefore I listen into it and respond according to the guidance of my Divine Essence.

- Because I am in a Good State of Being I am the source of my joy.

- I am a beacon of light shining loving-kindness for all including myself.

- I live in trust of myself and therefore move forward in a good way.

- I am a lifelong learner and as such I allow myself to risk succeeding or failing and to always learn.

I am in a Good State of Being.

A GOOD STATE OF BEING

Being in a Good State of Being is to be in relationship with all that there is. To be without any sense of separation from each other, the plants, animals, and even the rocks as well as all the other things and beings that exist. Any sense of me versus you, us versus them or I versus it, is separation. We must relearn and find our way back to our knowing of this fundamental truth.

THE ONENESS OF US

You have no doubt heard the words that we are all one and wondered what that really means. We are born as one with our mother. As we leave the womb and enter this worldly life, we immediately start to forget what that Oneness was, in our natural process of individuating our Selves. This process is what allows us to survive and develop our Selves throughout our life. We then have to relearn what it is to be One. In Part One, I wrote about the experience I had of dying. In that experience, I was able to be in connection with the Oneness of all there is. I was held in a field of energy that I can only describe as love. It is a field of energy that runs through us all, along with everything that we create. It holds us like a web. It responds to our thoughts, words, and actions. It is the Divine.

As we learn to live through our Divine Essence, we get closer and closer to the Divine. As long as we are in this life, we can only experience the Divine through the context of being a human. Even when fully open to our Divine Nature, we come so close. We are always held in our human experience, so we are never quite the Divine. At best, we can be our Divine Essence. Through opening and allowing our Divine Essence to be out in front, we can be in relationship with the Divine, we can be one with the Divine. Simultaneously we will never know what it is to be The Divine.

Our human capacity cannot fully comprehend that. We can, however, have glimpses of it and we can get very close if we choose to and do the work necessary to attain that state of One.

Nature is our greatest teacher on this attainment. By putting your Self into prolonged experiences with nature, it is possible to drop into deeper and deeper levels of connection. What we are talking about here is you learning how to open your heart fully, to still your mind, and to soften to the vulnerability of your body.

To start to get a sense of the immensity of this truth, sit quietly for a few moments. Then as a living practice of this, expand your Observer out and open it through all three intelligences of mind, body, and heart. Allow your intuition and your imagination to inform you about what the state of the collective experience is for everyone in the room all at once. Expand that out to include the surrounding community, then pull it out wider and wider. While doing this, imagine that you can feel into each being and have a sense of how they are. Now imagine that they are an expanded sense of you, an aspect of you. As you do this, you are moving from your Subjective Observer to the Interrelated Observer. You are moving closer and closer to experiencing, and then being, One.

Now imagine that you are sending them loving-kindness like a radiant bath of light energy. You can imagine this light in any color your intuition tells you is beneficial.

Practice this often, noticing anything that catches your attention.

BEING WITH THE WISDOM FIELD

As you slow down and fully connect to your Self first—and from there out and into All—your state of being shifts from an isolated island of a human to being a part of the great web of life and consciousness. In order to be this, you must allow your heart to become fully open, your mind to be available, and your body to let go and have this experience.

From that state you will experience a deep connection to the Wisdom Field. It is in that state that the Wisdom Field is most open to you. Remember that you and everyone is a part of it anyway. What we are talking about is how to tap into it, open to it, hear it, feel it, and have it move you.

WALKING THE WALK OF BEING

A Good State of Being also refers to how you are physically, mentally, and emotionally. It takes into consideration the quality and nature of the relationships you have in your life, including the relationship you have with your Self.

Being in a Good Sate of Being indicates that you have developed the ability to check in with each of your three intelligences, using your Observer to gather in the reports and to respond in a good way according to the wisdom of your Divine Essence.

That level of awareness will inform you on a continual basis as to how you are doing at living a life of integrity in accordance with your values. Integrity is personal because only you can establish what it means for your life. Society has a lot to say about how we are expected to behave, but at the end of the day it comes back to you and what is right according to your value system and the wisdom of your Divine Essence.

When you are congruent with your Divine Essence's wisdom, you will experience a deep inner peace, even if things aren't always going the way you would like.

As you move through each day of your journey in a Good State of Being, you will be holding a good balance between the various intelligence systems of the mind, body, and heart.

Your actions will come from a place of connection to your Self, the people around you, and to the planet itself. In order to have that level of connection, you must learn to walk with an open mind and an open heart. You must be willing to listen to those who disagree with you and be able to hold respect for all beings.

The primary relationship you have in your life is the one between you and your Self. How you think about your Self, talk to your Self, and act with regards to your Self is critically important to the quality of life you are experiencing. It is essential that you develop a relationship with your Self that is founded on respect, compassion, and life-giving energy.

Every thought you choose to give energy to shapes and influences the way you show up. Every single thought of self-doubt or self-criticism is like a pebble of sand added to your karmic backpack. So too is every thought of self-appreciation, love, and compassion, except that these thoughts create lightness of being.

As the weight of your karmic backpack goes up or down according to your thoughts, words, and deeds, the experience you are having in each moment of your life is influenced likewise.

Clearly it makes sense to be filling up on love rather than on all that negative stuff, and yet people move through their lives while laying distorted trips on themselves. These trips are of judgment, shaming, guilting, or spinning stories of worst-case scenarios about all the things that could or are going wrong for them.

None of that type of energy comes from your Divine Essence. If your behavior is creating any kind of negative self-view about the kind of person you are, then you are engaging with your Distorted Self. This is also true if you are creating a view of your Self that has you feeling superior to others. This is just a distorted insecurity pushing you higher so that your ego feels defended against its fears.

Each of us has this distorted aspect of us inside always ready to lay in a knock or two. We must learn to recognize it when it shows up, and to then be self-responsible and respondable according to our Divine Essence's wisdom.

It is the distorted part of us that criticizes, puts down, or instills fear when we consider moving our life forward. The good news is that you can learn how to manage your Distorted Self. Distorted Self will stand by forever waiting for opportunities to jump in, so you have a responsibility to your Self to be vigilant.

One of Distorted's common tricks is to use some moment of your life that didn't go well against you. In fact, Distorted is so clever that it keeps track of all the moments in your life that didn't go well for the sake of using them against you when the moment is right.

One example of this is when someone sincerely tells you something nice about you. Take notice. Does your Distorted Self push away the nice thought, disbelieving the person who said it and quickly countering it with a deflection or a negative counter-thought?

Ker chink, ker plunk, and the old karmic backpack just got heavier. People more connected with Divine Essence in that same example will allow the compliment to land. They'll say thank you to the person who paid the compliment and feel a sense of fullness at being recognized by another. For these people, the karmic backpack just got a little lighter. Through Divine Essence you can accept your gifts without getting inflated and big headed by them.

DIVINE FAILURES

Another classic moment when Distorted Self likes to take over is when you try something and perhaps it doesn't go according to plan. Well, welcome to the life of a human. Each one of us is subject to the occasional failure. That is part of what we risk when we dare to create change in our lives.

Divine Essence is willing to risk being in situations that support your learning. These are situations that are too big for you to control. They will stretch you, grow you, and you will fail often. Divine Essence honors the courage it takes to stay in these situations.

But Distorted Self takes these failures and uses them against us by having us doubt that we are smart enough or good enough to try again. Your responsibility to your Self in these moments is to activate your Divine Essence. As the self-authority of your life, you take that very same experience, regardless of the fact that it didn't go according to plan, and learn what there is to learn. When you approach it the next time around, you'll do it in a different way according to what you learned.

From the place of your Divine Essence, you begin with celebrating that you took a risk with that decision, whatever it was.

You remind your Self what it was that you were trying to create in your life through that action, and why it was and may still be important to you.

You then ask your Self how you contributed to the idea not working out. This is not so that you can beat your Self up for it, but rather so that you can find out what there is for you to take away from this experience. The next step is to ask your Self what you can learn from what happened.

You then ask your Self what is needed now and you activate your will to follow through according to the wisdom that was revealed through this process.

Life is an adventure that calls us out to risk for the sake of something important. Success is managing the distorted energies that would otherwise pin us down, while continuing to move forward from risk to risk.

Remember that you are not a bad person because you might have made a bad decision. Bad choices do not make bad people; they are just bad choices. Your job as an awakened human is to learn from what works and what doesn't, and to then carry the learning forward.

Again, you must always be vigilant about what aspect of your Self you are putting in charge of the learning department. Your Divine Essence will find a completely different learning than what your Distorted Self will find. You are always in charge of what aspect of your Self you turn to in every situation.

It helps to understand how normal a part of the human journey it is to have a Distorted Self and for it to get engaged.

Three years ago, I was invited to Thailand along with a colleague to offer some training to a group of monks and nuns. I was thrilled and somewhat nervous about bringing training to these inherently wise people.

At one point during the workshop, we were doing an exercise that required some of the participants to voluntarily come up to the front of the room to practice. After the exercise was over, we were all discussing the experience as a group, when one of the monks who had been sitting quiet for a while finally spoke up.

He generously shared his experience, telling us that he wanted to get up during the exercise to practice but his Distorted Self wouldn't let him. He found himself stuck in his chair, afraid to get up. We were stunned by this sharing because he had been a very active contributor up to that point—and because he was an accomplished monk. It hadn't occurred to us that he, too, would be managing his Distorted Self.

I was thrilled by what I was hearing, however, for a couple of reasons. By naming what he was experiencing, he was finding the power to manage his Distorted Self in the future. Also, I felt his sharing gave a message of hope because it showed the rest of us how normal it is to have a Distorted Self—even this monk was still learning how to manage his. It was an example that this is just a normal aspect of life and therefore something we all get to work through each day, one day at a time. There is nothing wrong with you because you have a Distorted Self speaking to you often. You are just a brilliant human having a normal human experience.

BEING IN RELATIONSHIPS

To be in a Good State of Being means that you value other beings as highly as your Self, and that you value your Self highly. What are those other beings? By "being" I mean anyone or anything that you have a connection with. The truth is that we are all connected in a great web of life to everyone and everything.

In the Delicate Lodge teachings, we are taught that our relations include every aspect of this Universe, including animals, plants, minerals, the stars and planets, and much more. It could be a friend, relative, or stranger, and it could also be something like a forest or a computer or a house. The possibilities include anything that is, regardless of whether or not you have an existing relationship.

Being in a Good State of Being means that you and the other have a clean and bright energy between you. So your job is to look into the nature and quality of each of your relationships with any and all beings and to be aware and respondable for how you are doing.

THE RELATIONSHIP TRIANGLE

For an easy way to see how our contributions are affecting our relationships, refer to the triangle below. On one corner is where you sit. Next, think of anyone or anything in your life and place them on the second corner of the triangle. Now, on the third corner, imagine the relationship that you have as though it was an actual entity that exists. It has its own wants and needs, it has its own Divine Essence. It even has its own Distorted Self. As soon as you create awareness of another being, you have realized your relationship with them or it.

Figure 11: The Relationship Triangle

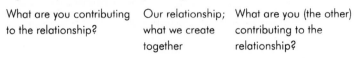

| What are you contributing to the relationship? | Our relationship; what we create together | What are you (the other) contributing to the relationship? |

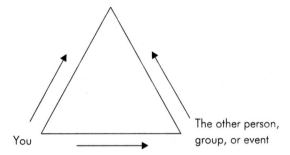

You   The other person, group, or event

How would you describe the nature of your relationship? Is it full of life, vibrant, and beautiful? Imagine it as amazing as it can be. Is this far away from the way it is? Or perhaps it is close? What is needed to improve the quality of this relationship?

Now, along the line that rises up between you and the relationship, write down all the things that you are contributing to the relationship. Perhaps you have been appreciating it and giving it time, or it may be that you are not enjoying it and are avoiding participating in it.

Next, look at the horizontal line along the bottom between you and that other being. Along that line write down all the thoughts, expectations, spoken words, and things you have done with regards to that person. Be specific.

For example, you might be loving them, enjoying them, and telling them so, or it may be that you are angry with them and thinking that they are not behaving in the way you want them to be.

You will start to get a sense of a map of the contribution that you have made, not only to the other person, but also to your relationship with them.

Assign a plus (+) to everything that adds positive energy to the relationship and other person, and assign a minus (-) to every thought, word, or action that is negative towards the relationship or other person.

Now compare this score to how you view the relationship. You will start to get a clear picture of what you are contributing to it.

Ask your Self: What is needed here? And adjust accordingly.

A relationship with another has a life of its own. It has an age; it has hopes and desires; and it has needs, just like a human being, to be nurtured and cared for.

You start to get a clear sense that you are a very big influence on that relationship. You will also start to realize that what you are putting into it is what you are getting out of it. That relationship is an outer reflection of you and your thoughts, words, and actions towards it.

CLEAN AND BRIGHT

No matter what is going on between you and another, you have had a big part in creating the dynamic. To truly clean up your relationships, you must be willing to find your part in what is taking place.

The objective is to have all of your relationships be clean and bright. There is a metaphor from the Buddhist tradition of working your relationships like a goldsmith works on gold. First they need to clean up the gold and remove the impurities. Then the gold is shaped through a wide variety of processes according to the goldsmith's vision for it. The metal is rubbed and polished and brightened. The mission of the goldsmith is to bring out the highest potential that can be imagined from the gold.

What is the highest potential you can imagine for your relationships?

What is the highest potential you can imagine for your relationship with your Self?

Creating and projecting blame, shame, negative judgments, or thinking less of anyone is not getting to your part of what has been created. Those are your Distorted Self's ways of making you right at the expense of another.

It is equally destructive for you to project any of those harmful thoughts back onto your Self as well.

If you notice any repeating themes in the relationships of your life, you can bet that there is some way that you are a significant contributor to what is going on. The only way to break out of such a cycle is to change how you are behaving by checking in with your Divine Essence, then acting accordingly.

If you find you are caught up in a situation and your Distorted Self is having its way, you must do whatever you can to get clear of that negative energy.

Life can change very quickly for the better when we ask the right questions and respond with new behavior.

HUMAN PROJECTORS

We humans are projection machines. Imagine that every thought you have about another person or organization is a projection that you beam out towards them. Of course when you shine such a light, they start to align with your projection. They become that for you.

It's really no more complicated than how a real projector works. When you use a projector to show a presentation, you hook your computer up to it. That computer sends specific images into the projector. The projector provides light and the images shine onto a screen or a wall. That is simple and obvious.

Think about this. If you left that projector on long enough, eventually that image would burn itself onto the wall. That is what we do to people when we project our ideas of who they are onto them.

We have a big impact on others, and with that comes a responsibility for that impact. We are that goldsmith who is constantly shaping our relationships according to how we choose to influence them.

Therefore, it is very important to get clear about our projections on others. You will be amazed at the shift that can take place just from changing critical thoughts about other people to thoughts of how beautiful and wise they are. And then to add even more magic, try only speaking words of beauty and honoring and respect. From there the actions that follow will be congruent with those thoughts and words.

Begin now and witness the transformation of magnificence. It will create the blossoming of the most beautiful flower.

Then it will be important to keep it up. As this way of being becomes more and more natural to you, the world around you will start responding accordingly. Be patient with those around you as it may take some time for them to catch up to this new way of being and acting. Especially if this is a big shift.

Be patient, tenacious, and compassionate with your Self as well, for this may indeed be a big shift of habit for you, too. And, yes habits do change. It takes what it takes to make that happen.

FROM DOING TO BEING

What we are talking about here is a way of doing things, such as only speaking beautiful words, in order to attain a Good State of Being. Though doing such things is beautiful, the point is really twofold. Of course, one impact of speaking and moving through the world in this way is the magnificent contribution it is in and of itself.

The bigger benefit, however, is that you start to intrinsically become this contribution the more you practice and the more you shift your state of being. You alter your Self and become the light of beauty. You are then Beauty. When you attain this state, you will notice a profound shift in how the world responds to you.

Doing is a good start. Becoming is a process. Being is the point.

AGREEMENTS

As you look into the nature of your relationships with the world around you, there is much to consider. One important aspect of relationships is the agreements that exist within them.

Every time you make an agreement, you have created a string of energy between you and that one you made that agreement with. Even lightly held agreements have strings of energy. Eventually if these strings are not cleared, they start to weigh you down and entangle you. At the lightest end of the agreements are flip remarks like, "I'll call you." When you speak an agreement like that, you attach a string of energy between you and the other. If you say that you will call someone, then you must call and follow through. If you don't, the agreement lives on. Eventually, you could become completely knotted up in "I'll call you" agreements to the point of getting energetically stuck and entangled.

At a bigger level of agreements are those that involve exchanges, such as with money or delivering goods and services. Any unpaid obligation is a thick and heavy string of energy to carry around.

It is easy to see how important it is to be awake and intentional with such agreements. It is much cleaner not to say you will call someone if you don't intend to. Find another way to say goodbye that doesn't create an energy string.

If you do promise to call someone, do what you have to do to ensure that you will follow through with that promise, such as writing a reminder on a sticky note and posting it on your phone.

The point is if you speak it, follow through. If you don't really want to do it, don't speak it.

Agreements around money are treacherous to relationships if they are not kept clean and clear.

If someone (and this seems more challenging for many people when it involves family and friends) asks to borrow money, listen to what your Divine Essence is telling you. Perhaps it's clear that your Divine Essence says it is not a good idea, and upon further inspection you see that there is no good way to make this loan. In this case, a clean No is a lot better than a distorted Yes. If it is a good clean Yes, then you have got to be clear about what the agreement with the borrower really is, because once it is made, you are both held to it.

It may be that a creative loan is the only way this is going to work. If you are in a position to enter into such an agreement, be very clean about all the arrangements. Be sure that all arrangements are clear and fair and understood by everyone.

If you owe money to someone and are unable to honor your agreement, the best thing you can do is talk to them and explain the situation, and together find a solution.

Many years ago I found my Self buried in debt as a small business owner. Every time the phone rang, it was a supplier looking for money. That was a very painful time in my life. At first I tried negotiating time with them—without being completely transparent about my situation. That could only work for so long. Then I tried to avoid their calls, but that didn't work well either. One day I decided to call them all up and place all my cards on the table. I felt stuck in the circumstances of my life and business, and I could not see a good way out.

Almost without exception they responded with great ideas and flexibility that helped me get through that terrible time.

What I heard from them over and over was gratitude for being forthcoming about my situation. They all seemed excited about their part in supporting and guiding me through that time.

No less important are the agreements that you make with your Self. We will discuss that further in A Good State of Practice.

JOY

From a Good State of Being it is easy to be in-joy in every aspect of your life. Joy comes from the appreciation for the perfection of what is. That means being able to appreciate what is, regardless of whether or not you like it. As long as you stand in judgment of your Self or others or a situation, you are putting screens between you and being in-joy.

There is a perfect nature in every moment, no matter how bright or dark it seems to be. There is joy in a good laugh with a friend, or the passing of a loved one. There is joy in physical pain, and there is joy in a grass field or in a child's laughing moment.

Joy is not found by changing the world to look a certain way, but rather from looking and finding appreciation for the way it is.

This does not mean settling for things the way they are. By all means, change what you can, if it makes this world more beautiful. Just try doing it from joyful appreciation. See what is different about that process itself. For most of us, it is easy to find joy when things are pretty or perfect in some way. But those are fragile conditions that will pass. If perfection is what's necessary for joy, then joy will always be elusive. It is sometimes from the greatest depth of despair that we are finally opened up to the experience of sublime Oneness with this Universe. In that experience we are opened to a light of love that lives beyond any condition of this human experience. That Oneness is shining through in every moment. It just is. It lives right there in the center of all. It is only our willingness or ability to find it that wavers.

As joy exists in each moment regardless of the circumstances, it follows that each of us is our own source to opening to it. To fully open to joy, you must be able to transcend any separation you think exists between you and a given moment. You must reach out into it with love, appreciation, and unconditional openness to whatever it is. You look into it, you see that it is of you, you of it, and that all is perfect. Then, just allow the joy that was there anyway to wash over and through you. Now that is a Good State of Being.

The path to developing the ability to receive joy is revealed through every turn around this wheel. As you understand more of the nature of this Universe. As you learn to shape your thoughts and intentions that you give energy to in a better way. As you speak words that are in accordance with your Good State of Words.

As you act in a good way, and in accordance with your Divine Essence, you will be your own source of joy. The world you create will reflect the same back to you.

We humans are lucky enough to be life-long learners. Every day opens new opportunities for us to bring forward a new way of being in this world. It is never too soon or too late to become the artist, shaping your own creation of this life.

We can keep learning as long as we stay soft and flexible and willing to risk letting go of the very things that we played a role in creating in the first place.

I have had my moments of being mean and angry, or trying to be right about something. All that did was wear me down and push others away. It was the opposite of what I wanted. I decided one day to live a life of openness and light and the shift happened for me right in that moment. Of course, learning how to do that is a day-by-day process. Being able to stay with it is also a learning process. We must find the joy in failing to stay in-joy, as much as celebrating the moments that we have attained it. There is no destination where joy lives. It is a way of moving and it is a Good State of Being.

COLLECTIVE ASPIRATIONS FROM A GOOD STATE OF BEING—A NOTE FROM THE FUTURE

We move through each day now in full connection with our heart wisdom, mind wisdom, and body wisdom. Divine Essence is apparent in everyone, since the wave of the Great Awakening swept over us all. We now tend to move with more attention on the present moment. Our feet touch the floor when we walk and we know it. We are aware of our body and our heart as we move.

The same is true for our emotional status. We have learned how to check in often, to know the emotion that we are experiencing, and to embrace that emotion rather than block it out or push it away. We have learned how to support each other in keeping the channels of emotional awareness open.

Now, when one of us is in a very low state, we know how to be with that person, how to support them in facing into the emotion directly.

The same is true when we are in high emotions as well. The adults have learned how to be in levels of happiness that previously were known mostly only to young children.

We are integrated with all the different aspects of our Selves, and we welcome them. Now when I am angry or afraid, I know it is okay, it's human. I get support from those around me to be with the angry or afraid one inside me, and to discover what it needs. Of course, anger and fear don't happen as much anymore, it's just that it is still a normal part of being human.

Now when we play, we play as children, bringing joy to each moment of our lives. We have learned how to sustain joyous open states of being. It really is infectious. Now it is most highly encouraged in the places where we work.

Our relationships with each other are bright and clear because we have learned how to work through our differences. Because we now live through our heart wisdom, when we speak or act the results are much better for everybody.

We have learned how to manage the voices of doubt with compassion. Even though those voices still lurk, always at the ready, they don't hold the same power they used to. Now we know that those voices let us know when something needs attention and we get to keep moving forward steadily and easily.

We still have many differences among us, but we have learned to appreciate each other in our differences, to celebrate and laugh as those differences show up.

It was interesting that as soon as we got clear with our Selves and each other, we also got clear about how to be in relationship with the planet and all the other beings in the Universe.

We learned how to invite in and open to the Wisdom Field. Through that we were able to establish a much deeper relationship with the plants, animals, and other beings, and we discovered how much support there had always been for us. We just couldn't see it before. I guess we were too scared of not having enough to open up to all there was.

That is over now. The more we let go, the more we discovered how much there is and, paradoxically, how little we need.

Now we understand that we are in community with all the other beings in the Universe. We move about this world easily, because everywhere we go we are greeted as brothers and sisters on a journey together. We know what it is to be One.

PRACTICES FOR A GOOD STATE OF BEING

Practice Suggestion 1

Sit quietly for a few moments and then, as a living practice of this, expand your Observer out. Open it through all three intelligences of mind, body, and heart. Allow your intuition and imagination to inform you about the state of the collective experience of everyone in the room all at once. Expand that out to include the surrounding community, then pull it out wider and wider. While doing this, imagine that you can feel into each being and have a sense of how they are. Now imagine that they are an expanded sense of you, an aspect of you.

As you do this, you are getting close.

Now imagine that you are sending them loving-kindness like a radiant bath of light energy. You can imagine this light in any color that your intuition tells you is beneficial.

Practice this often and keep noticing anything that catches your attention.

Practice Suggestion 2

Identify a relationship you have in which the energy between the two of you is not completely clean and bright.

Ask your Self what you are contributing to this situation and stay open to any insight that comes through.

Approach them and ask them if they are interested in a better relationship with you.

If so, say what you discovered about your contribution to the situation, and ask them if they are willing to look into the same question. If so, give them forty-eight hours to do so.

Meet again and discuss.

Both of you together can now look forward, setting a Good State of Intention for what kind of relationship you would like to have together.

Practice Suggestion 3

Look into the condition of your mind, heart, and body. Ask your Self what is needed to improve each of these for the sake of a good relationship with your Self and a better quality of life.

A GOOD STATE
OF PURPOSE

I am in a Good State of Purpose.

- I am well-used in each day.

- I listen to the yearning of my heart, and I am respondable according to the wisdom of my Divine Essence.

- I am non-attached to any particular direction on my path. Therefore I am available to my dreams, purpose, and to the Universe's dream for me.

- I honor the gift of this life and I unfold my purpose daily according to the wisdom of my Divine Essence.

- I understand that the ultimate purpose of this precious life is a great mystery.

- I give my Self over to the moment-by-moment unfolding as authored by my Self as I dance with the unfolding story of the Universe.

- I allow my purpose to be revealed to me in each moment.

Therefore I remain flexible to the wisdom and call of my Divine Essence and the Universe.

- As I am in a Good State of Purpose, my livelihood is congruent with, and honors, the values of the wisdom of my Divine Essence.

- I unfold my purpose in a good way as the author of each moment of my life.

- I choose to activate my Divine Essence to guide my journey.

- My success is not measured by the quantity or size of my impact, but rather by the beauty that is created as a result of how I responded in each passing moment.

- I unfold my purpose simply through each breath and sweep of the broom.

- In each moment I am in-joy and therefore on purpose in a good way.

I am in a Good State of Purpose.

A GOOD STATE OF PURPOSE

As I walk through the day I am aware of the immensity of the Universe of which I am a part. Let's consider the unfolding of the story, at least to the extent we know it to be true at this time.

First, there was a time before time. Then there was an event that kick-started the forming of the stars and the planets. Galaxies were created and the passage of time began.

Eventually, the Earth was ready to bear life, and after much development of many different forms of life, the humans came to be. There is still a lot of mystery about exactly how this happened and I am not attempting to answer that question. I am, for now, quite content to sit in the mystery and the question of how we came to be.

Now imagine that you are God and that you have manifested this great Universe. You have a desire to have it unfold and to become something. What is it that you would want from all of this? What is the point of it all?

In my own life, the moments in which I've felt the closest to God were those moments when I was struck by the greatest beauty. And the times that seemed like the lowest points, when everything was being stripped away from me—when I was alone, struck down. These moments allowed the veils of separation between my human experience and knowing the Oneness of the Universe to disappear. In those moments I was struck by the beauty of All. I was filled with the joy of being. There was nothing to do about it but witness the truth that All is of beauty.

I have also had this experience when faced with moments of profound connection with other humans, when I've let my guard down and experienced between my Self and another nothing but love and joy. Also in nature, when I have allowed my Self to be touched by it. When faced with the extraordinary magnificence of a mountain lake. When being approached by a great whale while kayaking. Upon hearing an eagle scream out in its joy at having caught a salmon. When I looked into the eyes of a snow leopard that found me on a trail in the Himalayas and graced me with its stunning presence.

In all of these moments I felt the presence of God. In all of these moments I experienced a particular joy that was ignited by being touched by the beauty of the world around. My ongoing learning is to know this same rapture in the ordinary moments of life. In every precious moment lies the potential to know, to feel, to be in-joy.

When we allow our Selves to be so touched that our hearts are overwhelmed and our minds are shattered, we our Selves are the fuel of joy in the Universe. We then emit the wave of joy, we become the beauty, we create a field of energy that is good in this world. That is why, after all is said and done, I believe the ultimate purpose for us all is to be beauty, to be in-joy.

The pathway to that is through the allowing of everything that separates us from it to fall away. The big cosmic joke is that we are All, we are Joy, but we just forgot. We are on a path of remembering. To remember is to claim back our wholeness. That is our life's work. That is the ultimate way of being, and the direction of the unfolding of the Universe's story leads us back to our own beauty. It was there all along.

WALKING A PURPOSEFUL WALK

The question of what is a Good State of Purpose can be looked at from at least a couple of different points of view. If the Universe were to ask the question, "What is our purpose?" it's answer would likely be, "Your purpose is to be in-joy."

HOW CAN WE BE IN-JOY?

We're in-joy by creating beauty, by being beauty, and by discovering the beauty that is in every moment. There are many ways to be in-joy.

Everything else we can say about purpose will trace itself back to this ultimate point. When we are in–joy, we are in the present moment with a fully open heart in the energy field of Divine Essence.

Being on purpose is also an aspect of living from a Good State of Being. From that state of being we make choices about how to do or how to express our purpose in each moment of our lives. You are the author of your own unfolding story. It is the choices you make every day that shape your journey.

Living a life on purpose is a way of being and walking that is akin to the way of a spiritual master. A master lives their way in every moment, and has infused the practices of their discipline into the cellular level of their body and being. A master holds a consciousness about their way in every moment. Paradoxically, they can let it go and just be it at the same time. A master is one who has moved from knowing about something to experiencing it and being it.

An awakened one expresses their purpose as much with each sweep of the broom as with an amazing career that makes the best use of who they are.

IT IS ABOUT SOMETHING BIGGER THAN YOU

We are all connected to our purpose. Our life is always about something bigger than us. When we are gifted with an inspiration, when we have been touched by the Universe and our hearts are activated to draw us forth towards the fulfillment of our sacred mission, we do so on behalf of All.

For some, it is being called to the life of an entrepreneur with the latest and greatest offerings, while for others it is being an agent of change in an organization, pointing the way for others who may or may not see or feel what you do. Or it may be the desire to pull out your checkbook and send support to a cause that has caught the attention of your heart's desire. In these cases, what you're doing is being a part of something bigger than just you.

Even if your actions are self-serving, they can still be of benefit to the greater good. I would even argue that you must be willing to be self-caring; that is, willing to take care of your Self, in order to sustain and grow your Self and your resources in a way that ultimately allows you to offer back.

For some, the resources that are offered might be that of heart energy, while for others it may be the contribution of finances. It is all needed. When you feel inspired to act, when you feel anything, ask your Self what is reaching you—and why you? Imagine that you are the one who is needed, and imagine that there are others out there, as well, wondering where you are. Make your Self known, so that you are easier to find.

I assure you that there will be nothing convenient about making your Self known in this way. In my life, such callings seldom came at times of convenience. So be prepared to have your life shift according to your own wisdom. Even the anonymous donor has had her life shifted through the reflection of her generosity, as the impact of her gift came back through an improved world.

YOU ARE A GENIUS

We are all gifted with our particular genius. That is our specialty and the gift that we bring into this world. It is encoded in our DNA and is of our Divine Essence. Our genius is sublime. Therefore there is nothing in the life of a human that absolutely touches or expresses the purest form of it. This also means there are always a variety of ways we can manifest and bring forth our purpose through the expression of our genius.

For example, someone who is a naturally gifted musician and is able to learn ever higher skillful levels of creating music is actually using their music as a way of fulfilling a higher purpose, which might be opening the door to joy. Playing their instrument is the earthly way of fulfilling their greater purpose.

Great music often has the effect of opening and connecting people to their hearts. Opening hearts may be that person's purpose.

That same person could have found other ways of fulfilling their purpose. In fact, sometimes we see great musicians who put down their instruments and go off to express their gifts in other ways.

YOUR MISSION, SHOULD YOU CHOOSE TO ACCEPT IT

Even if you don't know it consciously, your purpose is shaping you, working on you, calling you forth to realize it. The Wisdom Field is speaking to you. The Universe is recognizing you and how to use you in the highest and best way.

Once you know this, then your purpose shapes who you are and what you do more consciously. As I respond to a call, I find my Self changing according to what is needed. It may be that I take some training to be better able to respond. It may be that I talk to people and am shifted as a result of those conversations. I find that the more willing I am to learn, to adapt, to be flexible according to what is needed, the more current I can be in answering the particular call that is coming through.

YOUR PURPOSE AT THIS TIME

Purpose is the Universe's assignment for how it wants you to be used at this time. The key phrase here is "at this time."

As the Universe moves its story forward, it will have different requirements for us humans according to what is needed in each moment. As the state of the world changes, so will our assignment. Purpose is not a static destination that we discover—and then we are done. It is an ever-shifting response according to what our Divine Essence realizes is needed. Some people might find a full expression of their purpose that continues to serve throughout their human life, while others may be called to shift the form of it from time to time.

A lot of people ask, "What can I do to fulfill my purpose?" That is always a fair question to hold. Every day may provide a new answer. This opens you up to new and evolving ideas about expressing your purpose.

Another good question to ask is, "How can I express my purpose through what I am doing today?"

What I like about this question is that it points us to look deeper into how we are leveraging the moment we are in now. It has us look at the job and the task at hand, and connect our purpose to it.

As an entrepreneur, I have owned and been involved in a wide variety of businesses and projects. One thing that has always worked out well for me is connecting what I am doing to a higher purpose.

Here are a few real life examples from my own past experience:

Expression: Being an electrician.
Purpose: Bringing power and light to make people's lives better.

Expression: Being a jeweler.
Purpose: Connecting people to beauty and gems that could bring them happiness and balance their energy.

Expression: Being a consultant to businesses.
Purpose: Supporting others as they discovered and fulfilled the calling of their genius.

Expression: Selling cars.
Purpose: Guiding people through a good buying decision. A good decision supports their life fulfillment.

Expression: Being a coach.
Purpose: Providing an environment in which clients are called forth to live more fully through their Divine Essence.

Expression: Founding Awakened Wisdom Experiences™ (AWE).

Purpose: To play my part in awakening humans and my Self.

This partial list shows a developing story of ways in which my purpose has been expressed.

We have the opportunity to express our purpose through every breath we take. How you articulate your purpose is helpful to a point, but it is not essential that you name it in order for you to express it. Trust the wisdom of your Divine Essence to guide you in each moment.

You are fulfilling your purpose in every moment that you are sending out energy from a Good State of Intention or whenever you are speaking from a Good State of Words.

LISTENING TO THE WISDOM OF HEART

Our heart intelligence is a portal to Universal Wisdom. When we allow our Selves to stop and listen to our heart intelligence, we are connecting to a much larger field of knowing that is the Wisdom Field. Heart intelligence is of the Universe, but it moves us in ways that can often be confusing or challenging for our minds to comprehend.

Sometimes we just have to follow the yearning of the heart and be with whatever confusion and resistance the mind kicks up until we come to understand what a particular situation is all about. If we ever come to understand.

After all, our minds are usually playing catch up, trying to put context around a heart-based wisdom, when very often there is no logic or vocabulary that can translate heart intelligence accurately.

Those are important times to be vigilant about keeping the energy of Divine Essence activated. As long as you keep holding the questions in front of you, you will courageously traverse an important part of the path on your journey.

Be aware that the path of heart will very often activate Distorted. As far as Distorted is concerned, there is nothing safe or predictable about heart wisdom. Following heart wisdom will often mean that you will risk disappointment or public attention or getting your feelings hurt. It's Distorted's job is to protect you from all of that. In fact, heart wisdom will quite often challenge the status quo of your life, which is just about a worst-case scenario for Distorted. Therefore, you must be ever-vigilant and watch who is in charge of your Purpose Department. Is it Distorted Self or Divine Essence?

As people get more and more attuned to a Good State of Purpose they are often inspired to walk a walk that won't initially make sense to them or the people around them.

It takes a good measure of courage to follow the path of heart wisdom. Fortunately, Divine Essence is a deep well and the source of amazing courage.

VALUES AND CONGRUENCY OF LIVELIHOOD

The path of an awakened human is the path of Divine Essence. That means that when it comes to how one makes their personal livelihood, that it be congruent with the wisdom of Divine Essence.

The value system of Divine Essence includes ideas that we have previously mentioned, such as creating beauty, holding good intention, and being life-giving. There will be many other considerations that will vary from person to person. What will not vary is the level of resonance that comes from a livelihood that is consistent with Divine Essence, versus one that is not.

Some livelihoods are harmful to others, while others may be harmful to other aspects of this Universe—such as work that harms forests or animal populations. For those people who do work that involves or affects other forms of beings, such as forests, oceans, and related populations, it is absolutely essential that

Divine Essence be brought front and center into the process, and that listening into the Wisdom Field be included as well.

No matter what the needs of a group of people are, there is always a solution that does not require that irreparable damage be done to someone or something else. All that is needed is the will to find a better way.

No one should ever feel trapped into a job or into making decisions in a job that are inconsistent with the value system of their Divine Essence. There are many roads to walk and many decisions to make along your journey.

When you know you are compromising your value system, no matter how much you think you need that job, there is a way to create a change of direction towards doing what is right. It may require you to take a stand. It most likely won't be easy. It might even get you fired. But there is no fire as hot as the one of compromised ethics and values and selling out.

The path of awakened living winds its way through many a dark forest. At every turn there is a choice to follow the wisdom of Divine Essence or to go another way. Some will keep to the path, while others will compromise just a little for the sake of a shortcut or two.

As we walk along, we hear the shouts of those lost ones entangled in the stickiness of that forest, caught in a desperate maze of unhappiness and numbed consciousness. Some are trying to find their way back to the awakened path, the path of joy, while others have completely turned away from it.

For some, the weight of their karmic backpacks may be too heavy to bear. They will have to lighten them before they will be able to move on. For others, their karmic load is getting lighter by the moment as they have begun to set right what they once set wrong. It is never too late to lighten your load. There is always a light along the path to help you find your way back.

IT IS NEVER TOO LATE

When I was a monk in Burma, I was often around one particular monk who caught my attention. Even though I spent a lot of time around him, we didn't speak for months. I mistakenly assumed he could not speak English, and he waited for a few months until he had something to say.

When I first saw him I was awestruck by a bright light that glowed from within him. He resonated with such peace and harmony that just standing next to him raised my own vibration.

Finally, one day he approached me and struck up a conversation. I was pleased and surprised to discover that he could speak English quite well.

I asked him how long he had been a monk. He told me a few decades, which didn't seem possible because he looked so young.

Without any further prompting, he volunteered his story to me. He explained that as a young man in India, he had been drawn into the life of a murderer and a thief. At that time, he thought he was lost for eternity. He was caught in a life of hopeless despair. He could see no way out. The things he had done were so bad that he had given up on the idea of redemption. As he had no hope anyway, he saw no reason to change his ways.

One day, he met another monk who explained to him that it was never too late to begin the walk back to a life of light. That monk's message touched him deeply. His heart cried out for him to change his ways immediately. He felt a tiny opening of hope, enough to give him the courage to change. And so he did, one day at a time.

He joined a monastery, became a monk himself, and committed the rest of his life to correcting the wrongs he had committed. He had a heavy bag of karmic weight to clear. He told me that it may take many lifetimes for him to get clear of what he had done, or perhaps it could be in this lifetime—but either way he was on a good path.

As he told me his story, it was as though the telling activated the light within him. I felt awash in the compassion of his heart. The truth of what he spoke was evident in his personage. I felt as though I had received a transmission of energy from him. It has stayed with me to this very day.

I thanked him for sharing his story and we each wandered our separate ways.

Every one of us has done things that we would probably take back if we could. Perhaps it was speaking unkindly to or about someone, or perhaps you carried out some serious crime.

The point is that the path of this life is walked one step at a time, and each step requires new choices. Choosing well from now on is a great way to walk. Today is a good day to be Divine.

SYNCHRONICITY AND PURPOSE

Imagine the Universe now and see your Self as you walk through each day held in the Wisdom Field, moving in a Good State of Being and walking on purpose. Now you understand that there is a greater intelligence behind it all. That is the intelligence of the Universe developing itself moment-by-moment towards its expression of greater and greater beauty. Imagine that you are the Universe and you have these beings, known as the humans, living within you. You want to guide them towards the creation of joy through beauty. The humans have free will because, as the Universe, you knew that their free will was essential to the ultimate unfolding of the Universe's highest dream. So you don't attempt to control them. Humans, after all, are not preprogrammed robots—they are Divine Essence and potential.

Each human has been gifted with a variety of talents and genius. Individually and together they are whole in their ability to serve you, the Universe.

While you don't want to control the humans, you do want to support them. So you communicate with them in ways that they can receive. You whisper in their ear, you meet them in their dreams, you send in signs and signals, hoping that they will notice, listen, receive, and respond.

Carl Jung wrote about synchronicity as coincidence with a meaning. The meaning here is to fulfill your purpose through the highest expression of your inherent gifts, your personal genius.

As the Universe sends in synchronistic experiences, your job is to notice and get curious about what messages are being offered. You are never alone and you are totally supported. The only question is how available you are going to be to the Universe and all the wisdom that is holding you.

What do you have to let go of to be fully available to your purpose?

WHEN YOU CAN'T FIND IT

There will be times in your life when you will feel inspired and on purpose. There will be other times when knowing it will elude you, frustrate you, and perhaps even scare you because you can't find it. Till then, explore and stay curious. Chances are you are expressing your purpose, whether you realize it or not.

LISTEN CAREFULLY

Listen carefully to the whispering of your heart as you are guided moment-by-moment along a path of purpose. Notice what catches your attention, especially if the same theme calls you over and over. Know that even the simplest gestures can have long-lasting impacts.

It may be that the expression of your purpose is simply to live in-joy. As you walk down the street your smile touches someone exactly at the moment they were praying for help.

It may be that you are called to completely and radically change your life, or it may be that you are already walking a good path, and all that is needed is a little more intention behind what you do.

If you are called to give up your career and set off on a great adventure of purpose, then get on with it. I have never regretted the times I turned my life upside down on a hunch or a whim. I have found those times to be very challenging, and it was in that challenge where I met my Self in ways that the easy times do not quite reveal. No one said it would be easy, and for a life well-lived, such times are inevitable.

Make a pact with the Universe that you will respond to its beckoning whisper, that you will follow its signs like the wind, and that you will answer to the call.

This life is too precious to pass up such callings. If you are called, it is because what you have to offer is exactly what is needed. Your calling may be to go into public service, to start your own company, or to go backpacking and discover for your Self the truth of what is out there. The Universe will meet you in the most extraordinary ways when you let go of yesterday's ideas and leap into the present moment of inspiration.

We get to the essence of our purpose when we can express it simply in a few seconds with a stranger in an elevator, or in passing on the street. If you are called to a bigger and more elaborate expression of purpose, then that is welcome. Remember, it is not the grandness of your purpose that is the measure of it. It is the heart and the Divine Essence in it.

COLLECTIVE ASPIRATIONS FROM A GOOD STATE OF PURPOSE—A NOTE FROM THE FUTURE

Now the time has come in which we are all freed from the fears and concerns that had previously trapped some of us into jobs we would rather not have had. Because the world shifted into a Good State of Purpose, all organizations hold as their highest directive that all members and employees make decisions based on the wisdom of their minds and hearts and according to the guidance of their Divine Essence. We understand now that every job has purpose in it, and we are fully connected to that.

Now every job in every organization has become aligned with a Good State of Purpose because the organizations themselves are operating in accordance with Divine Wisdom.

We are all encouraged to sit in stillness each day and to tune our Selves into the Wisdom Field. Now we are so skilled in attunement that it seems strange to think there was ever a time when we didn't do this.

As a result, all decisions respect the well-being of all the entities that are impacted, including the plants and animals. The good news is that it turned out to be easy to prosper and to make profits in a good way. In fact, it turned out to be so natural and easy that no one can quite remember why it was ever any other way. "What were we afraid of back then?" is a common musing.

As a result, the resonance of each person while at work and at home is at a very high level, and that light is passed on to their families and communities.

The intellect of the mind is still valued highly, only now it is balanced with heart wisdom and intuition.

Each person is nurtured according to their inherent genius— and the level of creativity and breakthroughs are startling. People still create a lot of wealth, only now it is for the sake of contributing back. Each person's purpose is honored and valued in a good way.

Schools work with children in ways that foster the nurturing of talent and heart-based wisdoms. It is recognized that each person is blessed with a personal genius, and the entire educational system thrives on nurturing and revealing what the genius is. Teachers are happier and more fulfilled than ever, as they facilitate the blossoming of human potential in ways that we used to hope for but couldn't quite get to with this much consistency.

The universal healthcare system no longer requires as much funding. Because as we learned to live more on purpose, illness has declined to never-before-seen lows. In general, the happiness quotient is at an all time high and there is an overall increase in well-being. Additionally, much more funding is available for holistic learning programs. One aspect of everyone's purpose is to be a vibrant source of light.

As this wave of the Great Awakening swept the planet, crime rates and violence in general plummeted to never-before-seen lows as well. There is such an ease and well-being everywhere now that the power of distortion has lost its hold. The presence of Divine Essence is the norm—everywhere. Now people move about consciously, so we are always on purpose—because we learned how to use the power of our heart and mind wisdom to shift the conditions of the world in each moment. Now we know that even as we take a walk consciously, we are expressing our purpose in the simplest ways. What a relief it was to discover that. As a result, each person's contribution is valued and openly appreciated. It is no longer about important jobs and big salaries, but rather about contributing and being awake and intentional.

We learned that it is okay to do what brings us joy, and to bring joy to everything we do. The result is beauty.

PRACTICES FOR A GOOD STATE OF PURPOSE

Practice Suggestion 1

Make a list of the jobs you have had in the past.

Ask your Self, "What purpose did I serve through that job?"

Notice the pattern that has run through your life.

What does this tell you about your particular genius?

Practice Suggestion 2

In the morning, look at the activities that are planned for your day. What purpose can be expressed through those activities?

Practice Suggestion 3

Notice if you have a nagging voice that tells you it is time to change some part of your life.

Ask your Divine Essence what change is recommended. What connection does this have to your purpose?

Practice Suggestion 4

Right now activate your Divine Essence and ask it this question: What group of people or other beings need your support today?

Then ask this question:
What does Divine Essence want to be different for
_____. *(Fill in the blank with the name of someone or group you thought of.)*

Listen for an answer.

Now close your eyes and see, hear, and imagine that person or group.

Now imagine that the idea that occurred to you has become true for that person or group. Now ask your Self, "What else is needed?"

By sending out an intention in this exercise, you have served others, and it may be that you are called to doing more. If that is so, then stay in conversation with Divine Essence and ask what is next for you in response to this question.

Practice Suggestion 5

Wonder about what purpose or mission you can happily serve today.

Notice any and all thoughts that come in.

A GOOD STATE OF EFFORT

I am in a Good State of Effort.

- Because I am in a Good State of Effort, I am mindful in each moment of my life.

- I hold effort and mindfulness with ease and delight.

- I choose to act or be still according to my Divine Essence's wisdom.

- As I am at choice, I apply my will to follow through and move forward according to my choice.

- Did I say that I hold effort with ease and delight?

- As I am at choice, I choose to live from the wisdom of my Divine Essence.

- I use my will easily to follow through on my choices.

- I summon up the will and commitment to hold the energy of mindfulness lightly.

- I apply the right measure of energy to follow through and complete what I intend—with ease, delight, and respect for cycles and timing.

- I actively appreciate and approach each moment with ease and delight.

- I am actively grateful for every being and every thing that I have attracted into my life.

- I am actively compassionate and forgiving to all including my Self.

- I honor the cycles and timing, remaining at choice about when to act and when to be still.

- I look into each moment and ask, What is needed? I then respond according to the wisdom of my Divine Essence.

I am in a Good State of Effort.

A GOOD STATE OF EFFORT

Moving through the world in a Good State of Effort will have the most profound impact on your life, if practiced well. You have no doubt heard the expression that life is about the journey, not the destination. That's at the center of a Good State of Effort.

It is important to be present as you move through each moment and each task of your day. When you move with presence you are aware of the quality of the moment that you are in, while moving forward with the objective in mind. Both of these ideas must be present at the same time in order to be and remain in a Good State of Effort. Be in the present moment and be aware of the effort that you are putting forth.

A Good State of Effort begins with being in a Good State of Being, and from there, moving through each day with the right touch of effort, joy, ease, and delight. Even when the work at hand seems very difficult, when you approach it with a sense of joy, it will be accomplished in a much better way.

THE EFFORT OF THOUGHT

Our minds are like wild animals that prefer to run wild rather than be disciplined into a Good State of Effort. Take any thought at all and try to hold it for two minutes. Try focusing on the thought: chair. Hold the word chair or the image of a chair in your mind. Have it be the only thought you have, keeping it right in the front of your attention. Don't allow it to drift away or change in any way. As soon as it has drifted away or changed into anything else, the game is over. In fact, if you are thinking about doing it, then you have already lost the game, as thinking about holding a thought is not the same as just holding the thought itself. How did you do? If you even made it a short amount of time, you did well. Our minds are not practiced at holding a thought for any amount of time. It is more likely that your mind let chair go. You might have thought, "I'm doing it!" While in that thought, you are already not doing it anymore. Then you may have remembered the game and you brought the thought, chair, back into your mind. Now it's here; now it's not.

These moments of non-presence are abundant—when we drift off to a new place. At first don't even know we have done it. We are essentially catching up with our mind. It goes to some thought, and then we realize it and catch up with it. This process is called drift.

DRIFT

Drift allows the lies of Distorted to slip in. We are going along, perhaps creating a good intention for something to happen, when suddenly we are in another thought, perhaps one of judgment about our ability to succeed with a given intention.

Who invited the judgment in? Not you? Then what is it doing here? It takes constant effort to watch out for each thought that arises, and then to assess whether it's one that we should be giving energy to. Or whether it's a message from Distorted that we must release as soon as it has been detected.

In order to make this discernment, you must first activate your will. You must choose to engage in this practice. Distorted most likely will attempt to discourage you from this practice by having you believe that it is too difficult, or perhaps not really important. More lies.

This effort is very important. It is not only doable, but in fact can be engaged in lightly, with ease, delight, and compassion.

THE AMPLITUDE OF ENERGY

Effort is an important consideration in living an awakened life, yet something that is easily misunderstood. One aspect of effort is the amount of energy that is applied in any particular moment or event in your life. It functions like a volume switch—you can rev up or down the amount or the amplitude of the energy that gets applied.

I have had the experience of this teaching while driving formula racecars and sports racing cars, where every move the driver makes results in a quick and direct response from the car. These cars only do what the driver tells them to do, so the feedback from the car is honest and clear. Spinning off the track if the brakes are applied too hard, accelerating, or steering inputs that result in a rough transition are all direct results of driver behavior. If it all goes well, you get the perfect exit off a corner, enabling you to pass the other cars. This also has to do with timing and measurement from the driver.

Let's make our example in an ordinary four-door car you'd drive around day-to-day. Let's say that your task is to drive a car, and your objective is to get around the block. Let's imagine two different examples of amplitudes of effort.

In the first example, you get into the car and grip the wheel with all your might. You are going to apply maximum amplitude of effort. Holding the wheel as tightly as you can, you approach each corner with intense pressure, turning the wheel with a vice-like grip. When it is time to apply the brakes or the accelerator, you do so with the same level of intensity.

If you actually try this, you will find that your driving becomes jerky and abrupt. The car will do everything you ask it to do, but it will do it all poorly. You are expending far more energy than the task requires, and even though you are trying harder, if something happened that required you to respond quickly, such as avoiding a pedestrian who stepped unexpectedly into your path, your reaction would be ineffective and possibly even dangerous. You might overreact and slam on the brakes too hard, or steer to avoid the pedestrian only to find your Self facing a new problem.

For even more fun, imagine that you have passengers. They are doing their job as passengers with just as much over-efforting. As passengers who are trying so hard, they might think that their job is to keep the driver from making any mistakes. Now you are a car full of people who are over-reacting and keeping each other in this ineffective state of trying too hard. Not only is this not joyful, but it could get nasty, as the likely thing to transpire would be the passengers' attempts to control the driver. The harder they try to control the driver, the more likely the attention of the driver is drawn away from driving.

Now it is less likely the driver will see the pedestrian when he steps into the path of the car.

When we check in on the three intelligences of heart, mind, and body, we find that the mind of the driver in this case was filled with trying so hard that it shut out a lot of helpful information. The heart was closed and isolated, as the driver needed to defend in order to hold all together. The body intelligence was ignored, resulting in the over-powering of the steering wheel and the pedals.

Now let's take the same drive, only this time you, as the driver, remind your Self to approach this drive with ease and delight and with just the right amount of effort. You invite your passengers into an experience that is fun. As they sense your Good State of Effort, they relax into their job, which is to empower you as the driver and to support the overall success of the drive.

Now you grip the wheel lightly with just enough pressure to hold it steadily and safely. When you use the brake and accelerator, you apply a smooth pressure according to what is needed in each moment. Your input into the driving controls is measured and applied according to the amount of amplitude that is needed. The car moves according to what you are asking it to do. Now it rolls smoothly and quickly. The experience of traveling so smoothly supports everybody in being in-joy and available as needed.

Suddenly, a person steps off the curb into your path. You are alert and your attention is on the road ahead, so you have the maximum amount of time to respond. Your passengers see this as well and respond with helpful inputs of information. One says, "Pedestrian ahead," while another says, "Left lane clear." You turn the wheel smoothly as you double check the left lane for availability, and with just enough steering input you easily drive around the pedestrian. Everyone is calm and engaged with a Good State of Effort.

Now when we check in with the three intelligences, we see that the mind intelligence was clear and focused, the heart intelligence was open and connected to everyone around, and the body intelligence was informing the driver of the correct amounts of input into the steering, braking, accelerating. The overall experience was very positive for everyone.

The correct level of amplitude is available to us in every situation. Sometimes a great exertion of energy is required, so the message here is not that you will never have to apply a lot of energy. Rather that you can measure the energy required in each situation and apply it as needed.

THE EMOTION OF ENERGY

When you consider the energy it takes to accomplish something, not only is the amplitude important, but so too is the emotional quality of energy that you are creating. Energy is available to be transformed by you and put to use according to your wisdom. You can affect the energy by shifting it in an emotional way. You can approach any task and determine in advance what type of energy you will apply to it. You can make it fun and easy or hard and challenging. You can activate your heart intelligence to influence the energy according to what you choose. Most of us do this out of habit, unconsciously, and therefore we often find our Selves repeating the same emotional quality of experience over and over. The task changes, but not the experience of it.

Now imagine the same two drives around the block, picturing each of them with two choices of emotional quality. In the first drive, you choose an amplitude that is very intense. The emotional quality that goes along with it is very serious. The message here is that the drive is hard and dangerous, and we must be prepared for trouble. There certainly is no joy in this experience.

In the second drive, the emotional experience is joyful and full of ease. The message here is that we be alert and respond to what is needed while we enjoy this experience.

Effort, as you can see, has these two different aspects to it: the amplitude or amount of effort and the emotional quality of the effort in the experience. We must learn to be conscious of what we are choosing with regard to both of these considerations.

These examples are a simple way to show you that you have a big impact on your experiences in each moment according to the choices you make around amplitude and the quality of the effort.

HOW DO WE CREATE OUR HABIT OF EFFORT STYLE IN THE FIRST PLACE?

I grew up on the Canadian Prairies. It was a beautiful environment in which to experience childhood. The prairies are a place where people are open, friendly, and fair-minded. The prairie work ethic is to put in a "hard day's work." That stems from the requirements of an agricultural-based society where the wisdom that gets passed down is to "make hay while the sun shines." This ethic makes a lot of sense, and it's what is needed to be a successful farmer.

The reason I bring this up is to tease out the idea of a hard day's work. For some people, a hard day's work goes along with the choice that the work itself be experienced as hard. As such, I am not voting for or against this practice, but rather pointing to how people experience effort. Many people set out each day of their lives using a certain habit of effort regardless of the situation. In the community where I grew up, however, it is the measure of "hard" that is used to determine whether or not someone has been doing good, or has made good use of a given day.

Consider the expression, "He tried real hard!" Again we have an example of the value of hard being used as the standard for how things should be done.

If you have attached the quality of hard to your personal value system as a measure of worth, then it makes it challenging to appreciate accomplishments in your life that happened to come easily.

Many cultures develop value systems around effort without knowing it. Then we get caught in the pressure of the culture to align with the expectation. A culture of work hard influences people to keep at their work in a way that allows them to belong and be accepted. I have seen some very serious cases of corporate burnout created by cultures that advocate working too hard.

The same can be on the other side, too, when a culture is so identified with fun and easiness that when someone wants to work harder in order to accomplish something, they find themselves meeting all kinds of resistance from the surrounding people.

The point is not to find a particular ethic better than the other, but rather to be conscious of the choices you could make. Choosing a Good State of Effort is an important consideration. We must choose according to the wisdom of our Divine Essence.

We tend to go to sleep around our choices of effort. When we do, we create a habit that becomes our default.

When you approach any situation in your life from a place of habit, you are no longer using your Divine Essence to guide you. The habit will work some of the time—that is how it got to become a habit in the first place—but it won't be highly effective all of the time.

CALIBRATION

When you are living in a Good Sate of Effort, you are able to calibrate the amount of energy to apply according to what is needed, rather than overpower every situation or fall short. Sports are a great metaphor for this. Consider a football player who is praised for having a light touch. This athlete understands that even in a game that requires force and strength, applying too much energy into a situation is not going to get the best result.

Calibration is a matter of learning, and learning comes from practice. Great athletes stay open moment-by-moment, responding according to what their practice has taught them. Though many athletes are naturally gifted with a wisdom that supports them in their particular sport, I am sure that every great athlete would also credit their practice for providing the experiences through which they learned how to respond according to the situations they face in each moment.

WE GET WHAT WE ASK FOR

We have already discussed how words set up our experiences in life. Here we can see how we, as a culture, collude with one another in measuring our worth—in this case, according to how hard we try.

I had a direct experience of this when, as a teenager, I applied for a job with the local gas company. To say I applied overstates what it took to get the job. I simply convinced the manager that I would work real hard and that I could learn any job.

I got hired and was taken out the next morning to what seemed like the middle of nowhere along with a shovel and my lunch. I was dropped off with the instructions to dig a trench between two stakes in the ground. They seemed impossibly far apart. The rest of the crew drove off chuckling as they abandoned me to this assignment.

It felt odd to be left out there alone on my first day. Being the optimist that I am, however, I grabbed that shovel and struck the pointed end of it onto the hard-packed earth, expecting at least to make a dent. The earth met the shovel with steeled resistance and a quiver traveled up the handle of the shovel, moving me more than the ground. The impact of the shovel hitting the hard earth created a heart-breaking clunk, and the ground didn't show any sign of being willing to be opened up.

As the morning went on, I jumped on that shovel, twisted it into the cracks of the baked earth. All the while, the words I had spoken only the day before kept running through my head. I had asked for the hardest job and the gas company had complied, always ready to serve.

The excruciatingly hot prairie sun shone bright that day, jeering at me, no doubt, as the only witness to this ordeal. I made little progress over the next few hours. I am quite sure that if I had had a vehicle I would have left to at least find more and better tools. Perhaps the crew was testing me, though more likely it was the Universe that was teaching me most directly.

At the end of the day the crew returned to pick me up. I could see by the looks on their faces that they weren't too happy by the poor result of the day's effort. I guessed it would mean that I'd be back the next day.

I dragged my sore body home that night. Later a friend of mine, who had also had his first day on the job with the same gas company, came over for a visit.

He was laughing and celebrating what a great job he'd landed, telling me how happy he was going to be that summer with it. He was quite surprised to see how beat I was, so we exchanged the stories of our day. His assignment had been to walk around a beautiful neighborhood with a gas sniffer looking for leaks around people's homes. He was filled with stories of the people he'd met, the lemonades he'd shared with some of them, and, to add insult to injury, he had even met some cute girls our age.

I was struck by the disparity between our two experiences. I asked him what he said in the interview the day before.

He happily explained to me that he had told the manager that he did not want to work too hard. He asked if they had a job that might be easy and fun. They assured him that they did in fact have such a job.

I was floored. Each of us had walked through the same door and each of us had received exactly what we had asked for. I asked for hard effort and got it; he asked for fun and easy effort and that's what he got.

The quality of experience that we have in each moment of our life is in accordance with how we approach it. When we approach a job or an event, we have an opportunity to choose, then to respond according to how well that choice is working out. As awakened beings, we are responsible for how we approach each moment.

WHAT IS THE QUALITY OF EFFORT AND MINDFULNESS THAT WE CHOOSE TO APPLY TO ANY GIVEN EXPERIENCE?

When I was a monk in Burma, one of my fellow monk friends would often invite me along on walks or trips to someone's home, or to a ceremony of some kind.

He would approach me with a big smile and ask, "Would you like to join me for a walk, happily?" or "Would you like to attend this ceremony, sincerely?"

I noticed that he approached everything with an intentional tone that he would choose according to his wisdom of what was needed.

Along with creating the experience according to the quality of effort, he also taught me a lot about the mindfulness of being in a particular experience. Even an experience as simple as walking became an exercise in mindfulness.

I started noticing the amount of effort it took to stay mindful about walking. As I practiced this more and more, I played with a wide range of effort. I practiced with a very light touch of effort at times, similar to how a sticky note attaches to something. It holds with just enough effort to stay connected to the surface.

I also practiced with the effort equal to a spike being nailed through something to keep it in place. I tried very hard and got quite forceful with my attention. In each case, I found my experience to be quite different.

When I practiced mindfulness with a light touch, I found the experience to be sustainable and enjoyable. Whenever I found that my attention had slipped, I gently brought it back with ease and delight. When I tried with great force, I got worn out, tired quickly, and found that I experienced a great deal of frustration.

SOMETHING IS TRYING TO HAPPEN HERE

Effort is not concerned with particular results. Life is not about trying harder and getting more done. In each moment there is something that is trying to happen and our job is to read the Wisdom Field and support what is trying to happen, as long as it is in accordance with our Divine Wisdom.

In order to do that, not only must we be able to listen carefully to the emerging inspiration of creativity, but we also must be flexible, as this will most often require a change of plans.

I was invited into an organization to do some coaching with the senior leadership team. The plan was to support them as they moved through a process of decision-making. They were looking into decisions that would structurally change the leadership of the organization in major ways, and they brought a lot of worry, resistance, and tension with them.

As we began the process, it became apparent that the plan was not unfolding as we had hoped. They seemed unable to get clear about their choices, and I could feel that there was something going on beneath the surface that was trying to happen but had not yet been revealed.

As I checked in with them, it became clear that there was a lot of resentment among the members of this team. They had been tolerating each other for a long time, rather than addressing the relationship issues between them. We had to shift away from our original plan. The session became one of clearing out the old energies and recreating a workable relationship between them.

I could have tried to ignore that, pushing harder, with more effort, to stick to the original plan, but it was a wiser course to be flexible. As I aligned with the energy that was trying to emerge, things moved quite easily. It was not fun as they cleared out some very upsetting things, but the energy itself flowed like a river that had to be released to follow its course.

Resisting it would have been possible, as we are always at choice. Had I done so, however, it would have taken more and more energy on my part to hold to the plan.

So with a Good State of Effort, notice when things are being difficult and get curious about what is really trying to happen. You can then align with the flow of energy to direct and influence the energy rather than try to control it.

It is always important to understand the nature of what you are working with, so that you can learn how to use the energy that is already present in a way that supports your wisdom.

CONTROL SELDOM WORKS
When you are confronted by a situation, there are a variety of

choices about how to respond. If you choose to confront, control, or dominate, then your energy will need to be much bigger than the energy of the situation itself. This could be very difficult if the circumstances you are trying to change resist your efforts. When two or more people get distorted with each other, it becomes a misguided contest of domination over each other or over the situation. This is a very ineffective approach and can even be destructive.

REDIRECTING ENERGY

It takes much less energy to redirect. Remember that everything, every situation, every task, is just about moving the energy according to the purpose and intention in your mind and heart. When you understand that you are just working with energy, then you can consider how to align with it and turn it towards a new point, according to a blend between your intention and the intention that the energy itself has.

When you meet a situation, be curious about what is trying to happen in this moment. Then consider how to blend your intention with the intention of the energy that you are meeting. Remember that energy can be transformed.

CYCLES AND TIMING

Ask any farmer in Saskatchewan, Canada why they don't plant their seeds in January to get a head start. The answer would seem too obvious, or the question itself too ridiculous, to even consider. Why, it's winter. It is clearly not the right time for planting.

It is easy for us to see that there is a cycle of seasons. There is a good time to plant and a bad time to plant. Working against the cycles of the seasons would be a fool's game. This concept of cycles and timing is just as true for everything in our lives.

Interpreting the seasons and cycles can be a bit tricky, though.

Growing up in that part of Canada, I remember that the adults would consider the best time to plant their gardens. The choice usually pivoted around what is informally known as the "May twenty-fourth long weekend." Should we plant before May 24, thus taking advantage of a longer growing season but risking a late-May frost, or should we plant after May 24, and have a shorter growing season but no risk of frost?

In his book *Outliers*, Malcolm Gladwell presents some fascinating insight into timing where sporting leagues are concerned, and into the influence of timing on entire industries. He leads us to conclude that timing is perhaps more important than having the best of plans. He points out how being in the right place at the right time takes many people to great success, oftentimes even before they know the path that they are walking.

It is important that we learn how to look more deeply into the timing of our ideas. Many people have had the next great emerging idea early on. But after a few attempts to move it forward, they give up only to have someone else succeed afterward. It is commonly stated that the three most important keys to success are location, location, location. I would add timing to that list.

When you notice that an idea is possessing you and you are struggling to move it forward, consider if the timing is correct. It may be that what is needed is the effort of patience and persistence to see it through.

THE DANCE OF LIFE

Life is a dance with many people and factors all wanting to lead at the same time. When you dance with the effort of mindfulness, listening to the beat and what is hidden between the notes, you will develop a great sense of rhythm with the Universe. When you learn to dance with life in this way, you will find a great joy in each moment. It is not the kind of joy that relies on things being a certain way—that joy is too fleeting and fragile. It is instead the kind of joy that is available in every moment, no matter how good or bad things look. Here you will know that you are a great dancer with life because you are meeting life from a place of awakened awareness with a Good State of Effort. Therefore you will treasure the very chaotic, fertile, and promising nature of life itself.

Go now and travel according to the direction of your dreams and with the speed, ease, and delight of a Good State of Effort.

COLLECTIVE ASPIRATIONS FROM A GOOD STATE OF EFFORT—A NOTE FROM THE FUTURE

We move in a good way now. We finally learned how to maintain a constant and easy mindfulness as we go about our days. There are times when we rest, and we do so with ease and peace. And there are times when we put in longer hours according to the cycles of timing, the seasons, and the various stages of our projects. It's all quite fulfilling.

As we learned how to respect Divine timing, life got a lot simpler. We remembered how to read the tides, and to go when the timing was right. Of course, we had to let go of thinking that our demand to have it all now was the right way. Since the Great Awakening, we finally learned to hear the whisper of the Universe as it spoke to us through the Wisdom Field about what was needed from day-to-day, season-to-season, year-to-year.

In order for this to happen, we had to learn how to put in good effort to listen. The wisdom and inspirations wash over and through us in each moment. All it took was the willingness to stay open and present and to be unattached to how we thought things would come about.

We activate our Divine Essence now. Through that we receive so much insight into what is needed, that the way has become more effective, happier, and joyful.

This allowed us to ease up. Now when we realize we are working too hard, we look into what is taking so much effort. When more effort is needed, we adjust quickly and wisely. More often than not, as soon as we let go, things move right along.

Who knew we could accomplish so much and have so much time to play, be with each other, tell stories, and listen! Even the Earth breathed a sigh of relief as we humans became her partners rather than her dominators.

This all takes a steady effort of consciousness, and that is okay. It turns out that it took more work to tune out than it now takes to stay tuned in.

People accomplish more now. They follow through because we learned how to apply the correct measure of will to our intentions. We also collaborate better, knowing when to step up and when to recognize that someone else is in a better position to do the task—or we revisit it and find a better way.

Our kids are taught mindfulness exercises in the first few years of school, so the practice of being present is fully established everywhere. It seems that was key to regrounding us in our resourcefulness and heart wisdom.

We still work hard and strive when our Divine Essence guides us to do so. It is just that now our energy is blended more with the energy of others. The result is a cooperation among us that supports everybody more fully.

A Good State of Effort has put everything into alignment, and through that good things happen.

PRACTICES FOR A GOOD STATE OF EFFORT

Practice Suggestion 1

Take a moment before any activity in this day and ask your Self these questions:

- What is my habit with regards to the amplitude and the emotional quality of effort in this activity?
- What is another style of effort I could approach this task with?
- Make a list of five different efforts, naming the range of possible amplitudes and emotional qualities that could work for you in a given situation.

Choose one as a starting point.

Remember to switch amplitude and qualities of effort moment-by moment as the experience unfolds.

Practice Suggestion 2

Go for a walk in nature. As you walk, select a few objects, like a tree branch, a blade of grass, or a variety of rocks. Practice applying just enough effort to move them ever so slightly. Experiment with moving them in a confronting way or in redirecting ways. Use different aspects of your body to do this. For example, experiment moving things with your fingers, your feet, even your breath, and any other aspect of you that comes to mind. Add in a variety of emotional tones, noticing how the quality of the experience changes.

A GOOD STATE OF PRACTICE

I am in a Good State of Practice.

- I create my day consciously, and care for my state of being.

- I design my day according to my Divine Essence's wisdom, and am flexible according to the call of the unfolding mystery in each moment of the day.

- I care for my physical body, my mind, my emotional body, and my spirit daily.

- In each day I have a time of stillness, a time to listen to the beating of my heart, to my breath, and to the breath and call of the Universe around me.

- I consciously appreciate all that shows up in the unfolding of my journey, including the things that seem unpleasant or inconvenient.

- I check in with the Wisdom Field each day and ask what is needed. Then I listen, responding according to the wisdom of my Divine Essence.

- I actively honor all the beings that are present in my life each day, including my Self.

- I actively create beauty each day, and all my thoughts are life-giving to all beings.

- Each day I play, I laugh, I cry as a good response to what is unfolding around me.

- I practice the paradox of flexibility and intention as I move through each moment.

- I keep the agreements I make with others and my Self.

- I keep the relationships with others and my Self clean and bright.

- Because I am in a Good State of Practice each day, I create beauty.

- I apply my will and a good measure of effort to honor and fulfill my practice.

I am in a Good State of Practice.

A GOOD STATE OF PRACTICE

A Good State of Practice is key to keeping the wholeness of who you are in balance and in the best possible condition. Having a daily practice is like tending a garden. To have a good garden it is important to care for the soil, the seeds, as well as the plants that have already begun to thrive.

WHAT IS A PRACTICE?

A practice is a regular event that you have chosen to be a part of your life. Practices could have a wide variety of frequency, such as several times a day, weekly, monthly, or any other cycle, according to what the intention behind the practice is.

It is good to have a variety of practices that tend to the wholeness of who you are in this stage of your life. The intention of your practices is important to know, so that their benefits can be realized. It is likely that a practice will also provide a range of benefits beyond the ones you are asking for.

Practices can be intended to care for your body, your mind, your spirit, your relationships with Self, loved ones, friends, and God.

At the heart of a practice is the intention you hold and the agreement you have made with your Self or others who might join you in your practice.

RITES AND RITUALS

A rite is a formal or ceremonial act that holds an intention of some kind. The ritual is the procedure for carrying out that rite.

We have many rituals in our daily lives that are so customary, we take them for granted. In the beginning, however, these procedures carried a particular intention. For example, in much of the world the handshake is considered a good gesture to use when meeting someone.

It's thought to originally have been a way for two people to show one another that they carried no weapon. The handshake is such an important ritual that, today, turning down a handshake is considered very poor manners.

It is important to ritualize the activities you do regularly. By ritualizing I mean consciously creating an intention for the activity and approaching it with a sense of sacredness or a higher level of consciousness than you might bring to the usual moments of your life.

For example, if it is a day when I am going to be coaching people, I will use the activities of getting up and preparing my Self in the morning to call in a powerful day for my Self and each of my clients. When I shower and shave, I call my Self forth to being the best coach I can be that day. When I eat my breakfast, I eat as a great coach. After breakfast, I will sit for a few moments and become still. I check in with the Wisdom Field. I ask, "What is needed for these people through my coaching?"

As I do all that, I can feel my mind, heart, and body align around the purpose of the day. It is a powerful experience. Nothing is taken for granted. A ritual might also be your exercise routine, and setting an intention or a prayer to begin and end each exercise session. The intention to begin might be a spoken wish that the exercise session contribute to you having a healthy body. If you are healing some aspect of your body, you could include that in your prayer, asking that the exercise session bring about that healing. At the end of the session, it is always good to offer a prayer of gratitude for the opportunity of this life, for the great body you do have, and for any healing that was received in that session.

PRAYER

Prayer is itself an important practice. In its simplest form, prayer is an appeal that is sent out to God. I use the words Universe, God, Goddess, and Great Spirit interchangeably.

Including a prayer heightens the attention you are holding and calls in the Universe to join you, according to what you have spoken.

A prayer is often a request or a gratitude that is sent out. Praying regularly has many benefits, such as offering your daily struggles over to a higher authority and activating the Universe's energies to move according to the prayer or wish that you have offered. Prayer also helps the one who is praying get a perspective on what they want. It also helps people give up the illusion that they can control everything themselves without some assistance from God and others in their life.

I offer prayers of gratitude on a regular basis as a way of sending the energy of compassion into the world. It is especially useful to offer prayers of gratitude for things that may have happened that you do not particularly like or easily appreciate. When someone has made you angry or hurt your feelings, offering a prayer of gratitude is a powerful way of getting to the learning that is available for you in that experience.

As I am writing this paragraph, it is 6:00 AM and I am in Istanbul. I can hear the morning call to prayers coming from a nearby mosque. Prayers can remind us of what is important and what guiding principles we want to live by. When we gather with others to pray, we are reminded that we are never alone in this journey.

PRACTICES FOR THE THREE INTELLIGENCES

When you choose your practices, be sure to consider all three intelligences. Here are a few ideas to inspire your own thinking in these three areas:

What Practices Will Refresh Your Mind?

- Opportunities to be still, such as taking time to sit in a garden and just hang out

- Stretch your capacity by offering a challenge to your mind in the form of puzzles or solving math questions
- A practice of listening to the Wisdom Field daily

What Practices Will Open Your Heart?
- A practice of keeping all your relationships clean and bright as discussed in a Good State of Being
- A practice of checking in with your emotional state
- A practice of reaching out and connecting with nature

What Practices Will Take Care of Your Body?
- Exercise
- A better diet

AGREEMENTS TO PRACTICE

Every time you tell your Self that you are going to practice something, such as exercising or dieting, you are essentially making an agreement or a promise with your Self. Or, if spoken to another person or to God, you have made that promise with another.

Many people make agreements easily, without considering what it means to make them—nor what it could mean to not follow through. Every time you break a promise, you are loading your karmic backpack with the pebbles of broken agreements. If you had a friend who told you every day that he or she will show up to exercise with you but they rarely do, you would likely stop believing them when they made that agreement with you. It would possibly become an issue between you, especially if you were counting on them to show up. If left unaddressed, this behavior could easily cause a breakdown in the fabric of the friendship.

The same thing happens when you break these agreements with your Self. Eventually, you would probably stop believing your Self, and the energy of being let down so often would start to discourage you from even wanting to try. Or, just as bad, you won't believe your Self when you want to do something about it.

This is the time to get real about what is needed. You are responsible for your life and for your choices. First, you must get your Divine Essence present, then check in about what is needed. If you know that doing a certain practice is needed in your life, for whatever reason, then you either choose it or let it go and get it off the list. If you do choose it, then you must activate your will and follow through. It can be useful to ask for help from people around you, but that does not make it their responsibility. It is your life, your responsibility, to follow through.

This is also a good time to remember that you could also approach this practice from a place of lightness, delight, ease, and a Good State of Effort. If you feel that a certain practice is like a punishment of some sort, then you will be carrying an energy with it that could have unintended negative consequences. For example, approaching exercising with a heavy dread and worry will probably stress you out more than the benefit of the exercise.

It can be very helpful to find ways to make certain practices fun and compelling, rather than have them be chores and difficult.

There is a real paradox here of holding your Self to an agreement with ease and delight. If it turns out that you fall out of the agreement, be compassionate with your Self. Reground in the commitment to get back into it, as long as it remains the best choice for you.

Maintaining a Good State of Practice puts a steady heartbeat into your life. It provides a structure that ensures that you are taking care of your Self, that you are honoring your Self, and that you are being present to what is needed for a sustainable life ahead.

COLLECTIVE ASPIRATIONS FROM A GOOD STATE OF PRACTICE—A NOTE FROM THE FUTURE

When we as a people went through the Great Awakening, it was shocking at first because so much of what we thought was important fell away. Once we realized that we were going to make it after all, we collectively found a new set of priorities that easily emerged for us.

Since then we live according to what supports our well-being, and having enough is enough.

With all that worry about keeping up gone, we are more available now to live in the moment, to honor and care for our Selves, our families, and our communities.

Each day we routinely check in with our mind intelligence and ask what is needed to care for our state of mind. Play is honored along with work, and contribution can look like a lot of different things according to the inspiration of our Divine Essence.

Each day we check in with our body intelligence. We care for our bodies in ways that support health and well-being. Diet is about good foods that are healthy, and when eaten, are accompanied with good intention.

Each day we check in with our heart intelligence. We address what needs to be addressed regularly in order to keep our connections with each other and the planet clean and bright.

It is no longer a challenge to work, to tend to the fields. This has instead become our pleasure. Rituals have become regular parts of each day. Through the rituals of exercise, storytelling, and listening circles—which are also provided where we work—life now includes our careers in a way that it never had before. We are living on purpose, so everything just fits together nicely. We don't miss that old hurried busyness that used to push us around so much.

Inevitably, there are still challenges, but now we all look out beyond our immediate circle, and we can always see what is needed. Since the practice of generosity and appreciation became important to everyone, it has been a lot easier to create sustainable innovations and ideas that support our lives in a good way.

The daily time of sitting has become so important, it is hard to understand why we didn't do it before the Great Awakening. It is still amazing to me how this simple practice of listening to the Wisdom Field keeps us all so clear about our present condition and what is needed.

Speaking of clear, we are so excited about the practice of relationship cleansing. It still happens that we sometimes say and do things that get misunderstood in some way—only now it is standard procedure to seek each other out with loving-kindness to clear the air. To think that we used to carry those heavy little peeves around.

We all feel and look younger now, and there is no question we are healthier. It's true that when we get to the causal levels and shift the factors that create negative stress, our bodies have a natural disposition to being healthy. Now it seems that when things in life challenge us, we are invigorated rather than worn down by them. Now we really understand that caring for the wholeness of who we are is an essential idea.

PRACTICES FOR A GOOD STATE OF PRACTICE

Practice Suggestion 1

Each day routinely check in with your mind intelligence and ask what is needed to care for your state of mind.

Practice Suggestion 2

Each day check in with your body intelligence. Care for your body in ways that support health and well-being. Consider your diet and exercise programs according to what is needed to support your healthy body.

Practice Suggestion 3

Each day check in with your heart intelligence. Address what needs to be addressed regularly, in order to keep your connections with your Self, others, and the planet clean and bright.

Practice Suggestion 4

Look for places where you can meet like-minded people who can support your ongoing development and interests. Consider going to book clubs, exercise clubs, meditation centers, or any other place where you will be exposed to people with similar interests to yours.

Practice Suggestion 5

Take walks regularly.

Practice Suggestion 6

Journal to check in and get clear about life's experiences.

Practice Suggestion 7

Create rituals that add consciousness into your life.

Practice Suggestion 8
Have a daily practice of appreciation and gratitude.

Practice Suggestion 9
Create a regular practice of generosity.

Practice Suggestion 10
Send loving-kindness intentions out to the world daily.

Practice Suggestion 11
Plan and take vacations.

Practice Suggestion 12
Play every day. Have hobbies that you enjoy.

Practice Suggestion 13
Read regularly.

Practice Suggestion 14
Send letters to friends as they come into your heart and mind.

Practice Suggestion 15
Have a daily practice of checking in with the Wisdom Field.

A GOOD STATE OF DOING

I am in a Good State of Doing.

- My thoughts and words are congruent with my intention of creating beauty, they are life-giving, so it follows that my actions are in alignment.

- The actions that I consciously move into in each moment are well-intended.

- I am moving forward steadily, while respecting the cycles and timing of the Universe around me.

- Informed by the wisdom of my Divine Essence, I choose when to move and when to be still.

- The moments in which I choose stillness as my doing are grounded in connection with my Divine Essence.

- My actions are called forth and inspired through my deep listening to the Universe around me, to my heart wisdom, and to the wisdom of my Divine Essence.

- I take risks according to my Divine Essence's wisdom, and move forward in a good way.

- When I act, I move in a conscious and intentional way. I do so lightly with ease, delight, and with good effort.

- I play and I release my Self to the joyfulness of a child who, by blowing the dandelion seed, releases and scatters joy to the world around, then delights in the unfolding dream that each seed holds.

- I move as one, as one of the people, as one of the many beings, so every breath, every action, adds beauty and forwards the unfolding dream of the Universe in a good way.

I am in a Good State of Doing.

A GOOD STATE OF DOING

You move through each day with a busy schedule and so much to do. You are pulled from task to task. The hours turn into days and the days into weeks. A lifetime happens. You wonder where all the time goes. You know that you are not really honoring your Self or your life as you could. Somehow it seems that you have been hypnotized by the action of your life. You may be getting a lot done, but this is not a Good State of Doing. It doesn't have to be that way.

In a Good State of Doing you are present to each passing moment of the day. You move with time as your friend, a resource that informs you of your coordinates, so that you may be in good relationship with your commitments and other people. Time is not your master now. You approach the day with an abundance of space and you are aware of your Good State of Being.

DOING WITH PRESENCE

It is important to living an awakened life that we be present to every moment. Being present is both a state of being and a way of moving in the world. As a present one, you are conscious in each moment, present to what is here, present to your Self, using your three intelligences as ways of checking in and being present to others and to the Field.

From this state of presence your actions are guided by your Divine Essence. As your Divine Essence is One with the Universe, it follows that your actions will be in connection to, and as One with, the Universe.

That will include times of lightness and play, as much as it does times of more focused and concentrated activity.

DOING AND PLAY

Play is an important part of an awakened life. Play is a way of keeping young in spirit and allowing your creativity to come through. It is a time to bring out your inner child and just play.

Nature teaches us once again here. Coyotes are amazing animals that are much maligned, as their interactions with humans do not always go well. They have a brilliant ability to adapt to the changing conditions around them. Coyotes have appeared to me many times in my life. Often literally as well as in visions. If you could follow a pack of coyotes around, you would see them play a lot. Then when it is time to be more serious in order to accomplish something, they align around their task and carry it out with great intention.

I had the amazing privilege once of witnessing these amazing animals at play. I had wandered off into a Canadian forest for a hike. I reached a spot in the woods where I decided to sit and be still.

I had only been sitting there for a short time when a pack of coyotes came along. They were roaming and playing joyfully, yipping to each other with what appeared to be expressions of happiness and excitement. It was as if I was invisible to them, yet they were within a few feet of me. It seemed that they might have been hunting as they were poking around in the underbrush. At the same time, however, they were jumping around, playing and cajoling. I just sat there in silent appreciation and watched. Their joy was so contagious that it was all I could do to avoid laughing aloud at their antics. Then one of them gave out a more significant yelp and they immediately became serious. They then continued along and wandered off through the forest.

We need to learn the balance between playtime and work. The more we can bring play into our work, the better the results become.

This is especially true when we want to solve a problem or accomplish a task that we consider important. So often when we are facing something that we view as important, we tighten up and shut our Selves off from our greatest creativity. Learning how to stay loose and playful is an important aspect of living an awakened life.

DOING AND RELATIONSHIPS

When we make action too important, we cut our Selves off from the people and the world around us, including the Wisdom Field. When we do that, it is as if we were trying to sail a boat towards a particular destination while we disconnect our Selves from our awareness of the winds and the underlying currents. Instead, we pull out our charts and maps, create a brilliant plan, and push on with it no matter what.

What is needed instead is for us to be open and in connection to the people, environment, Wisdom Field, and Universe as a whole.

Only then will our actions be guided by our own wisdom.

Action that comes from this level of connection will be more effective and honoring of the whole. These actions will be carried out in relationship with the world around.

DOING WITH TIME

Imagine that you and time are in a relationship together. Who is leading whom?

For many people, there is never enough time. It is as if they are being pushed around by time and they can never run fast enough to keep up. Others simply don't participate with time at all. They push it away, and in so doing they cut themselves off from the relationship.

Go back to imagining being in a relationship with time. You get to be in connection with time, so both of you are honored in the relationship. From this space you will find that there is flexibility in the field of time, a spaciousness that bends and opens for you. Time can be sped up or slowed down according to what is needed.

You may have had an experience of being in slow-motion time. This is usually brought on by an experience of great intensity, but that is not the only way to create this.

By playing with your relationship with time, you can learn to slow down while being in what seems to be a fast-moving experience. I have practiced many fast-moving sports in my life, including skydiving, car racing, motorcycling, and downhill skiing. Through these experiences I have learned that, regardless of how fast my body is moving, I can learn to engage with the experience at my own pace—a pace in which I do not feel rushed or pushed by the speed, but rather in which I am responding with what is needed a hundredth of a second at a time. In order to accomplish this, I bring my heart and body intelligence more to the front, releasing my mind from being in charge of the experience. To do this, it is important to focus and keep your attention on the task at hand. Learn to keep your body responding to what is needed and your mind pointed to where you intend to be next.

This also translates to tasks that are less intense and more of the everyday variety.

Begin by identifying what you want to accomplish. It might be writing a report or creating something. It helps to design your relationship with time by deciding how long you will allow for the task. You might give your Self one hour of uninterrupted time. It helps to set an alarm to monitor the time, so you do not have to think about it. Turn off your phone and really allow your Self to have this opportunity.

Now practice breathing before you start moving into the task. Sit and allow your breathing to be deep and regular. While you breathe, imagine the task and how you would like it to go. At this stage you are not moving yet. You are using your imagination to go ahead of you. You may feel some pressure to get into it. Just allow your Self the opportunity to imagine it first.

Imagine your Self moving through the task easily and wisely. Imagine the finished product and see your Self smiling, enjoying both the process and the result.

Keep your heart open and courageous. It might be an important task that carries some pressure to do it really well. Perhaps some clients are counting on you to perform at a very high level. This pressure could start to shut down your heart in this situation. Assure your Self that you can do what's before you very well. Imagine your heart being open and beating in a slow and regular way. Keep your breathing going evenly and feel your heart beating steadily, not rushing.

Now is the time to begin to move into it. Allow your body to respond to what is needed. Grab the materials or go to the keyboard, and just start moving. Trust that your body knows how to do this. Allow it to move steadily through this task.

If anything distracts you, practice the art of refocusing by bringing your Self back to the task. Notice that it is getting done with ease and delight. Now you are in the flow of it. This is a Good State of Doing.

The same goes for a period of sitting in stillness. Often when I first sit down to be still, I am coming from a faster-paced event in my day, moving quickly even at a cellular level. I activate the stillness using all three of the intelligences. I use my mind intelligence to give my Self permission to slow down. To do this I might even speak the words out loud, so that my whole being can hear them. I might say, "I am going to sit and be still for the next fifteen minutes now."

I then open my heart to the experience by noticing and acknowledging how I feel. It helps to note the feeling with your Observer. There is nothing that needs to be done about it. Just noticing it is a very powerful experience. Then I imagine that my heart is beating easily, steadily, and happily.

After that I activate my body intelligence by breathing deeply and regularly. I scan my body. Wherever I feel tension, I direct my breath to that part of my body and allow the tension to be released. If necessary, I might stretch that part of my body or tense and loosen it a few times to move the energy that is being held there.

I can feel my mind, heart, and body all come into alignment. Then I am available to drop into the moment to a very deep level.

As I drop, I experience a shift. When I am busy, it's as if I am a stone skipping over the surface of the water; when I allow my Self to slow down, I am the stone dropping into the depth of the lake. I might travel far or I might feel like I am floating in one spot. Either way, very little time seems to pass. It is as if I become a light traveler for whom there is no passage of time. There is only now.

While in this experience, I may travel the cosmos, and my body is being rested, my heart is reopened, my mind is at peace. Sometimes it seems that I have gone far and deep, when I return I might find that only fifteen linear minutes has passed by.

In everyday life, we are generally living somewhere between these extremes—being very still and moving quickly. When we are in a conscious relationship with time, we can design our experience with choice and intention, according to what our Divine Essence informs us is needed.

WHAT IS NEEDED?

For each task of the day you may take the opportunity to consider what is needed before you start moving through it. If you are at liberty to accept or decline tasks as they are directed towards you, choose what you are doing wisely. For most of us, there are things we cannot say no to, due to work obligations or family situations. In these cases, be sure to remember the Ring of Power, and choose a state of being from the place of your Divine Essence.

As you accomplish your tasks, remember to remain in a Good State of Effort. You move with the right amount of energy, with ease and delight, and you remain conscious about the quality of the experience you are having.

DOING AND LIFE PURPOSE

Earlier we discussed life purpose. One of the ideas about purpose is that we can express it through every breath we take and through any event that we are in. While we are doing whatever we are doing, it helps to hold the question, "How am I expressing my purpose through this moment?"

Even what might seem like the most mundane tasks have purpose in them. All we have to do is to become conscious of what it might be.

When I walk down the street on my way to the market, I remind my Self that my purpose is to serve the awakening of all. Then as I walk along, I accomplish this just by holding the intention, seeing through the intention, listening through the intention, and smiling at strangers through the intention. It does not have to be an exercise that requires huge concentration. I hold it with ease and delight, so I am available to have fun with it and not take it too seriously. It is just there, guiding and informing what I choose to do.

DOING AND GOALS

Quite often in life we can find our Selves running along, being quite busy keeping up with all the myriad stuff of life and forgetting why we are doing what we are doing in the first place. When we make the goal more important than anything else, we can lose touch with the essential experience of moving towards accomplishing the goal. It is through the quality of the experience of the movement that we touch and influence the world around us.

You can move through a day with force and anger to accomplish your goals, but the damage that is done to the relationships of that day will certainly add weight to your karmic backpack. Alternately, you could move through the same day with ease and delight, still accomplish your goals and objectives, and have a very positive impact on all those you touched.

A goal is just a static point in time that helps us realize where we are on the path. It is never the point of the walk. Goals are important and useful, but we have to keep them in context.

We are in relationship with our goals. There is a tension that gets created between a goal and us. A goal is something that we have created the intention to accomplish. It is the intention that sets up an attractive force that draws you and the goal towards each other. You are in relationship with it. In a good relationship, you hold your goals in a wise way and they do not have a distorted power over you. You remain flexible in relationship to them, constantly reevaluating whether or not they are still wanted in your life. When a goal no longer serves you, you then release it from your commitments.

When a goal is added to your commitments, make sure you have looked into it and added it only after you have determined through your Divine Essence that it is truly needed. Then the actions you choose in order to attract that goal in are being informed by your own wisdom.

It is our will that determines the resolve and strength of our commitment to what we do. It is by activating our will that we stay in the action of life.

Through our body intelligence we can check in and notice how our will is being used. When we are moving well, we are flexible and willing to bend according to what we are meeting in each moment. Our will allows us to continue along the journey. It is like the horsepower of our engine. The will to follow through, to move, keeps us going.

I am not suggesting that everything will be easy, or that if something is not going smoothly there is something wrong. I am only suggesting that we have a responsibility to be aware. From that awareness we get to choose our response to the way our doing is being carried out.

DOING AND BEING STUCK

At times we may feel stuck. When this happens, it is important to notice and to check in on what is going on. When you know what is needed and yet you seem unable to move forward, you can check into a variety of factors that might be impacting you.

First is the possibility that the environment you are in is holding you back. There are external forces that can hold us and keep us down, making it difficult to get going. Homeostasis is one of these forces. As we discussed earlier, this is when the present situation is resisting change and is therefore holding you back. If you're experiencing this, it's a good time to activate your will to start the movement. Often the greatest effort is needed for the first three steps of a journey. Then the momentum begins, the world starts to align with you, and the going gets easier.

DOING AND CYCLES AND TIMING

If you are finding it difficult to get moving, it could be that the timing is off. Look into what you are trying to do and ask if this is the right time. It may be that this is, instead, a time for patience and waiting, rather than pushing on. If all the signals seem to indicate that moving forward is timely, yet you are still challenged to get it going, then it could be that you are in an internal struggle of some kind.

It may be that you don't feel able to move forward with new ideas at this time. It is not unusual to have periods like this. Or, you may be zooming along so fast that you feel like you are barely keeping up with the tidal wave that threatens to pull you in. These cycles are quite normal at different times in our lives. What you want to watch out for are extended lengths of time during which you are not engaged in the doing side of life, or extended periods of time in which you are just running full out.

A PLAN CAN BE HELPFUL

I don't believe that everything benefits from advance planning. But of course there are times when creating a plan is a great place to start. If you are having trouble getting going, creating a plan could start the wheels turning for you. If you are running so fast that you can't keep up, a plan might provide you with a useful strategy that will support you in slowing down.

WHO'S IN CHARGE OF THE ACTION?

As we well know by now, we have a choice about who within us to put in charge of the action of our life: Divine Essence or Distorted. Since we're in a place of practicing choosing Divine Essence, it's good to know that from that choice, there are a variety of other choices about what aspect of your being you can put out in front.

From old teachings, we are given the archetype of the warrior. The warrior moves forward with courage, which is activated from heart wisdom. The warrior of Divine Essence holds good intention for all. They are about creating beauty, and are respectful and resourceful. This warrior is kind and benevolent, and because they are in touch with their strength, they have no need to prove it or make a show of it.

In the Beauty Way teachings, the warrior energy asks you to determine what resources are needed, to assemble them, to create a strategy, and then to get into action. It is important for us as humans to be in balance between a Good State of Being and a

Good State of Doing. The warrior or warrioress knows this, moving through the world in a good way.

It is easy for us, in this extremely fast-paced world, to get caught up in rushing forward without taking any time at all to check in each day, to recalibrate our direction, nor to shift our priorities because something has shifted in the world around us.

The warrior knows to take a few moments of stillness each day as one of the most important steps in moving forward in a good way. What a great paradox that choosing to be still is an important step to move forward.

The Universe is always in conversation with us, so our responsibility is to check in on a regular basis. The act of stopping for a few moments and then listening may be the single most important thing you will "do" in each day. Again, this is a time to return to the important question, "What is needed?"

In this case, the question is posed from the warrior to the Universe to inform us about what is needed in order to move forward in a good way. The Wisdom Field holds a lot of information for us. It is our responsibility to check in.

When asking what is needed, you must first be grounded into connection with your Divine Essence rather than your Distorted Self. It is easy to imagine how differently each aspect of the Self might answer this question.

As much as our thoughts and words have impact on the world around us, it is our actions that have the most obvious impact. You have probably heard the expression that actions speak louder than words. That expression teaches us of the wisdom and importance of choiceful action.

Inaction is a form of action, too. When we choose not to do something, we set up a consequence, good or bad, as a result of that choice. Quite often inaction might be the wisest choice. Sometimes waiting to see what will happen next can save us from a lot of unnecessary movement and running around.

Therefore, it is important to check in on the impact of your action or your inaction, then to choose what is needed accordingly.

WHAT ARE THE CRITERIA THAT INFORM YOU ABOUT HOW YOU ARE DOING?

For me, some of the most important questions are:

- Is the result of this action/inaction life-giving?
- Is this action/inaction creating beauty?
- Does this action/inaction honor my personal value system?
- Does this action/inaction honor any and all agreements that I am holding with another person or group?

There are undoubtedly some other important questions for you to consider according to the wisdom of your own Divine Essence. Listening is an important action. Listen to the Field. Allow it to inform us. Adjust as needed.

BE FLEXIBLE

When we are considering moving forward on some idea, we must listen to learn how we are doing as we carry it out. What we are listening for in this case is feedback from the world around us about what our impact is. Quite often we intend a certain result, yet as we move forward we are not getting the result that we had anticipated. In this situation, if we listen, we will realize this and we can then adjust according to what is needed.

In order to listen and to gather in the information about how you are doing, activate your Observer. Remember to activate your personal Observer to gather in your report through the three intelligences. Then activate the Interrelated Observer and imagine what is going on in the other aspects of the Universe around you.

What does not work is not listening or not checking in at all, and then being inflexible with our plan. That usually sets us up for a hard time, as we may be moving in the wrong direction or we may be running over other people in a way that is damaging our relationship with them. If we are listening, we will be able to adjust. And when the people and the world around us get that we are listening to their feedback, they are much more likely to support us, even if they don't necessarily agree with what is going on.

WHOSE IDEA IS IT?

As we discussed in Part One, many ideas are originating and being passed around through the Wisdom Field. You may be quite inspired, so you start into the doing of the idea. You dream into it, discuss it with people, check around and look for the wisdom of it. At times things will move quickly and easily. You will feel blessed to be in such a groove.

Or it may be that you are not quite ready to further that idea until you yourself develop more—perhaps through some experience or training. If you are out of touch and not listening, then you could spend a lot of money, energy, and time very ineffectively, while someone else who is asking these questions and listening is going to succeed where you might have.

Again, it is important to check in with each of your three intelligences to determine what there is to pay attention to.

I have had great ideas that, for reasons I never fully understood, I simply had to put down for a period of time. When that has happened, I come back to the idea later, from the being state of curiosity, and ask if the idea still has merit for me in particular. If it does, I then ask if now is the time to pick it up again. If the answer is no, then I put it down again until a later time.

When the answer is yes, I ask what is needed to pick this idea up again in a good way.

This process has saved me a lot of grief and has seen some very good things come true, in their time.

We are in a dance with this amazing Universe. It is not our will that controls and prevails above all, but our ability to listen to what is needed and then to respond accordingly.

When we think we can drive anything forward regardless of others around us, then we are trying to control. When we are trying to control, we are operating from a distorted place of fear. When we give up control and listen to the world around us, responding according to our Divine Essence's wisdom, we are able to influence what is happening in a good way. From a Good State of Doing, our path becomes a much more beautiful dance and collaboration that attracts in resources, support, and Universal guidance.

COLLECTIVE ASPIRATIONS FROM A GOOD STATE OF DOING—A NOTE FROM THE FUTURE

We move as one people now. We have been fully opened to the wisdom of our Divine Essence and the most amazing levels of intuition that come along with that. We still have plans, but they live more as guides than strict policies. We have learned to do things with a high level of consciousness, a presence, and a flexibility, which has us in the most beautiful moment-by-moment dance and collaboration with the Universe.

Since the Great Awakening, we are more aware and understanding of the interrelatedness of All. As such, we have learned to become one with the Wisdom Field. It guides us and we inform it. It is a vibrant and deep connection that every being has access to. The way in which it impacts our ability to move and accomplish things in a good way that honors All is abundantly evident.

Creating beauty has become a leading standard for how we are doing. Now we look at the quality of the experience and at the result, from the point of view of beauty and life-giving energy. If what we are doing is adding beauty and is life-giving, then chances are we are doing quite well. It is interesting to notice that as our organizations embraced this idea they actually became more profitable and sustainable.

It is amazing how life-giving our actions are now. We have learned how to find a joy in our daily actions in a way that was fleeting before, but is now quite a constant experience.

Today, at work, we all gathered around a new important project and we created together in a way that was like generating music. When it is done, we will have partnered with every constituency in a way that has everyone feeling completely heard and respected.

Every person's ideas are heard and considered, and everyone is unattached to their part in the project. It doesn't mean that everyone gets their way. It is just that it is no longer important to win at the cost of others, so everyone looks at the big picture with a generous attitude and wisdom.

Here is the cool thing. As we do things, we are so spacious with each other and with our Selves that every task, from the simplest to the most complex, is like a spiritual experience. Of course, there is still a lot to do. We are busy, but the difference is that we respect the timing of it all. And because we are so connected to each other through our heart wisdom, everything seems to unfold itself.

The level of excitement about each day's work, play, and activities is fun to notice. People just move around through their day with this joy and a giggle living just below the surface. Of course those giggles quite often break out, and then we have a good laugh rippling around in every direction. Doing things with such a present-moment consciousness, as we have learned to do, has not only made the experience of doing things better, but the results much more resonant, too.

Turns out it really was about the journey, and yes, the end also matters.

One other big shift from the old ways is that now, instead of everything in a way that's intended to help us go faster, we have created a lot of willingness and support to slow down. Now we regularly visit still points where we are encouraged to reflect and nurture. Don't worry, we still go fast when it is needed, only now it is a part of every day to be still, to not even think about what needs to be done. At first it was challenging because most of us had forgotten how. We remember now.

It is so important to us now that when we move, we move happily, with ease and delight. Then we stop, listen, and be present fully. We humans were always meant to do things in a good way. We just had to learn how.

PRACTICES FOR A GOOD STATE OF DOING

Practice Suggestion 1
- Be clear of the result you are wanting in a project.
- Determine what resources are needed.
- Assemble those resources.
- Design a strategy to move forward in a good way.
- Get into action around that strategy.

Practice Suggestion 2
When things are going easily, ask your Self, and others who are involved and who support you, the following questions:
- What is working?
- What can I learn from this?
- What is needed?

Practice Suggestion 3
When things are going slowly and feel hard, ask your Self, and others who are involved and who support you, the following questions:
- What is working?
- What is my state of being? (Use the three intelligences to inform you.)
- What is not working?
- What can I do differently?
- What is needed?

Practice Suggestion 4
When things seem stuck, ask your Self, and others who are involved and who support you, the following questions:
- What is my state of being? (Use the three intelligences to inform you.)
- What cycles and timing are influencing this idea and me?

- What is not working?
- What can I do differently?
- What is needed?

Practice Suggestion 5
Regardless of how things are going each day, stop, be still, and listen. Ask the following questions:
- What is my state of being? (Use the three intelligences to inform you.)
- What is needed?

Be unattached to the plan, and dance with what shows up.

Practice Suggestion 6
Create accountabilities with people around you to hold you to each step, including timelines and reporting.

Practice Suggestion 7
Each day, create a practice of intentional happiness. Do an activity that makes you happy and that intentionally shifts you to a happier state of being.

In Conclusion

There is much more to be said about all of this, and I am going to stop here. Thank you for taking the time to read through these ideas. I hope that this book has supported you in tapping into your own wisdom and into the Wisdom Field.

There is a change drawing near. I don't know what it will look like or how or when it will happen. I believe we are in it right now. It involves a paradigm shift of a global scale. I expect that it will disturb a lot of the old systems that are dependant on a more naïve and robotic population. Large organizations will have to align with the wisdom of people like you and me. As a population, we don't have to be available to go along with the hypnotic trance of these ways that no longer serve us. These ways of thinking have us believe that if we just go along with the status quo, everything will be fine.

Welcome to the age of personal responsibility—not for the sake of Self, but for the sake of Universal well-being. We are entering a time when we together, as a global people, will participate in the directions of evolution according to our collective wisdom, rather than according to what a few well-financed industries tell us to believe.

I am talking about a peaceful cosmic revolution, a full awakening to the Divine which will bring us into alignment with what our beautiful indigenous teachers call All Our Relations. That means we will take our place alongside all the other beings in a good way, and in partnership we will navigate together. We will do this because we have to. We will do this because if we don't we will be held accountable for our resistance to this idea. We will do this because it is a beautiful way to move forward. And we will do this because we want to. The more people who get tapped into the Wisdom Field and access their Divine Essence wisdom, the more inertia this shift will carry.

What is in it for you? Everything.

You are being invited into a dream in which your full beauty, brilliance, and purpose will be expressed according to your Divine Wisdom. When you really get how amazing you are now, today, you will be brought to your knees in awe of the extraordinary nature of God and the Universe as revealed through you.

There is some work to do. We'll do it together. Now is the time to engage even more fully into that work, that play. The steps will be known to you. All you have to do is to activate your will and follow through on it.

Yes, of course there are challenges. The biggest are the ones that will come from within your Self. Distorted is a persistent force. One with much good intention, yet not aligned with where you need to go. Distorted will try to have you doubt that any of what I'm saying is possible or even good. Don't worry. It is natural and even healthy to question. Just keep putting your Divine Essence in charge of the question department and you will be fine. We will be Fine.

Be compassionate with your Self. The only perfection that exists for humans is the perfection of acceptance for who we are. You will have breakthroughs on some days, and grow by the inch on others. You will also have days in which you may feel that you have slipped backwards. It is all part of the journey. I have failed often in living this work. Yet after each setback, I've looked at what I might learn, and then I've regrouped and begun again.

It is never too late, so no matter where you are in your path, today is exactly the right time and place to begin again. Every day, begin again.

You can keep it simple. It is not about grand and complex plans, except when it is. Simple steps with good intention can shift the world from where you are now in this moment.

Remember that you are the crystal of wisdom, and just by being connected to your Divine Essence, you are having a beautiful impact on this world.

You can do it. You are the one to do it. In fact, in your life you are the only one. We are all the only One. It is as One that we breathe together. Our hearts beat as one, calling Divine Wisdom into each moment.

Nobody said it was going to be easy, but it doesn't have to be so hard, either. Remember that every process will be interrupted. This is a good thing, not a problem. Your job is to trust and to stay on the path you choose.

Believe, because it is your belief that the Universe is using to construct itself according to what you really intend. It is your belief that will inform the world how to organize itself.

Remember that the beliefs of others, even when different, are not in competition with yours. We are all just catching up with each other and with the Universe itself. We are all heading towards a point of alignment. It is just that there are many roads that will get us there. That is also a good thing. This is a diverse Universe, and it is all good.

Do your part. That is all we can ask. Stay in the action of it, according to your own best guidance. I always say that you can probably create anything you want by sitting on your chair and doing enough intentions. But it will come a lot faster if you pick up the phone and make a few calls.

Don't take it all too seriously, though. After all, all we are doing is shaping and reshaping the fabric of the Universe. Have fun and play with these ideas. Make it a big experiment. Learn for your Self and share what you are learning with all of us, so that we may also benefit from your wisdom.

As I mentioned in the beginning with regards to the ideas presented here, "Take what works and leave the rest here."

I love you and I love this life.

Thanks for your part in it.

ADDITIONAL INFORMATION ABOUT AWAKENED WISDOM

*V*isit us at www.AwakenedWisdom.com and at the virtual online Awakened Wisdom Center for information on all our programs and offerings and to learn more about what is needed for us all to create great lives and great organizations in ways that are aligned with awakened wisdom.

HOW DOES AWAKENED WISDOM EXPERIENCES DO THIS?

Workshops and Retreats

Through our highly-acclaimed 10-week program, "Reclaiming Your Brilliance," a three-day live workshop that is followed up with a ten-week online program which is delivered through the Awakened Wisdom Center.

Advanced Coach Training (ACT)

The Awakened Wisdom ACT Program offers leading-edge training for professional coaches. For over a decade, Patrick has been training coaches all over the world and he is now offering Part 1 of the ACT program by tele-conference.

The Awakened Wisdom Center

At every AWE event the one thing that everyone wanted was a place to gather so that they could carry on the process of learning in a community of great people interested in awakened wisdom, so Patrick has created the online Awakened Wisdom Center.

You can join for free by visiting www.AwakenedWisdom.com and becoming a member.

The Awakened Wisdom Center is a virtual online center that

has been built on a leading-edge on-line platform that enables Awakened Wisdom to deliver interactive training.

Join now and receive, for free, the audio recordings of the 16 visualizations for living an awakened life.

Work with an AWE Coach
Now for the first time you can work with an AWE Coach. AWE Coaches are available to work with you either on- on-one or in an Awakened Wisdom Circle. You choose the program.

Awakened Organizations
Now it is more important than ever to be sure that your organization is operating according to awakened wisdom principles. Patrick has been developing leaders in organizations for over ten years and has developed leadership training, executive leadership coaching and relationship skills training for people in organizations.

As well, Patrick has assembled a dynamic team of highly experienced professionals ready to discuss the challenges and opportunities that your organization is facing now.

Says Patrick, "It is essential that we learn new ways of operating in this complex environment in order to bring out the best in the people, the culture and the world."

Other Offerings
Life Purpose Training, Living the Eight States of an Awakened life.

These are just some of the offerings of online training available through the Awakened Wisdom Center. The courses not only guide you through your own learning but also support you with a community of others that are also in the program.

Connect with these amazing teachings and with a global community and find out for yourself why these teachings are changing people's lives the world over.

About the Author

©ROB BOSSI

Patrick Ryan is an executive coach, leadership trainer, author, and founder of Awakened Wisdom Experiences™ Inc. Patrick brings twenty-five years' experience as CEO, owner, and general manager of several successful businesses. As a former Buddhist monk in Burma (now Myanmar), he practiced the path of awakened living, according to Buddhist philosophy. Patrick works with executives and entrepreneurs, focusing on questions of personal effectiveness and leadership. He powerfully integrates his rich life experiences with ancient teachings and modern applications to help deepen his clients' understandings of their own experiences.

Find out more about Patrick Ryan and Awakened Wisdom at www.AwakenedWisdom.com.

CPSIA information can be obtained at www.ICGtesting.com
Printed in the USA
LVOW051816290712

292038LV00001B/6/P